Distributed Computing Java 9

Make the best of Java for distributing applications

Raja Malleswara Rao Pattamsetti

BIRMINGHAM - MUMBAI

Distributed Computing in Java 9

First published: June 2017

Production reference: 1290617

Published by Packt Publishing Ltd.
Livery Place
35 Livery Street
Birmingham
B3 2PB, UK.

ISBN 978-1-78712-699-2

www.packtpub.com

Credits

Author
Raja Malleswara Rao Pattamsetti

Copy Editors
Charlotte Carneiro
Gladson Monteiro

Reviewer
Yogendra Sharma

Project Coordinator
Vaidehi Sawant

Commissioning Editor
Aaron Lazar

Proofreader
Safis Editing

Acquisition Editor
Denim Pinto

Indexer
Francy Puthiry

Content Development Editor
Anurag Ghogre

Graphics
Abhinash Sahu

Technical Editor
Jijo Maliyekal

Production Coordinator
Shantanu Zagade

About the Author

Raja Malleswara Rao Pattamsetti is a Java expert, focusing on enterprise architecture and development of applications with Java and related technologies. He is a certified Java and web components professional with deep expertise in building enterprise applications using diverse frameworks and methodologies. He has a thorough knowledge of the distributed system setup and developing applications that support distributed computing. He is an active participant in technical forums, groups, and conferences. He has worked with several Fortune 500 organizations and is passionate about learning new technologies and their developments. He has also authored a book, *Spring Batch Essentials*, for Packt previously.

I would like to thank my family and friends for their love and support, especially my wife, Bhargavi, for encouraging me through this stint.

I should thank my reviewers and editors, for their valuable suggestions in improving the quality of the book, my colleagues, and the Java community, for sharing great thoughts that helped me a lot in keeping myself updated.

About the Reviewer

Yogendra Sharma is a Java developer with a Python background, with experience mainly in middleware development. He has completed his bachelor's degree of technology in computer science.

He is currently working in Pune at Intelizign Engineering Services Pvt. Ltd as a software development engineer. He constantly explores technical novelties, and he is open-minded and eager to learn about new technologies and frameworks.

Yogendra was also the technical reviewer of the books, *Mastering Python Design Patterns*, *Test-Driven Development with Django*, and *Spring 4.0 Microservices*, and the video courses, *Python Projects*, *Learning Python Data Analysis*, and *Django Projects: E-Learning Portal*, by Packt.

I would like to thank my parents for allowing me to learn all that I did.
I would also like to thank my friends for their support and encouragement.

www.PacktPub.com

For support files and downloads related to your book, please visit www.PacktPub.com.

Did you know that Packt offers eBook versions of every book published, with PDF and ePub files available? You can upgrade to the eBook version at www.PacktPub.com and as a print book customer, you are entitled to a discount on the eBook copy. Get in touch with us at service@packtpub.com for more details.

At www.PacktPub.com, you can also read a collection of free technical articles, sign up for a range of free newsletters and receive exclusive discounts and offers on Packt books and eBooks.

https://www.packtpub.com/mapt

Get the most in-demand software skills with Mapt. Mapt gives you full access to all Packt books and video courses, as well as industry-leading tools to help you plan your personal development and advance your career.

Why subscribe?

- Fully searchable across every book published by Packt
- Copy and paste, print, and bookmark content
- On demand and accessible via a web browser

Customer Feedback

Thanks for purchasing this Packt book. At Packt, quality is at the heart of our editorial process. To help us improve, please leave us an honest review on this book's Amazon page at `https://www.amazon.com/dp/1787126994`.

If you'd like to join our team of regular reviewers, you can e-mail us at `customerreviews@packtpub.com`. We award our regular reviewers with free eBooks and videos in exchange for their valuable feedback. Help us be relentless in improving our products!

Table of Contents

Preface

Distributed computing is a way of improving the system processing ability by splitting and sharing the effort with multiple smaller systems and collating the results from them to get the desired process output. In this book, we have tried our best to put together the concepts of distributed computing, from the thought they started and how trends have changed from single-computer processing to modern distributed computing on cloud portfolio.

While we describe each of the concepts with detailed explanations and handy diagrams that rightly represent the systems and flows, we bring appropriate examples and code snippets to help you understand how they can be implemented with the help of Java 9.

There are numerous improvements to the concepts, and additional features have enriched Java's ability to support distributed computing in Java 9. We have discussed the era of distributed computing along with latest improvements and application in Java 9 through the separate chapters. This should cover the design thoughts and security aspects as well, which, we believe, lets you concentrate on that specific topic and understand it a step further with the right combination of explanation, diagrams, and code snippets.

This book took about 6 months for me to write, and it was a great journey. The design and development experiences with multiple enterprise integrations and distributed systems with the support of solution architecture teams helped me go through the on-ground challenges and improve the design standpoint of system integration. You will see in multiple places that I start talking about design perspectives and patterns before the solution implementation specifics. Also, care has been taken to help you with the concepts in such a way that you should feel like being part of a detailed technical conversation right from the start, where your knowledge and past skillset help you go through them and improve along the depth of the chapters.

Most concepts are imbued with an everlasting perception of reusability and thorough engineering, and I believe some parts of this will remain with you, being the reader, as useful techniques to reuse in your application development.

Finally, while I have made sure to complement every chapter with several images to illustrate the desired output, I think it is paramount for you to review every concept along with practice, which helps you learn and build confidence in working with such systems. Have fun building great things!

What this book covers

Chapter 1, *Quick Start to Distributed Computing*, reviews the basic concepts of distributed and parallel computing, what it is, why it is required, and how Java supports distributed computing, along with their architecture.

Chapter 2, *Communication between Distributed Applications*, covers different ways of communicating with remote systems in a distributed architecture, the concept of sockets, and stream programming with examples and URL-based communication.

Chapter 3, *RMI, CORBA, and JavaSpace*, teaches what the components of message-based systems are and how architectures such as RMI, CORBA, and Java Spaces complement it.

Chapter 4, *Enterprise Messaging*, explores the concept of enterprise integration patterns and the concepts of synchronous and asynchronous messaging, with technologies such as JMS and web services.

Chapter 5, *HPC Cluster Computing*, covers handling large amounts of data through parallel or distributed computing using HPC, cluster-computing architecture, and Java support for these implementations.

Chapter 6, *Distributed Databases*, covers the concepts and ways to set up a distributed database. It also explains how distributed databases help in performance improvisation with distributed transactions and XA transactions with examples.

Chapter 7, *Cloud and Distributed Computing*, explains how cloud and distributed computing go hand in hand. You will also learn the setup and procedure to configure your applications on market-leading cloud environments.

Chapter 8, *Big Data Analytics*, discusses big data concepts and how big data helps in distributed computing. The chapter covers the implementations of big data, along with methods and applications, including Hadoop, MapReduce, and HDFS.

Chapter 9, *Testing, Debugging, and Troubleshooting*, explores how to test, debug, and troubleshoot distributed systems, and the different challenges in distributed computing.

Chapter 10, *Security*, discusses different security issues and constraints associated with distributed computing and how to address them.

What you need for this book

To follow along with this book, you'll need a computer with an internet connection. You can choose to work online on the Cloud Java IDE to practice the examples. I recommend you have the Eclipse IDE with Tomcat/WebLogic container with the respective respective Maven/Gradle dependencies based on the concept you want to practice happily. For concepts such as cloud computing, you should have access to Cloud Foundry to practice.

Who this book is for

This book has been tested on people who have decent programming knowledge of Java. They picked up going through the chapters with practice, and in the end, they had a thorough knowledge of distributed computing and the design aspects of distributed computing. In this book, you will learn some tricks and tips that you probably didn't know about, or some wise suggestions that will help you along the way.

This book, if followed from cover to cover, will turn you into a proficient distributed system architecture expert. On the other hand, if you already are, it provides a good reference for many different features and techniques that may come in handy from time to time. Finally, this book is also a valid migration guide if you have already experimented with distributed system concepts and you feel overwhelmed by change.

Conventions

In this book, you will find a number of text styles that distinguish between different kinds of information. Here are some examples of these styles and an explanation of their meaning. Code words in text, database table names, folder names, filenames, file extensions, pathnames, dummy URLs, user input, and Twitter handles are shown as follows: "We can include other contexts using the `include` directive." A block of code is set as follows:

```
[default]
public static void main(String[] args) {
   System.out.println("Distributed computing with Java 9");
}
```

When we wish to draw your attention to a particular part of a code block, the relevant lines or items are set in bold:

```
[default]
public static void main(String[] args) {
   //Comments for the below statement System.out.println("Distributed
   //computing with Java 9");
}
```

Any command-line input or output is written as follows:

```
# cp /usr/src/main/java/distributed/target/Component.class
    /etc/distributed/classes/Component.class
```

New terms and **important words** are shown in bold. Words that you see on the screen, for example, in menus or dialog boxes, appear in the text like this: "In order to download new modules, we will go to **Files** | **Settings** | **Project Name** | **Project Interpreter**."

Warnings or important notes appear in a box like this.

 Tips and tricks appear like this.

Reader feedback

Feedback from our readers is always welcome. Let us know what you think about this book-what you liked or disliked. Reader feedback is important for us as it helps us develop titles that you will really get the most out of. To send us general feedback, simply e-mail feedback@packtpub.com, and mention the book's title in the subject of your message. If there is a topic that you have expertise in and you are interested in either writing or contributing to a book, see our author guide at www.packtpub.com/authors.

Customer support

Now that you are the proud owner of a Packt book, we have a number of things to help you to get the most from your purchase.

Downloading the example code

You can download the example code files for this book from your account at http://www.packtpub.com. If you purchased this book elsewhere, you can visit http://www.packtpub.com/support and register to have the files e-mailed directly to you. You can download the code files by following these steps:

1. Log in or register to our website using your e-mail address and password.
2. Hover the mouse pointer on the **SUPPORT** tab at the top.
3. Click on **Code Downloads & Errata**.
4. Enter the name of the book in the **Search** box.
5. Select the book for which you're looking to download the code files.
6. Choose from the drop-down menu where you purchased this book from.
7. Click on **Code Download**.

Once the file is downloaded, please make sure that you unzip or extract the folder using the latest version of:

- WinRAR / 7-Zip for Windows
- Zipeg / iZip / UnRarX for Mac
- 7-Zip / PeaZip for Linux

The code bundle for the book is also hosted on GitHub at `https://github.com/PacktPublishing/Distributed-Computing-in-Java-9`. We also have other code bundles from our rich catalog of books and videos available at `https://github.com/PacktPublishing/`. Check them out!

Errata

Although we have taken every care to ensure the accuracy of our content, mistakes do happen. If you find a mistake in one of our books-maybe a mistake in the text or the code-we would be grateful if you could report this to us. By doing so, you can save other readers from frustration and help us improve subsequent versions of this book. If you find any errata, please report them by visiting `http://www.packtpub.com/submit-errata`, selecting your book, clicking on the **Errata Submission Form** link, and entering the details of your errata. Once your errata are verified, your submission will be accepted and the errata will be uploaded to our website or added to any list of existing errata under the Errata section of that title. To view the previously submitted errata, go to `https://www.packtpub.com/books/content/support` and enter the name of the book in the search field. The required information will appear under the **Errata** section.

Piracy

Piracy of copyrighted material on the Internet is an ongoing problem across all media. At Packt, we take the protection of our copyright and licenses very seriously. If you come across any illegal copies of our works in any form on the Internet, please provide us with the location address or website name immediately so that we can pursue a remedy. Please contact us at `copyright@packtpub.com` with a link to the suspected pirated material. We appreciate your help in protecting our authors and our ability to bring you valuable content.

Questions

If you have a problem with any aspect of this book, you can contact us at `questions@packtpub.com`, and we will do our best to address the problem.

1
Quick Start to Distributed Computing

Distributed computing is the process of accomplishing a bigger task through splitting it into multiple subtasks, which can be performed by multiple components that are located in a network of computers termed as distributed systems. These distributed systems have the capability to communicate and coordinate their activities by exchanging the information and/or status of their individual processes. Having such distributed systems allows organizations to maintain comparatively smaller and cheaper computers in a network rather than having to maintain one large server with bigger capacity.

In this chapter, we will cover the following topics:

- Evolution of computing models
- Parallel computing
- Amdahl's law
- Distributed computing
- Parallel versus distributed computing
- Design considerations for distributed systems
- Java support

Let's begin our discussion by remembering the great Charles Babbage, considered to be the "father of the computer", who originated the concept of a programmable computer. He, who was an English mechanical engineer and polymath, conceptualized and invented the first mechanical computer in the early 19th century. While Alan Turing introduced the principle of the modern computer in 1936, modern digital computers were heralded to the world in the 1940s, and the **Electronic Numerical Integrator and Computer** (**ENIAC**) was among the earliest electronic general-purpose computers made. From there on, computers have evolved to be faster and cheaper at an astonishing rate, along with the operating systems, programming languages, and so on. The computers with such faster processing capacity were called supercomputers and used to occupy more than one big room years ago. Today, we have multicore processing capacity computers such as minicomputers and mobiles/smart phones, which can be carried in a pocket and are able to do most of jobs humans need in day-to-day life.

While a computer may be regarded as executing one gigantic program stored in its main memory, in some computers, it is necessary to have the capacity of executing several programs concurrently. This is achieved through multitasking; that is, the computer is enabled to switch rapidly between multiple executing programs to show them running simultaneously.

Next-generation computers are designed to distribute their process across numerous CPUs in a multiprocessing configuration. This technique was earlier available in huge and commanding computers, such as supercomputers, servers, and mainframe computers. Nowadays, such multiprocessor and multicore capabilities are extensively available on personal computers and laptops.

Although such high-speed computers are demonstrating delightful processing abilities, the next serious invention that transformed the world of processing was high-speed computer networking. This technique permitted an enormous number of computers to interact and established the next level of processing. The incredible fact about networked computers is that they can be placed geographically either within the same location connected as **Local Area Network** (**LAN**) or be situated across continents and connected as **Wide Area Network** (**WAN**).

Today, a new computer/smartphone is definitely expected to have multiprocessor/multicore capacity at an affordably low cost. Besides, the trend has changed from CPU to **Graphics Processing Unit** (**GPU**), also called as **Visual Processing Unit** (**VPU**), which can be installed in personal computers, mobile phones, workstations, embedded systems, and gaming consoles. Recent GPUs are very capable of computer graphics manipulation and image processing, and they are more efficient than general-purpose CPUs due to their highly parallel assembly.

The following diagram represents the evolution of computing models from mainframe to cloud, how each concern like availability SLA, Scaling, Hardware, HA Type, Software and Consumption are varied over the time with technology.

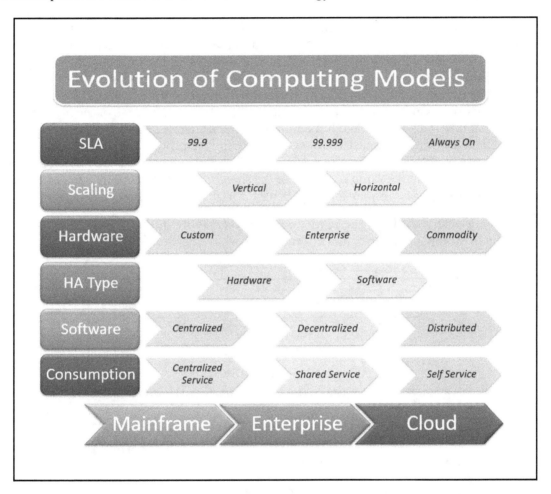

Early computing was a uniprocessor computing that was performed on a single processor, which can be called **centralized computing**. Later, **parallel computing** with more than one processor simultaneously executing a single program helped middleware processing. **Parallel processing** was achieved through either a single computer with *multiple CPUs* or *multiple network* connected computers (with the help of software).

Let us now learn in detail about parallel computing and how the trend moved toward distributed computing.

Parallel computing

A parallel system contains more than one processor having direct memory access to the shared memory that can form a common address space. Usually, a parallel system is of a **Uniform Memory Access (UMA)** architecture. In UMA architecture, the access latency (processing time) for accessing any particular location of a memory from a particular processor is the same. Moreover, the processors are also configured to be in a close proximity and are connected in an interconnection network. Conventionally, the interprocess processor communication between the processors is happening through either read or write operations across a shared memory, even though the usage of the message-passing capability is also possible (with emulation on the shared memory). Moreover, the hardware and software are tightly coupled, and usually, the processors in such network are installed to run on the same operating system. In general, the processors are homogeneous and are installed within the same container of the shared memory. A multistage switch/bus containing a regular and symmetric design is used for greater efficiency.

The following diagram represents a UMA parallel system with multiple processors connecting to multiple memory units through network connection.

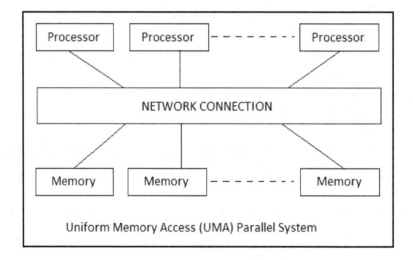

Uniform Memory Access (UMA) Parallel System

A multicomputer parallel system is another type of parallel system containing multiple processors configured without having a direct accessibility to the shared memory. Moreover, a common address space may or may not be expected to be formed by the memory of the multiple processors. Hence, computers belonging to this category are not expected to contain a common clock in practice. The processors are configured in a close distance, and they are also tightly coupled in general with homogeneous software and hardware. Such computers are also connected within an interconnected network. The processors can establish a communication with either of the *common address space* or *message passing options*. This is represented in the diagram below.

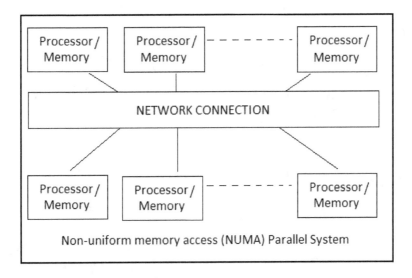

Non-uniform memory access (NUMA) Parallel System

A multicomputer system in a **Non-Uniform Memory Access (NUMA)** architecture is usually configured with a common address space. In such NUMA architecture, accessing different memory locations in a shared memory across different processors shows different latency times.

Array processor exchanges information by passing as messages. Array processors have a very small market owing to the fact that they can perform closely synchronized data processing, and the data is exchanged in a locked event for applications such as digital signal processing and image processing. Such applications can also involve large iterations on the data as well.

Compared to the UMA and array processors architecture, NUMA as well as message-passing multicomputer systems are less preferred if the shared data access and communication much accepted. The primary benefit of having parallel systems is to derive a better throughput through sharing the computational tasks between multiple processors. The tasks that can be partitioned into multiple subtasks easily and need little communication for bringing synchronization in execution are the most efficient tasks to execute on parallel systems. The subtasks can be executed as a large vector or an array through matrix computations, which are common in scientific applications. Though parallel computing was much appreciated through research and was beneficial on legacy architectures, they are observed no more efficient/economic in recent times due to following reasons:

- They need special configuration for compilers
- The market for such applications that can attain efficiency through parallel processing is very small
- The evolution of more powerful and efficient computers at lower costs made it less likely that organizations would choose parallel systems.

Amdahl's law

Amdahl's law is frequently considered in parallel computing to forecast the improvement in process speedup when increasing the use of multiple system processors. Amdahl's Law is named after the famous computer scientist Gene Amdahl; it was submitted at the American Federation of Information Processing Societies (AFIPS) during the Spring Joint Computer Conference in the year 1967.

The standard formula for Amdahl's Law is as follows:

$$S_{\text{latency}}(s) = \frac{1}{(1-p) + \frac{p}{s}}$$

where:

- $S_{latency}$ is the calculated improvement of the latency (execution) of the complete task.

- *s* is the improvement in execution of the part of the task that benefits from the improved system resources.
- *p* is the proportion of the execution time that the part benefiting from improved resources actually occupies.

Let's consider an example of a single task that can be further partitioned into four subtasks: each of their execution time percentages are *p1 = 0.11*, *p2 = 0.18*, *p3 = 0.23*, and *p4 = 0.48*, respectively. Then, it is observed that the first subtask is improved in speed, so *s1 = 1*. The second subtask is observed to be improved in speed by five times, so *s2 = 5*. The third subtask is observed to be improved in speed by 20 times, so *s3 = 20*. Finally, the fourth subtask is improved in speed by 1.6 times, so *s4 = 1.6*.

By using Amdahl's law, the overall speedup is follows:

$$S_{latency} = \frac{1}{\frac{p1}{s1} + \frac{p2}{s2} + \frac{p3}{s3} + \frac{p4}{s4}} = \frac{1}{\frac{0.11}{1} + \frac{0.18}{5} + \frac{0.23}{20} + \frac{0.48}{1.6}} = 2.19.$$

Notice how the 20 times and 5 times speedup on the second and third parts, respectively, don't have much effect on the overall speedup when the fourth part (48% of the execution time) is sped up only 1.6 times.

The following formula demonstrates that the theoretical speedup of the entire program execution improves with the increase of the number/capacity of resources in the system and that, regardless with the magnitude of the improvement, the calculated improvement of the entire program is always expected to be limited by that particular task that cannot benefit from the resource improvement.

$$\begin{cases} S_{latency}(s) \leq \dfrac{1}{1-p} \\ \\ \lim_{s \to \infty} S_{latency}(s) = \dfrac{1}{1-p}. \end{cases}$$

Consider if a program is expected to need about 20 hours to complete the processing with the help of a single processor. A specific sub task of the entire program that is expected to consume an hour to execute cannot be executed in parallel, while the remaining program of about 19 hours processing ($p = 0.95$) of the total execution time can be executed in parallel. In such scenarios, regardless of how many additional processors are dedicated to be executed in parallel of such program, the execution time of the program cannot be reduced to anytime less than that minimum 1 hour. Obviously, the expected calculated improvement of the execution speed is limited to, at most, 20 times (calculated as $1/(1 - p) = 20$). Hence, parallel computing is applicable only for those processors that have more scope for having the capability of splitting them into subtasks/parallel programs as observed in the diagram below.

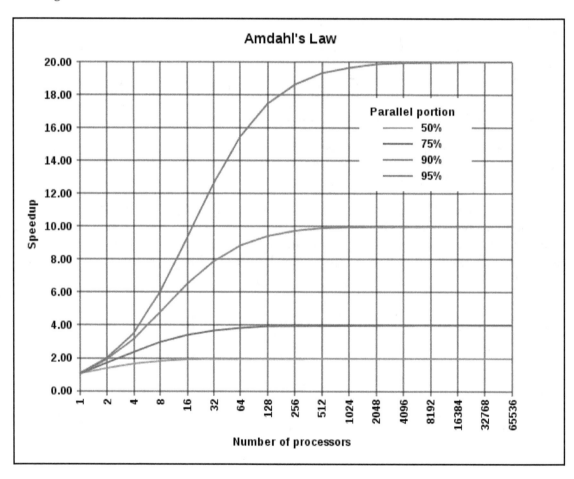

However, Amdahl's law is applicable only to scenarios where the program is of a fixed size. In general, on larger problems (larger datasets), more computing resources tend to get used if they are available, and the overall processing time in the parallel part usually improves much faster than the by default serial parts.

Distributed computing

Distributed computing is the concurrent usage of more than one connected computer to solve a problem over a network connection. The computers that take part in distributed computing appear as single machines to their users.

Distributing computation across multiple computers is a great approach when these computers are observed to interact with each other over the distributed network to solve a bigger problem in reasonably less latency. In many respects, this sounds like a generalization of the concepts of parallel computing that we discussed in the previous section. The purpose of enabling distributed systems includes the ability to confront a problem that is either bigger or longer to process by an individual computer.

Distributed computing, the latest trend, is performed on a distributed system, which is considered to be a group of computers that do not stake a common physical clock or a shared memory, interact with the information exchanged over a communication (inter/intra) network, with each computer having its own memory, and runs on its own operating system. Usually, the computers are semi-autonomous, loosely coupled and cooperate to address a problem collectively.

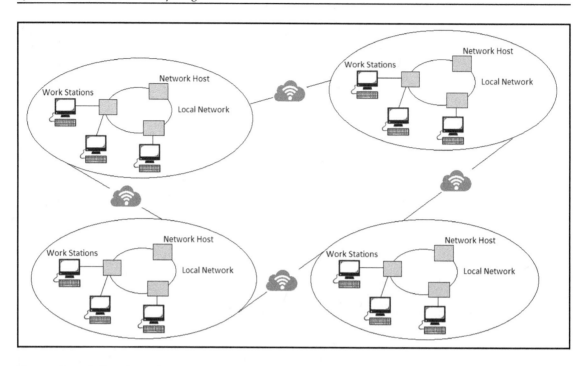

Examples of distributed systems include the Internet, an intranet, and a **Network of Workstations** (**NOW**), which is a group of networked personal workstations connected to server machines represented in the diagram above. Modern-day internet connections include a home hub with multiple devices connected and operating on the network; search engines such as Google and Amazon services are famous distributed systems. Three-dimensional animation movies from Pixar and DreamWorks are other trendy examples of distributed computing.

Given the number of frames to condense for a full-length feature (30 frames per second on a 2-hour movie, which is a lot!), movie studios have the requirement of spreading the full-rendering job to more computers.

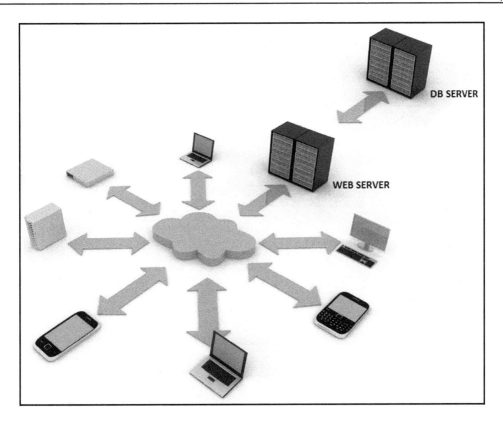

In the preceding image, we can observe a web application, another illustration of a distributed application where multiple users connect to the web application over the Internet/intranet. In this architecture, the web application is deployed in a web server, which interacts with a DB server for data persistence.

The other aspects of the application requiring a distributed system configuration are instant messaging and video conferencing applications. Having the ability to solve such problems, along with improved performance, is the reason for choosing distributed systems.

The devices that can take part in distributed computing include server machines, work stations, and personal handheld devices.

Capabilities of distributed computing include integrating heterogeneous applications that are developed and run on different technologies and operating systems, multiple applications sharing common resources, a single instance service being reused by multiple clients, and having a common user interface for multiple applications.

Parallel versus distributed computing

While both distributed computing and parallel systems are widely available these days, the main difference between these two is that a parallel computing system consists of multiple processors that communicate with each other using a shared memory, whereas a distributed computing system contains multiple processors connected by a communication network.

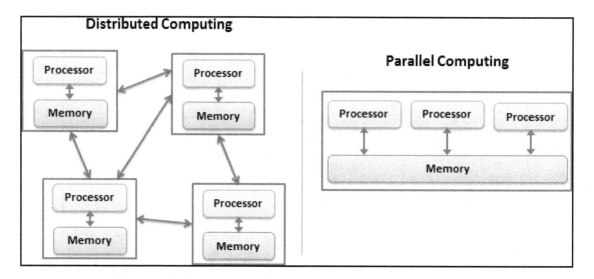

In parallel computing systems, as the number of processors increases, with enough parallelism available in applications, such systems easily beat sequential systems in performance through the shared memory. In such systems, the processors can also contain their own locally allocated memory, which is not available to any other processors.

In distributed computing systems, multiple system processors can communicate with each other using messages that are sent over the network. Such systems are increasingly available these days because of the availability at low price of computer processors and the high-bandwidth links to connect them.

The following reasons explain why a system should be built distributed, not just parallel:

- **Scalability**: As distributed systems do not have the problems associated with shared memory, with the increased number of processors, they are obviously regarded as more scalable than parallel systems.

- **Reliability**: The impact of the failure of any single subsystem or a computer on the network of computers defines the reliability of such a connected system. Definitely, distributed systems demonstrate a better aspect in this area compared to the parallel systems.
- **Data sharing**: Data sharing provided by distributed systems is similar to the data sharing provided by distributed databases. Thus, multiple organizations can have distributed systems with the integrated applications for data exchange.
- **Resources sharing**: If there exists an expensive and a special purpose resource or a processor, which cannot be dedicated to each processor in the system, such a resource can be easily shared across distributed systems.
- **Heterogeneity and modularity**: A system should be flexible enough to accept a new heterogeneous processor to be added into it and one of the processors to be replaced or removed from the system without affecting the overall system processing capability. Distributed systems are observed to be more flexible in this respect.
- **Geographic construction**: The geographic placement of different subsystems of an application may be inherently placed as distributed. Local processing may be forced by the low communication bandwidth more specifically within a wireless network.
- **Economic**: With the evolution of modern computers, high-bandwidth networks and workstations are available at low cost, which also favors distributed computing for economic reasons.

Design considerations for distributed systems

Following are some of the characteristics of distributed systems that should be considered in designing a project in a distributed environment:

No global clock: Being distributed across the world, distributed systems cannot be expected to have a common clock, and this gives a chance for the intrinsic asynchrony between the processors performing the computing. Distributed system coordination usually depends on a shared idea of the time at which the programs or business state occurs. However, with distributed systems, having no global clock, it is a challenge to attain the accuracy with which the computers in the network can synchronize their clocks to reflect the time at which the expected program execution happened. This limitation expects the systems in the network to communicate through messages instead of time-based events.

Geographical distribution: The individual systems taking a part in distributed system are expected to be connected through a network, previously through a **Wide-Area Network (WAN)**, and now with a **Network Of Workstations/Cluster Of Workstations (NOW/COW)**. An in-house distributed system is expected to be configured within a LAN connectivity. NOW is becoming widespread in the market with its low-cost, high-speed, off-the-shelf processing capability. Most popular NOW architectures include the Google search engine, Amazon.

No shared memory: An important and key feature of distributed computing and the message-passing model of communication is having no shared memory, which also infers the nonexistence of a common physical clock.

Independence and heterogeneity: The distributed system processors are loosely coupled so that they have their own individual capabilities in terms of speed and method of execution with versatile operating systems. They are not expected to be part of a dedicated system; however, they cooperate with one another by exposing the services and/or executing the tasks together as subtasks.

Fail-over mechanism: We often see computer systems failing, and it is the design responsibility of setting the expected behavior with the consequence of possible failures. Distributed systems are observed to be failed in integration as well as the individual sub systems. A fault in the network can result in the isolation of an individual or a group of computers in the distributed system; however, they might still be executing the programs they are expected to execute. In reality, the individual programs may not be able to detect such network failures or timeouts. Similarly, the failure of a particular computer, a system being terminated abruptly with an abrupt program or system failure, may not immediately be known by the other systems/components in the network with which the failed computer usually communicates with. The consequences of this characteristic of distributed systems has to be captured in the system design.

Security concerns: Distributed systems being set up on a shared Internet are prone to more unauthorized attacks and vulnerabilities.

Distributed systems are becoming increasingly popular with their ability to allow the polling of resources, including CPU cycles, data storage, devices and services becoming increasingly economical. Distributed systems are more reliable as they allow replication of resources and services, which reduces service outages due to individual system failures. Cost, speed, and availability of Internet are making it a decent platform on which to maintain distributed systems.

Java support

From a standalone application to web applications to the sophisticated cloud integration of enterprise, Java has been updating itself to accommodate various features that support the change. Especially, frameworks like Spring have come up with modules like Spring Boot, Batch, and Integration, which comply with most of the cloud integration features. As a language, Java has a great support for programs to be written using multithreaded distributed objects. In this model, an application contains numerous heavyweight processes that communicate using messaging or **Remote Method Invocations** (**RMI**). Each heavyweight process contains several lightweight processes, which are termed as **threads** in Java. Threads can communicate through the shared memory. Such software architecture reflects the hardware that is configured to be extensively accessible.

By assuming that there is, at most, one thread per process or by ignoring the parallelism within one process, it is the usual model of a distributed system. The purpose of making the logically simple is that the distributed program is more object-oriented because data in a remote object can be accessed only through an explicit messaging or a remote procedure call (RPC).

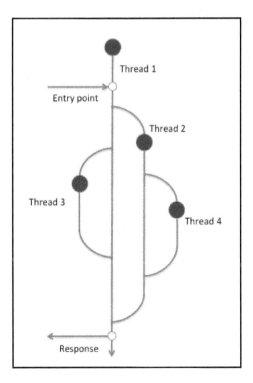

The object-orientated model promotes reusability as well as design simplicity. Furthermore, a large shared data structure has the requirement of shared processing, which is possible through object orientation and letting the process of execution be multithreaded. The programming should carry the responsibility of splitting the larger data structure across multiple heavyweight processes.

Programming language, which wants to support concurrent programming, should be able to instruct the process structure, and how several processes communicate with each other and synchronize. There are many ways the Java program can specify the process structure or create a new process. For example, UNIX processes are tree structured containing a unique **process ID (pid)** for each process. fork and wait are the commands to create and synchronize the processes. The fork command creates a child process from a parent process with a parent process address space copy:

```
pid = fork();
if (pid != 0 ) {
   cout << "This is a parent process";
}
else {
   cout << "This is a child process";
}
```

Java has a predefined class called `Thread` to enable concurrency through creating thread objects. A class can extend the `Thread` class if it should be executed in a separate thread, override the `run()` method, and execute the `start()` method to launch that thread:

```
public class NewThread extends Thread {
   public void run() {
      System.out.println("New Thread executing!");
   }
   public static void main(String[] args) {
      Thread t1 = new NewThread();
      t1.start();
   }
}
```

In the cases where a class has to extend another class and execute as a new thread, Java supports this behavior through the interface *Runnable,* as shown in the following example:

```
public class Animal {
  String name;
  public Animal(String name) {
    this.name = name;
  }
  public void setName(String name) {
    this.name = name;
  }
  public String getName() {
    return this.name;
  }
}
public class Mammal extends Animal implements Runnable {
  public Mammal(String name) {
    super(name);
  }
  public void run() {
    for (int i = 0; i < 100; i++) {
      System.out.println("The name of the Animal is : " + this.getName());
    }
  }
  public static void main(String[] args) {
    Animal firstAnimal = new Mammal("Tiger");
    Thread threadOne = new Thread((Runnable) firstAnimal);
    threadOne.start();
    Animal secondAnimal = new Mammal("Elephant");
    Thread threadTwo = new Thread((Runnable) secondAnimal);
    threadTwo.start();
  }
}
```

In the following example of Fibonacci numbers, a thread waits for completing the execution of other threads using the Join mechanism. Threads can carry the priority as well to set the importance of one thread over the other to execute before:

```
public class Fib extends Thread
{
  private int x;
  public int answer;
  public Fib(int x) {
    this.x = x;
  }
  public void run() {
```

```
      if( x <= 2 )
      answer = 1;
      else {
        try {
          Fib f1 = new Fib(x-1);
          Fib f2 = new Fib(x-2);
          f1.start();
          f2.start();
          f1.join();
          f2.join();
          answer = f1.answer + f2.answer;
        }
        catch(InterruptedException ex) { }
      }
    }
    public static void main(String[] args)  throws Exception
    {
      try {
        Fib f = new Fib( Integer.parseInt(args[0]) );
        f.start();
        f.join();
        System.out.println(f.answer);
      }
      catch(Exception ex) {
        System.err.println("usage: java Fib NUMBER");
      }
    }
  }
```

With the latest Java version, a `Callable` interface is introduced with a `@FunctionalInterface` annotation. With the help of this feature, we can create `Callable` objects using lambda expressions as follows:

```
Callable<Integer> callableObject = () -> { return 5 + 9; };
```

The preceding expression is equivalent to the following code:

```
Callable<Integer> callableObject = new Callable<Integer>() {
  @Override
  public Integer call() throws Exception {
    return 5 + 6;
  }
};
```

Following is the complete example with `Callable` and `Future` interfaces and lambda expressions for handing concurrent processing in Java 9:

```
package threads;

import java.util.Arrays;
import java.util.List;
import java.util.concurrent.Callable;
import java.util.concurrent.ExecutionException;
import java.util.concurrent.ExecutorService;
import java.util.concurrent.Executors;
import java.util.concurrent.Future;

public class JavaCallableThreads {

  public static void main(String[] args) {
    final List<Integer> numbers = Arrays.asList(1,2,3,4,5);
    Callable<Integer> callableObject = () -> {
      int sum = numbers.stream().mapToInt(i -> i.intValue()).sum();
      return sum;
    };
    ExecutorService exService = Executors.newSingleThreadExecutor();
    Future<Integer> futureObj = exService.submit(callableObject);
    Integer futureSum=0;
    try {
    futureSum = futureObj.get();
  } catch (InterruptedException e) {
    e.printStackTrace();
  } catch (ExecutionException e) {
    e.printStackTrace();
  }
    System.out.println("Sum returned = " + futureSum);
  }

}
```

Modern Java enterprise applications have evolved through messaging (through message queue), web services, and writing microservices based distributed application like docker with applications deployed on cloud computing services like RedHat OpenShift, Amazon Web Services (AWS), Google App Engine and Kubernetes.

We will discuss the Java 9 support for such application development and deployment in detail in the coming chapters.

Summary

Through this chapter, you learnt about the essential computing mechanisms including centralized, parallel, and distributed computing. You also learnt about the types of parallel systems and their efficiency through Amdahl's law. We finished this chapter with an understanding of distributed computing, and its strengths and the aspects that should be considered in designing a distributed system.

In the next chapter, you will learn about communication between distributed systems including Sockets and streams, URLs, Class Loader, and message-based systems in detail.

2
Communication between Distributed Applications

The emergence of the internet and **World Wide Web** (**WWW**) as global media for communication has revolutionized the fields of engineering, e-commerce, and scientific applications. Modern applications, such as the ones related to social media, entertainment, and banking, are no longer strangers to mobile operations carried out through smartphones. Organizations in these domains have been investing a lot into technology to find newer ways of providing services. Gone are the days when we use to make calls to receive services; we now have mobile applications for almost everything, including health, food, banking, and communication. Global organizations obviously chose distributed web applications over legacy/desktop applications, which helped distributed applications evolve; subsequently, communication between such applications became a vital area of concentration.

In this chapter, we will cover the following topics:

- Client-server communication
- Sockets and streams
- Socket programming for Transport Control Protocol (TCP)
- Socket programming for User Datagram Protocol (UDP)
- Multicasting
- Streams
- URLs, URLConnections, and the ContentHandler classes
- URL (base URL and relative URL)
- Practicality of URLs
- ClassLoader

Client-server communication

Client-server applications are configured on a network (internet/intranet). Clients send requests to the server for a resource and, in turn, receive responses from the server. A computer that can send such requests for a resource/service is called a client, and the computer that contains the program that provides the requested resource/service to more than one client is called a server. Both clients and servers can be connected through a wired/wireless network protocol:

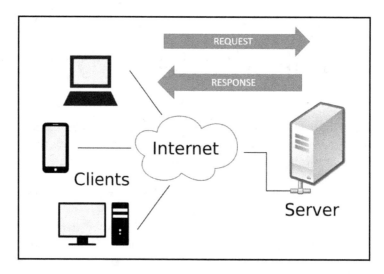

In the preceding figure, client-server communication can be visualized as a program running on the client machine interacting with another program running on the server machine. This communication through the network involves networking services offered by diverse communication protocols.

In a single processor system, applications can talk to each other through shared memory. The producer process writes data to the buffer or filesystem, and the consumer process reads the data from there. In distributed systems, there is no shared memory. In these systems, application communication is intense as they have to coordinate with each other and generate output in the shortest period of time for inter-process communication. As a result, computers engage in diverse methods of communication between distributed applications that may be remotely located from each other.

To address the issue, all communication systems are expected to comply with the **Open Systems Interconnection model (OSI model)**, which is a conceptual model that characterizes and standardizes the communication functions of a telecommunication or computing system, irrespective of their underlying internal structure and technology. This model partitions a communication system into seven layers: each layer serves the layer above it and is served by the layer below it. Among these, the data link layer is one of the most important layers as it serves the purpose of error detection and correction, thereby ensuring data quality. It groups bits into frames and ensures that each frame is received correctly. It puts a special pattern at the start and end of each frame to mark it; also, it computes a checksum by adding all the bytes to the frame in a particular order. To ensure defect-free transmission, follow these two strategies:

1. **Error detecting strategy**: In this strategy, the receiver receives limited information. It can only detect that some error has occurred and reject the message subsequently, but it cannot correct it.
2. **Error correction strategy**: In this method, the receiver receives duplicate information with each block referring to the previous block. If any error occurs, information from the following block can be used to correct the error at the receiver end itself. For example, if a frame consists of i data bits and duplicate d data bits, then the total length would be $i + d = n$. This total length n is called a **code word**. These code words are further compared to find the number of bits they differ by. The number of bit positions in which consecutive *code words* differ is called the **hamming distance**.

There are different methods of remote application communication available that you can use over a network, involving the following types:

- Network protocol stack
- Remote Procedure Call (RPC)
- Remote Method Invocation (RMI)
- Message queuing services (sockets)
- Stream-oriented services

We will discuss these in detail in subsequent sections. In this chapter, we will try to understand the basics of networking technology, how it evolved over a period of time, and how Java provides support for it. We will follow this up with different practical examples. Now let's look into the basics of networking:

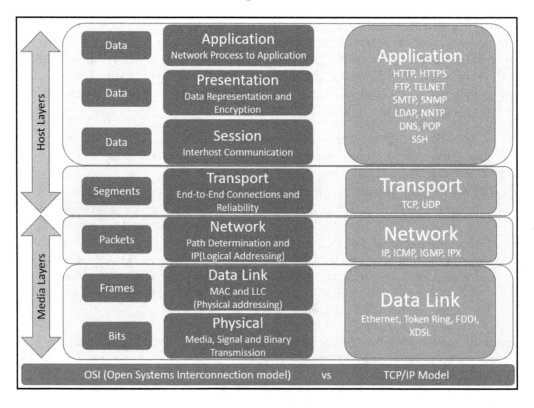

As depicted in the preceding diagram, **TCP** and **UDP** are part of the transport layer. Java supports programming in these protocols through API sockets. When we write a Java program, we do programming at the application layer. We do not worry about the TCP and UDP layers as they are internally taken care of by java.net packages, irrespective of the platform. However, java.net is an exhaustive package that contains many classes. In order to decide which ones to use, you need a basic understanding of networking and the difference between these two protocols.

When you speak over your phone, whatever you speak is delivered to the receiver in the same order without any damage. If any issue occurs during this transmission, the other person experiences voice disturbance. The TCP protocol is analogous to this kind of telephonic communication. This circuit-switching protocol ensures that data is delivered back and forth without any damage and in the same order. TCP is a two-way protocol; hence, data can be sent across in both the directions at the same time. TCP supports point-to-point channel functionality to foster reliable communication between interfaces. Well-known, high-level (application) protocols such as **Hypertext Transfer Protocol (HTTP)**, **File Transfer Protocol (FTP)**, and Telnet are some examples that are based on the TCP/IP protocol. While browsing internet sites, if data is not transmitted in the proper sequence, the user will see scrambled pages. Thus, TCP can be defined as a *connection-based protocol that provides a reliable flow of data between two computers.*

Analogous to our postal system, we don't require assured mail delivery every time. For example, if you are sending a business contract to your customer, you may look for assured delivery, but if you are sending flyers, you may not look for assured delivery. Coming to computers, let's say a customer sends a request for the price of a stock. But due to link failure, you are unable to deliver the stock price at that moment. In this case, it is not necessary that you retry sending the same stock price message again; this is because by the time the link is established again, the stock price could have changed. So, in this scenario, the customer will place a request again and the system will deliver the latest stock price. In these kinds of scenario, the system needs to manage the overhead of assured message delivery rather than execute the process again from scratch and send a new message.

In these scenarios, the UDP protocol comes in handy. It sends data in packets, and these packets are independent of each other and do not follow any sequence. If the application interfaces do not follow the TCP protocol for interacting and the interaction is not enforced, then such applications can interact using the UDP protocol.

This way, the UDP protocol can be defined as *a nonconnection-based protocol that sends independent packets of data, called datagrams, from one computer to another with no guarantee about their arrival.*

Many a time, UDP is not permitted by firewalls. If you face trouble in accessing a service, check with your system administrator and confirm that UDP is enabled.

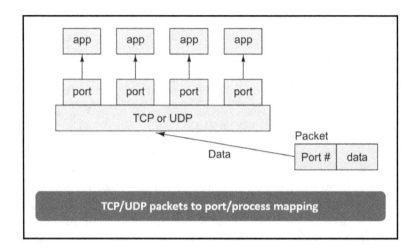

TCP/UDP packets to port/process mapping

The **TCP** and **UDP** protocols use ports to map incoming data to a particular process running on a computer. Each computer has a single physical connection to a network through which it sends/receives data to/from the network. To send data to a particular computer, 32-bit IP addresses are used. But once the data is received, how will the computer identify which application it pertains to? The answer is through ports. Thus, a **port** is the end point of communication in distributed systems. Though this is also used for hardware devices, here we are referring to a software construct that identifies specific processes or network services.

An IP-port-calling socket is never used on its own; it is always associated with an IP address and protocol type used for establishing communication. This way, it completes the destination or source address of a communication session. A port possesses a 16-bit number and ranges from 0 to 65,535; out of this range, 0 to 1,023 are reserved for HTTP, FTP, and other system services.

Transport protocols, such as TCP and UDP, provide the source and destination port numbers in their headers. A process that associates a port's input and output channels through an internet socket with a transport protocol, a port number, and an IP address is called *binding*.

This way, a port can be defined as a *channel for passing the inbound data passed to a specific interface on the host computer using either the TCP or UDP protocol.*

A port number can be assumed with a 16-bit positive integer. The following table shows a list of ports along with the processes they can possess with supported services:

Port Number	Process Name	Protocol	Description
20	FTP-DATA	TCP	File transfer – data
21	FTP	TCP	File transfer – control
22	SSH	TCP	Secure shell
23	TELNET	TCP	Telnet
25	SMTP	TCP	Simple Mail Transfer Protocol
53	DNS	TCP and UDP	Domain Name System
69	TFTP	UDP	Trivial File Transfer Protocol
80	HTTP	TCP and UDP	Hypertext Transfer Protocol
110	POP3	TCP	Post Office Protocol 3
123	NTP	TCP	Network Time Protocol
143	IMAP	TCP	Internet Message Access Protocol
443	HTTPS	TCP	Secure implementation of HTTP

Apart from these, any application- or user-defined service that is greater than 1024 will be able to consume a port.

When we send an e-mail to someone, how do we ensure that the e-mail will reach the recipient correctly? The answer is through the e-mail address, right? On the same lines, when a computer wants to talk to another computer, how does it ensure it's talking to the right one? The answer is through the IP address. Once the right computer is located, then which process to connect to is decided at the port number level.

An IP address can be defined as a numerical label assigned to every device (for example, a computer or printer) on a computer network that makes use of IP for communication. It serves two purposes: host or network interface identification and location addressing. Refer to the following figure:

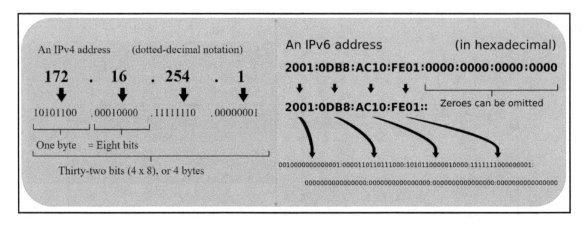

Two versions of IP are in use currently: IP Version 4 and IP Version 6. The IPv4 assignment started in 1980 and was 32 bits with a maximum limit of up to 4,294,967,296. However, due to heavy demand, IPv4 ran out on February 3, 2011, except for some small amounts of address spaces reserved until its transition to another system.

In 1995, IPv6 (the newer system) was devised, during the process of finding advanced technologies and improved mechanisms to generate an internet address, by **Internet Engineering Task Force (IETF)**. The 32-bit address size was increased to 128 in IPv6, and this seemed sufficient for the foreseeable future.

With the evolution of more networks that did not depend on preassigned identification-numbered networks, the early methods of host numbering proved to be insufficient in the case of internet addresses. In 1981, a classful internet network architect was introduced to replace the internet address mechanism, which changed the way of addressing. This network design permitted you to assign a higher number of separate network numbers in addition to the improved subnet designing.

Network Bits	Subnet Mask	Bits Borrowed	Subnets	Hosts/Subnet
24	**255.255.255.0**	0	**1**	**254**
25	255.255.255.128	1	2	126
26	255.255.255.192	2	4	62
27	255.255.255.224	3	8	30
28	255.255.255.240	4	16	14
29	255.255.255.248	5	32	6
30	255.255.255.252	6	64	2

Network and host separation can be observed in an IP address through either the subnet or CIDR prefix. IPv4 uses the subnet mask terminology, whereas the CIDR representation is used by both IPv4 and IPv6. This representation of an IP address is denoted with a slash followed by a number in its decimal position (bits). This representation of the network parts is denoted as the routing prefix. A sample value of the IPv4 address and the corresponding subnet mask are 192.0.2.1 and 255.255.255.0, respectively.

You may have noticed that every computer generally has a hostname and a numeric IP address. Both of these form the unique identifier of that computer in fully qualified form. For example, the URL of Google's home page is www.google.com and its IP address is 74.125.200.147, so you can access Google using both of these over an IP network. The identity of any computing device on a network is referred to as **Domain Name Services (DNS)**; it's a name and an alias for the IP address. In Java, an IP address is represented by the InetAddress class. Using the getHostName() method of this class, one can get the hostname; also, the getAddress() method provides the numeric address.

Sockets and streams

In distributed computing, network communication is one of the essential parts of any system, and the socket is the endpoint of every instance of network communication. In Java communication, it is the most critical and basic object involved. You may have seen browsers connect and communicate with the server through URLs over an HTTP protocol. Now, this is a high-level connection mechanism for accessing resources over the internet using **URL** and **URLConnection**. However, when huge amounts of data need to be exchanged in a secure way, then this method is not as performant as low-level data exchange. The reason is that every URL works on character streams, whereas low-level data exchange supports raw binary data exchange. Also, character streams are easy to hack and they pose security threats as the data is readable; you have to deploy heavy security frameworks to maintain the security standards. Sockets cater to low-level communication through which you can exchange binary data with other machines; the best example of this is either a client-server application or web server/app server communication.

Next to sockets, we have streams. It is through streams that data is passed in a defined sequence over the network. In this section, we will go through both sockets and streams in detail.

A socket is a handle that a local program can pass to the networking API to connect to another machine. It can be defined as *the terminal of a communication link through which two programs/processes/threads running on the network can communicate with each other. The TCP layer can easily identify the application location and access information through the port number assigned to the respective sockets.*

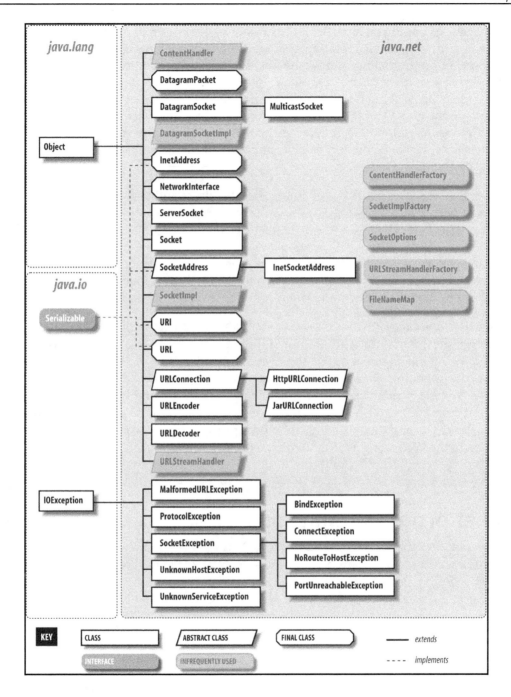

Any application running on a particular operating system can rely on the socket API supported by the respective operating system; this ensures seamless access and control over network socket programming. Across the internet, the socket programming API is, in general, *Berkeley-sockets-standard*-compliant. As per the standards defined by Berkeley sockets, sockets are nothing but a way of defining the description of a file (or can be treated as a handle to the file). Operations across sockets and files are observed to be quite similar (read/write/open/close). But, in general, they are treated quite differently, and people prefer to use interfaces, such as send and receive, on a socket. An internet socket is characterized by the following:

- A local socket address containing the IP address and port number
- A transport protocol, for example, TCP, UDP, and raw IP; this means that TCP port 53 and UDP port 53 are distinct sockets

During an instance of communication, a client program creates a socket at its end and tries to connect it to the socket on the server. When the connection is made, the server creates a socket at its end and then server and client communication is established.

The java.net package provides classes to facilitate the functionalities required for networking. The socket class programmed through Java using this package has the capacity of being independent of the platform of execution; also, it abstracts the calls specific to the operating system on which it is invoked from other Java interfaces. The ServerSocket class offers to observe connection invocations, and it accepts such invocations from different clients through another socket. High-level wrapper classes, such as URLConnection and URLEncoder, are more appropriate. If you want to establish a connection to the Web using a URL, then note that these classes will use the socket internally.

Socket programming for TCP

The java.net.Socket class represents a socket, and the java.net.ServerSocket class represents a server socket through which the server can listen to client sockets and establish a connection with them:

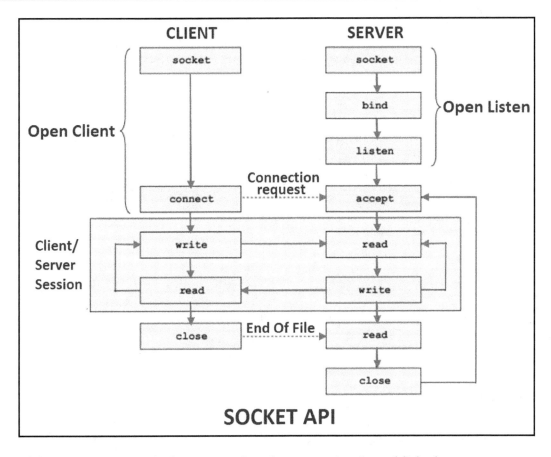

The following are the steps that occur when the connection is established:

1. The `ServerSocket` object is instantiated by the server with a port number for communication:

   ```
   ServerSocket server = new ServerSocket( PORT );
   ```

2. The server calls the `accept()` method of `ServerSocket` and waits until the client connects to a given port. This is called server listening on a given port:

   ```
   Socket serverclient = server.accept();
   ```

3. After this, the client instantiates `Socket` with the server IP address and port number:

   ```
   Socket client = new Socket(server, portid);
   ```

4. Then, the constructor of the `Socket` object tries to connect to the client with the server on a given port number. On successful connection, **CLIENT** has the `Socket` object through which it can communicate with **SERVER**.

5. The `accept()` method of the `ServerSocket` object on the server side returns a reference to new `Socket`, which is connected to the client's socket.

6. Once connected, the communication occurs through Java I/O streams; each socket has both OutputStream and InputStream. The server's `java.io.OutputStream` communicates with the client's `InputStream` string and vice versa. As said earlier, in TCP, data flows in both directions at the same time:

    ```
    DataInputStream ips = new
    DataInputStream(client.getInputStream());
    DataOutputStream ops = new
    DataOutputStream(client.getOutputStream());

    Client receive: String line = is.readLine();
    Client send: os.writeBytes("Hello World!n");
    ```

7. Close the socket when the data exchange is complete:

    ```
    client.close();
    ```

Reading from the socket

Now, let's check out an example where we will establish a connection to the server with the help of a socket. This will demonstrate how data can be sent and received between the client and the server. The following example is a server application making use of the `Socket` class to listen to clients on a port number specified by a command-line argument:

```
//Socket Server

import java.io.DataOutputStream;
import java.io.IOException;
import java.io.OutputStream;
import java.net.ServerSocket;
import java.net.Socket;
public class SimpleSocketServer {
  public static void main(String args[]) throws IOException {
    // A new service registered with the 1286 port
    ServerSocket ss = new ServerSocket(1286);
    //Accept the connection request made with the server socket
    Socket s=ss.accept();
    // Establish the output stream from the socket connection
```

```
OutputStream socketOutStream = s.getOutputStream();
DataOutputStream socketDOS = new DataOutputStream
(socketOutStream);
// Communicate with the socket data stream with a message
socketDOS.writeUTF("Hello world!");
// Cleanup
socketDOS.close();
socketOutStream.close();
s.close();
ss.close();
    }
}
```

In the preceding code, we have the `SimpleSocketServer` class when the main method constructor is invoked. This is where `ServerSocket` is instantiated with the given port. Further, when the thread starts, the `serverSocket.accept()` method is invoked and the server starts listening for requests on the given port. After that, when the client sends the request, the server responds and returns the response string to that call.

The following code is a `SimpleSocketClient` program that connects to `SimpleSocketServer`. Using the socket, send the test string and then wait for a response from the server that will contain the test string:

```
//Socket Client

import java.io.DataInputStream;
import java.io.IOException;
import java.io.InputStream;
import java.net.Socket;
public class SimpleSocketClient {
  public static void main(String args[]) throws IOException {
    // Establish a server connection through 1286 port
    Socket s = new Socket("localhost",1286);
    // Access the input stream of the server socket
    InputStream sIn = s.getInputStream();
    // Wrap the socket input stream with data input stream
    DataInputStream socketDIS = new DataInputStream(sIn);
    //Read from the socket data input stream
    String testString= new String (socketDIS.readUTF());
    //Print the data read
    System.out.println(testString);
    // clean up
    socketDIS.close();
    sIn.close();
    s.close();
  }
}
```

Using the `SimpleSocketClient` code, you can instantiate `Socket()` for a given server and port and also establish a connection. After that, the `InputStream` test string is read from the server socket.

Socket programming for UDP

Java supports both TCP and UDP through the `Socket` and `DatagramSocket` classes from the `java.net` package. Other components of this package foster communication between processes over the network using an IP address. A new `socket` object can be instantiated through the socket name or InetAddress and the port on which the process is running on the host.

As seen earlier, TCP is considered consistent in terms of receiving data in packets the same order as they are sent and with guaranteed delivery. If the next packet is not received in a defined period of time, then the receiver requests it again. The receiver keeps waiting until the packet is received and doesn't move further. In the UDP protocol, it's the other way round: it doesn't guarantee delivery of packets and doesn't even care about the order in which packets are received. UDP is used only when the entire information can be bundled into a single packet and there is no dependency on the other packet. Therefore, the usage of UDP is quite limited, whereas TCP is widely used in IP applications. UDP sockets are used where limited bandwidth is available, and the overhead associated with resending packets is not acceptable.

To connect using a UDP socket on a specific port, use the following code:

```
DatagramSocket udpSock = new DatagramSocket(3000);
```

If you don't care about the port number, then the default constructor can also be used for instantiation. In that case, an unused port will be used. We can find which port is used by referring to the following code:

```
int portNo = udpSock.getLocalPort();
```

A datagram is a self-contained, independent message whose time of arrival, confirmation of arrival over the network, and content cannot be guaranteed.

`DatagramPacket` objects are used to send data over `DatagramSocket`. Every `DatagramPacket` object consists of a data buffer, a remote host to whom the data needs to be sent, and a port number on which the remote agent would be listened. Here's sample code for doing this:

```
byte[] dataBuff = {'a', 'k', ' ', 'v', 'w', 'x', 'p', 'e'};
InetAddress inetAddr = InetAddress.getByName("www.google.com");
```

```
DatagramPacket dgPkt = new DatagramPacket(dataBuff, dataBuff.length,
inetAddr, 5100);
udpSock.send(dgPkt);
```

By invoking the `receive()` method on `DatagramSocket`, a remote process can receive data. `DatagramSocket` received by the remote process has the host address, port number, and the buffered data.

As a good programming practice, one should do proper exception handling while establishing a connection and sending/receiving data (for example, `IOException` could be thrown while you perform read and write operations to streams).

The following example is a program of the UDP server that accepts the request from the client, receives the data from the client as a datagram, and responds with the server response:

```
//UDP Server

import java.io.IOException;
import java.net.DatagramPacket;
import java.net.DatagramSocket;
import java.net.SocketException;

public class SimpleUDPServer {
  public static void main(String args[]) {
    DatagramSocket dgSocket = null;
    if (args.length <= 0) {
      System.out.println("Please pass the port number for UDPServer");
      // exit the program if no port number passed
      System.exit(1);
    }
    try {
      int socketNumber = Integer.valueOf(args[0]).intValue();
      dgSocket = new DatagramSocket(socketNumber);
      byte[] byteBuffer = new byte[1000];
      while (true) {
        DatagramPacket dgRequest = new DatagramPacket(
        byteBuffer, byteBuffer.length);
        dgSocket.receive(dgRequest);
        DatagramPacket dgresponse = new DatagramPacket(
        dgRequest.getData(), dgRequest.getLength(),
        dgRequest.getAddress(), dgRequest.getPort());
        dgSocket.send(dgresponse);
      }
    } catch (SocketException e) {
      System.out.println("Socket Exception : " + e.getMessage());
    } catch (IOException e) {
```

```
        System.out.println("IO Exception : " + e.getMessage());
      } finally {
        if (dgSocket != null)
        dgSocket.close();
      }
    }
  }
```

The following client program is used to create a datagram, send it to the preceding server program (in the server), and receive the response:

```
//UDP Client

import java.io.IOException;
import java.net.DatagramPacket;
import java.net.DatagramSocket;
import java.net.InetAddress;
import java.net.SocketException;

public class SimpleUDPClient {
  public static void main(String args[]){
    // pass the message, server host and port number as arguments
    DatagramSocket dgSocket = null;
    if (args.length < 3) {
      System.out.println(
        " Pass the arguments for SimpleUDPClient in the order :
        test message,
        Server Host name and Port number respectively");
      System.exit(1);
    }
    try {
      dgSocket = new DatagramSocket();
      byte [] bytes = args[0].getBytes();
      InetAddress serverHost = InetAddress.getByName(args[1]);
      int serverPortNumber = Integer.valueOf(args[2]).intValue();
      DatagramPacket dgRequest =
      new DatagramPacket(bytes, args[0].length(), serverHost,
      serverPortNumber);
      dgSocket.send(dgRequest);
      byte[] byteBuffer = new byte[1000];
      DatagramPacket dgResponse = new DatagramPacket
      (byteBuffer, byteBuffer.length);
      dgSocket.receive(dgResponse);
      System.out.println("Datagram Response: " +
      new String(dgResponse.getData()));
    }
    catch (SocketException e) {
      System.out.println("Socket Exception: " + e.getMessage());
```

```
      }
      catch (IOException e) {
        System.out.println("IO Exception : " + e.getMessage());
      }
      finally {
        if (dgSocket != null)
        dgSocket.close();
      }
    }
  }
}
```

Multicasting

In the previous sections, we learned how to establish a connection and exchange data between one machine and another; this is known as point-to-point communication. But, what if we want to broadcast data over the network to multiple clients? In that case, a subset of the OP protocol that supports multicasting comes in handy.

To broadcast over multicast IP addresses using multicasting, UDP packets are used. Any client listening to a broadcasting IP will receive a broadcasted data packet. A good example of multicasting is broadcasting a video as well as audio of special events over the internet.

Using the `java.net.MulticastSocket` class, multicasting is possible. This class is an extension of the `DatagramSocket` class. Any class can create a `MulticastSocket` object and invoke the `joinGroup()` method to be able to join the specific multicasted session, as shown in the following code:

```
MulticastSocket soc = new MulticastSocket(1400);
InetAddress grp = InetAddress.getByName("172.0.114.0");
soc.joinGroup(grp);
```

After the connection with the multicast session is established, the multicast channel will provide the broadcasted data that can be read by the program:

```
DatagramPacket pkt;
for (int i = 0; i < 5; i++) {
  byte[] buff = new byte[256];
  pkt = new DatagramPacket(buff, buff.length);
  soc.receive(pkt);
  String rcvdString = new String(pkt.getData());
  System.out.println("Quote: " + rcvdString);
}
```

Using the `leaveGroup()` method, one can disconnect from the session after the broadcast is completed or whenever one is willing to stop the multicast, as follows:

```
soc.leaveGroup(grp);
soc.close();
```

Using the `thesend()` method of MulticastSocket, data can be sent to other listening threads on the multicast channel.

Other examples where multicasting can be used are shareable whiteboards, synchronization tasks between application servers, and load balancing. Since a multicast IP is generally UDP-based, one should be ready for the possibility of losing partial/full data and deal with it gracefully. Also, if a client possesses the capacity to synchronize itself to the ongoing multicast at any time it wants to join, they can choose to join the multicast session at different points of time.

Streams

As we have seen, once a connection is established with the remote machine, data gets exchanged in the form of binary streams. To access binary data, the `java.io` package provides two basic types of classes: one for incoming and other for outgoing data, namely `java.io.InputStream` and `java.io.OutputStream`, respectively. Both InputStream and OutputStream support communication through bytes and expose the methods to read or write the information in the form of bytes or byte array. They have many subclasses meant for writing to different destinations and reading from different sources (for example, string buffers and files). But, if we want to send character data (16-bit), then one has to go for the `java.io.Reader` and `java.io.Writer` classes. They also have multiple subclasses specialized for different conditions. The class hierarchy of Java streams is shown in the following screenshot:

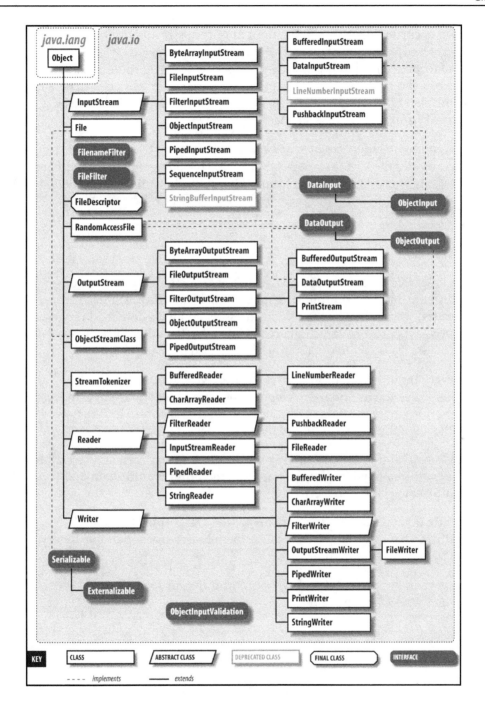

Once a socket is created, we can get the input or output streams from it using the `getInputStream()` or `getOutputStream()` methods, respectively; they return an instance of OutputStream and InputStream, respectively. If we choose to interact with the applications based on the character stream, then InputStream will need to be wrapped in **InputStreamReader** (the reader's subclass) and OutputStream will need to be wrapped in **OutputStreamWriter** (the writer's subclass).

Interprocess communication can also be established through the `java.lang.Runtime` interface. It provides the `Process` object that can be used to get both the input and output streams. This can be used to execute a local native subtask. Here's sample code of this:

```
Runtime rt1 = Runtime.getRuntime();
Process proc = rt1.exec("/usr/local/bin/performTask.sh");
InputStream in = proc.getInputStream();
OutputStream out = proc.getOutputStream();
```

If you want to transform data or provide additional functionality, then you can use **FilterInputStream** and **FilterOuputStream**. Using **BufferedInputStream** or **BufferedReader,** we can reduce the overhead associated with data read requests and also reduce latency as it performs large data reads into a buffer. Alternatively, we can use the `ProcessBuilder` class API to obtain InputStream and OutputStream.

Using **PushbackInputStream** or **PushbackReader,** we can push the data back to the stage where it will receive the information stream. This type of read-and-parse mechanism really helps in scenarios where the data of one level of the tree is parsed and reviewed to figure out the next level of the tree structure of the data reading process.

If you want to read and write information in the portal binary format, use **DataInputStream** and **DataOutputStream**, which are subclasses of the **FilterInputStream** and **FilterOutputStream** classes, respectively.

FilterInputStream and **FilterOutputStream** are the **DataInputStream** and **DataOutputStream** classes, respectively. Use them to transform portable binary data that can be used by any other system.

Different classes in the `java.io` package support different sources/destinations of data; they are given in the following table:

	Byte Based		Character Based	
	Input	**Output**	**Input (Reader)**	**Output (Writer)**
Arrays	ByteArrayInputStream	ByteArrayOutputStream	CharArrayReader	CharArrayWriter
Files	FileInputStream RandomAccessFile	FileOutputStream RandomAccessFile	FileReader	FileWriter
Pipes	PipedInputStream	PipedOutputStream	PipedReader	PipedWriter
Buffering	BufferedInputStream	BufferedOutputStream	BufferedReader	BufferedWriter
Filtering	FilterInputStream	FilterOutputStream	FilterReader	FilterWriter
Parsing	PushbackInputStream StreamTokenizer		PushbackReader LineNumberReader	
Strings			StringReader	StringWriter
Data	DataInputStream	DataOutputStream		
Data - Formatted		PrintStream		PrintWriter
Objects	ObjectInputStream	ObjectOutputStream		
Utilities	SequenceInputStream			

PipedInputStream is capable of reading data from **PipedOutputStream**, and **PipedOutputStream** is capable of writing data to **PipedInputStream**. Generally, a piped input stream and piped output stream are connected. **PipedInputStream** writes data bytes to **PipedOutputStream**. Typically, one thread reads data from **PipedInputStream**, and another thread writes data to **PipedOutputStream**. If both are required, having activities done from a single thread is not recommended, as it may lead to performance bottlenecks. **PipedInputStream** has a buffer that decouples the read operation from the write operation to a certain extent. If a thread that provides data bytes is no longer alive, then the pipe is called broken:

```
//Piped Server

import java.io.DataInputStream;
import java.io.DataOutputStream;
import java.io.IOException;
import java.io.PipedInputStream;
import java.io.PipedOutputStream;
public class SimplePipedServer extends Thread
{
```

```java
PipedInputStream pipeIn;
PipedOutputStream pipeOut;
public SimplePipedServer(PipedInputStream pipeIn,
PipedOutputStream pipeOut)
{
  this.pipeIn = pipeIn;
  this.pipeOut = pipeOut;
}
@SuppressWarnings("deprecation")
public void run()
{
  // Wrap piped input and output streams with
  // data input and output streams
  DataInputStream dataIn = new DataInputStream(pipeIn);
  DataOutputStream dataOut = new DataOutputStream(pipeOut);
  // Accept the client communication
  try
  {
     System.out.println("SimplePipedServer:
     Reading message from client : ");

     String clientMessage = dataIn.readUTF();
     System.out.println("SimplePipedServer:
     Client message: " + clientMessage);
  }
  catch (IOException ex)
  {
    System.out.println("SimplePipedServer: IO Exception :
    Couldn't read the
    message from the client.");
    stop();
  }
  try
  {
    System.out.println("SimplePipedServer:
    Writing response to the client : ");
    dataOut.writeChars("Message from the server.n");
  }
  catch (IOException ex)
  {
    System.out.println("SimplePipedServer: IO Exception :
    Failed to connect to client.");
  }
  stop();
  }
}
```

The following piped client program corresponds to the preceding server program:

```
//Piped Client

import java.io.DataInputStream;
import java.io.DataOutputStream;
import java.io.IOException;
import java.io.PipedInputStream;
import java.io.PipedOutputStream;
public class SimplePipedClient extends Thread {
  PipedInputStream pipeIn;
  PipedOutputStream pipeOut;
  public SimplePipedClient(PipedInputStream pipeIn,
  PipedOutputStream pipeOut) {
    this.pipeIn = pipeIn;
    this.pipeOut = pipeOut;
  }
  @SuppressWarnings("deprecation")
  public void run() {
    DataInputStream dataIn = new DataInputStream(pipeIn);
    DataOutputStream dataOut = new DataOutputStream(pipeOut);
    try {
      System.out.println("SimplePipedClient:
      Writing message to the server : ");
      dataOut.writeChars("Message from the
      SimplePipedClient to the Servern");
    } catch (IOException ex) {
      System.out.println("SimplePipedClient: IOException :
      Couldn't get the response from the server.");
      System.exit(1);
    }
    // Server responds
    try {
      System.out.println("SimplePipedClient:
      Reading response from the server : ");
      String response = dataIn.readUTF();
      System.out.println("SimplePipedClient: Server response : "
      + response);
    } catch (IOException e) {
      System.out.println("SimplePipedClient: IO Exception :
      Failed to connect to peer.");
    }

    stop();
  }
}
```

A similar program with PipeStream is given as follows:

```
//PipeStream Sample

import java.io.IOException;
import java.io.PipedInputStream;
import java.io.PipedOutputStream;
public class SimplePipeStream {
  public static void main(String[] args) throws IOException {
    final PipedOutputStream pipedOut = new PipedOutputStream();
    final PipedInputStream pipedIn = new PipedInputStream(pipedOut);
    Thread threadOne = new Thread(new Runnable() {
      @Override
      public void run() {
        try {
          pipedOut.write("Hello world, pipe!".getBytes());
        } catch (IOException e) {
        }
      }
    });
    Thread threadTwo = new Thread(new Runnable() {
      @Override
      public void run() {
        try {
          int pipedData = pipedIn.read();
          while(pipedData != -1){
            System.out.print((char) pipedData);
            pipedData = pipedIn.read();
          }
        } catch (IOException e) {
        }
      }
    });
    threadOne.start();
    threadTwo.start();
  }
}
```

URLs, URLConnections, and the ContentHandler classes

While surfing the internet, we use URLs extensively. As a result, many of us perceive URL as the names of files located on the WWW, but that is not true; a URL could also point to other resources on a network, such as a database query or command output and so on.

A URL can be defined as *an acronym for Uniform Resource Locator and is a reference (an address) to a resource on the internet.*

Every URL has two main components: a protocol identifier and resource name. Suppose we have `http://www.google.com`; in this case, HTTP is the protocol identifier and `www.google.com` is the resource name. They are joined together with a colon (:) followed by two slashes (//), as shown in the following screenshot:

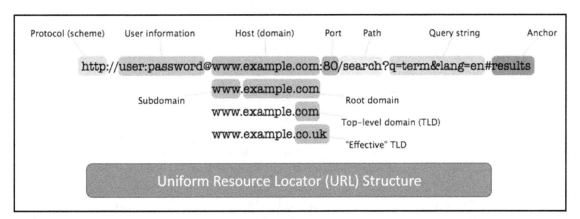

Protocols could be of many types, such as HTTP, HTTPS, file, gopher, FTP, and news. Here, the resource name represents the full address of the resource and contains the hostname, filename, port number, and reference. In many URLs, you might have seen that the hostname is mandatory, whereas the filename, port number, and reference are optional.

URL can be constructed in Java using the following syntax; note that URL addresses are passed in the form of a string to the URL class constructor:

```
URL urlHandle = new URL("http://example.com/");
```

The URL shown in the preceding code is the absolute URL where all the details are given. In addition to this, URLs could be relative to some already existing URL, as shown in the following example:

```
URL urlHandle = new URL("http://example.com/pages/");
URL firstPage = new URL(urlHandle, "page1.html");
```

URL (base URL and relative URL)

Every constructor looks for the base URL, and if its value is null, then it considers the relative URL as the absolute URL. Also, you can use a relative URL for creating URL objects for named anchors. There are other URL constructors available in which you can pass all the four preceding components given separately. If a URL contains any special character, then such URLs can get encoded first so that the address gets validated as the legal address; then, they are passed to the URL constructor (for example, the space character is encoded as %20).

While constructing a URL object, if the URL string passed to the constructor is *null* or is an unknown protocol, then it throws **MalformedURLException**. Therefore, one should handle this kind of exception without fail while building the URL.

The URL object helps the user to either connect, access, or download any of the URL-related pages containing information from that respective web server. To do so, the URL object has methods such as openStream(), getContent(), and openConnection(). The openStream() method returns a java.io.InputStream that is capable of reading the data contents directly. When openConnection() is called on a URL object, it provides URLConnection in return. URLConnection can be used to query the header information of the data to get the length of the data object, the data type it contains, the encoding of data, and so on.

The getContent() method downloads the data object and returns the data-containing object. This method has a content handler that can convert data into a Java object. When we invoke the getContent() method of the URLConnection or URL object, it queries *ContentHandlerFactory* for *ContentHandler* to request the information from the requestor. The responsibility of *ContentHandlerFactory* is to validate MIMEType along with the encoding of DataObject to supply the ContentHandler belonging to that MIMEType.

The returned *ContentHandler* is then used to get an object that represents the data by invoking its getContent() method with URLConnection. ContentHandler reads raw data provided through InputStream of URLConnection, then it formats it to the required object representations and returns the object to the caller.

Practicality of URLs

When we communicate over sockets, we don't know what type of data format we are dealing with. This may be an issue in a client-server environment where clients are not aware of the kind of data server that would be broadcasted. In this case, either both the parties should be in agreement about the kind of data that will be used for communication, or we should establish our own way of communicating metadata along with primary data that will tell the data type of primary data.

Using Java's classes for HTTP support makes it possible to serve and access data objects with ease in regard to knowing their type and format. To make a document available on a URL, we can deploy the document on the web server along with the respective MIMEType configuration. URLConnection is used to request the URL from any specific client. However, there are issues with this method, which we will discuss next.

First, it adds a lot of overhead to the data stream that leads to bandwidth reduction between communicating systems. The second issue is that the entire data should be serializable to send it over HTTP. The third issue is with respect to the resource naming that HTTP is going to provide, as LDAP and NIS follow the formal naming procedure.

Therefore, we can conclude that for distributed applications where bandwidth is severely limited or where support for complicated resource hierarchies is required, the use of an HTTP protocol is not recommended. Whereas, if you have some extra bandwidth for communication and the performance requirements are not that critical and are relatively simple resource groupings, then the data can be accessed using URLs.

ClassLoader

Java Runtime Environment executes platform-independent bytecodes for classes. Using a Java API, you can instantiate and load a class from its bytecode and integrate it with the runtime environment. When we compile Java files and when import statements are encountered, referenced classes or packages are loaded from bytecode files available in the classpath located in the local filesystem.

The ClassLoader class allows programmers to run the class load from the location. The ClassLoader subclasses should implement the loadClass() method to be able to locate and load the bytecodes for that class definition and, sometimes, find all the other classes on which this class is dependent (the resolving class) only after that class is constructed.

In distributed computing, ClassLoader plays an important role when data is exchanged in binary form. An example of this is an applet running on the browser. Unlike CORBA/RMI, you can use the ClassLoader client to convert incoming bytecode into an object containing data. Thus, using `java.io.InputStream`, you can transport instantiated class objects over the network and ClassLoader will convert them back into the data-containing object at the client side.

In the following example, the abstract `StreamClassLoader` class allows you to load a class from a given location using the simple `InputStream` by altering the `ClassLoader.loadClass()` method argument's semantics:

```
//StreamClassLoader

import java.io.IOException;
import java.io.InputStream;
import java.util.Hashtable;

public abstract class StreamClassLoader extends ClassLoader {
   Hashtable<String, Class<?>> componentCache =
   new Hashtable<String, Class<?>>();
   InputStream source = null;
   public StreamClassLoader() {
   }
   protected abstract String parseComponentNaming(
   String componentLocation) throws ClassNotFoundException;
   protected abstract void initializeStream(
   String componentLocation) throws IOException;
   protected abstract Class<?> readComponent(
   String componentLocation, String componentName)
   throws IOException, ClassNotFoundException;
   public Class<?> loadComponent(String componentLocation,
   boolean resolve) throws ClassNotFoundException {
     String componentName = parseComponentNaming(componentLocation);
     Class<?> component = (Class<?>) componentCache.get(componentName);
     if (component == null) {
       try {
         initializeStream(componentLocation);
       } catch (IOException e) {
         throw new ClassNotFoundException(
         "Failed opening stream to URL.");
       }
       try {
         component = readComponent(componentLocation, componentName);
       } catch (IOException e) {
         throw new ClassNotFoundException(
         "Failed reading class component from the stream: " + e);
       }
```

```
      }
      componentCache.put(componentName, component);
      if (resolve)
      resolveClass(component);
      return component;
    }
  }
```

The `URLClassLoader` class that extends `StreamClassLoader` parses the URL through stream loading:

//URLClassLoader

```
import java.io.DataInputStream;
import java.io.IOException;
import java.io.InputStream;
import java.net.MalformedURLException;
import java.net.URL;
import java.net.URLConnection;

public class URLClassLoader extends StreamClassLoader {
  URL urlClass = null;
  InputStream streamClass = null;

  @Override
  protected String parseComponentNaming(String componentLocation)
  throws ClassNotFoundException {

    String componentName = null;
    try {
      urlClass = new URL(componentLocation);
    } catch (MalformedURLException e) {
      throw new ClassNotFoundException("Bad URL " +
      componentLocation + " given: " + e);
    }
    System.out.println("File = " + urlClass.getFile());
    System.out.println("Host = " + urlClass.getHost());
    String filenameFromURL = urlClass.getFile();
    if (!filenameFromURL.endsWith(".class"))
    throw new ClassNotFoundException("Non-class URL given.");
    else
    componentName = filenameFromURL.substring(
    0, filenameFromURL.lastIndexOf(".class"));
    System.out.println("Classname = " + componentName);
    return componentName;

  }
```

```
@Override
protected void initializeStream(String componentLocation)
throws IOException {
  streamClass = urlClass.openStream();
}

@Override
protected Class<?> readComponent(String componentLocation,
String componentName)
throws IOException, ClassNotFoundException {
  URLConnection urlConn = urlClass.openConnection();
  int componentSize = urlConn.getContentLength();
  System.out.println("Class file is " + componentSize + " bytes.");
  DataInputStream dataInClass = new DataInputStream(streamClass);
  int isAvailable = dataInClass.available();
  System.out.println("Available = " + isAvailable);
  System.out.println("URLClassLoader: Reading class from stream...");
  byte[] clsData = new byte[componentSize];
  dataInClass.readFully(clsData);
  Class<?> component = null;
  System.out.println("URLClassLoader: Defining class...");
  try {
    component = defineClass(null,clsData, 0, clsData.length);
  } catch (ClassFormatError e) {
    throw new ClassNotFoundException(
    "Format error found in class data.");
  }
  return component;
}
}
```

Summary

In this chapter, you learned about client-server communication through different protocols and sockets; you also learned about Java support through the socket API for TCP and UDP programming. Then we discussed different data streams and Java API for supporting read/write content from different streams. We finished this chapter with an overview of URLs--base and relative URLs--and the ContentHandler and ClassLoader concepts.

In the next chapter, you will learn about CORBA and how it contributes to distributed computing and demonstrates the Java space support for such a programming model in detail.

3
RMI, CORBA, and JavaSpaces

Distributed computing has gotten stronger than before as it now provides the ability to handle communication over a network with distributed objects. Though there are a number of different ways to create distributed objects across a distributed network, distributed computing is preferred as it provides you the ability to access any component in a distributed system. In this system, the number of resources and the way to access them has enriched with the use of technologies that let you handle distributed objects effectively. The protocol through which these objects can be communicated is an essential concept to understand.

In this chapter, we will cover the following topics:

- Remote Method Invocation (RMI)
- What is RMI?
- Key terminologies of RMI
- RMI for distributed computing
- RMI programming

- Common Object Request Broker Architecture (CORBA)
- CORBA standards
- Inter-ORB communication
- OMG IDL samples
- CORBA services
- CORBA programming

- JavaSpaces
- How Java 9 adds value

Let's start our discussion with RMI. This is where we will establish interaction between applications as per the concept of remotely deployed Java applications.

RMI

When it comes to meeting high-performance system expectations, message-driven systems provide quite a few features; however, they have certain limitations. Remote-object-based systems have been considered an alternative for message-based systems for a while; however, the latest message-based-system implementation has improved in this regard.

What is RMI?

RMI is a Java-specific object-oriented extension of the **Remote Procedure Call** (**RPC**). It provides a mechanism to create Java-based distributed applications. It allows an object in one **Java Virtual Machine** (**JVM**) to interact with the object in another JVM by invoking the methods in that object. This is why an application built with an RMI is considered an application that could run across multiple JVMs.

RMI provides communication between applications that are deployed on different servers and connected remotely using objects called **stub** and **skeleton**. This communication architecture makes a distributed application seem like a group of objects communicating across a remote connection. These objects are encapsulated by exposing an interface, which helps access the private state and behavior of an object through its methods.

The following diagram shows how RMI happens between the RMI client and RMI server with the help of the RMI registry:

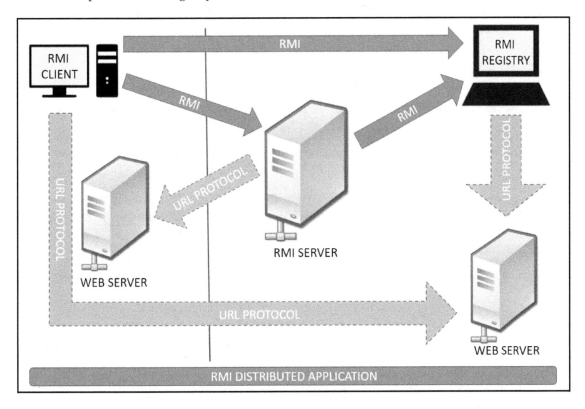

RMI REGISTRY is a remote object registry, a Bootstrap naming service, that is used by **RMI SERVER** on the same host to bind remote objects to names. Clients on local and remote hosts then look up the remote objects and make remote method invocations.

The following are some of the design considerations of applications built with an RMI:

- Seamless method invocation on objects created across multiple JVMs
- Ensuring the remote method invocation integrates easily with general programming logic with no external IDL while retaining most of Java's object semantics
- Setting up the ability to distinguish between a distributed and local object model
- Assisting in building reliable applications while maintaining Java's safety and security
- Extending support to multiple transport protocols, various reference semantics, such as persistence and lazy activation, and various invocation mechanisms

- Handling issues such as running in different memory spaces, parameter passing, data binding, and other failures of RPC
- Handling any additional problems, such as distributed garbage collection and distributed class loading

Key terminologies of RMI

The following are some of the important terminologies used in a Remote Method Invocation.

Remote object: This is an object in a specific JVM whose methods are exposed so they could be invoked by another program deployed on a different JVM.

Remote interface: This is a Java interface that defines the methods that exist in a remote object. A remote object can implement more than one remote interface to adopt multiple remote interface behaviors.

RMI: This is a way of invoking a remote object's methods with the help of a remote interface. It can be carried with a syntax that is similar to the local method invocation.

Stub: This is a Java object that acts as an entry point for the client object to route any outgoing requests. It exists on the client JVM and represents the handle to the remote object. If any object invokes a method on the stub object, the stub establishes RMI by following these steps:

1. It initiates a connection to the remote machine JVM.
2. It marshals (write and transmit) the parameters passed to it via the remote JVM.
3. It waits for a response from the remote object and unmarshals (read) the returned value or exception, then it responds to the caller with that value or exception.

Skeleton: This is an object that behaves like a gateway on the server side. It acts as a remote object with which the client objects interact through the stub. This means that any requests coming from the remote client are routed through it. If the skeleton receives a request, it establishes RMI through these steps:

1. It reads the parameter sent to the remote method.
2. It invokes the actual remote object method.
3. It marshals (writes and transmits) the result back to the caller (stub).

The following diagram demonstrates RMI communication with stub and skeleton involved:

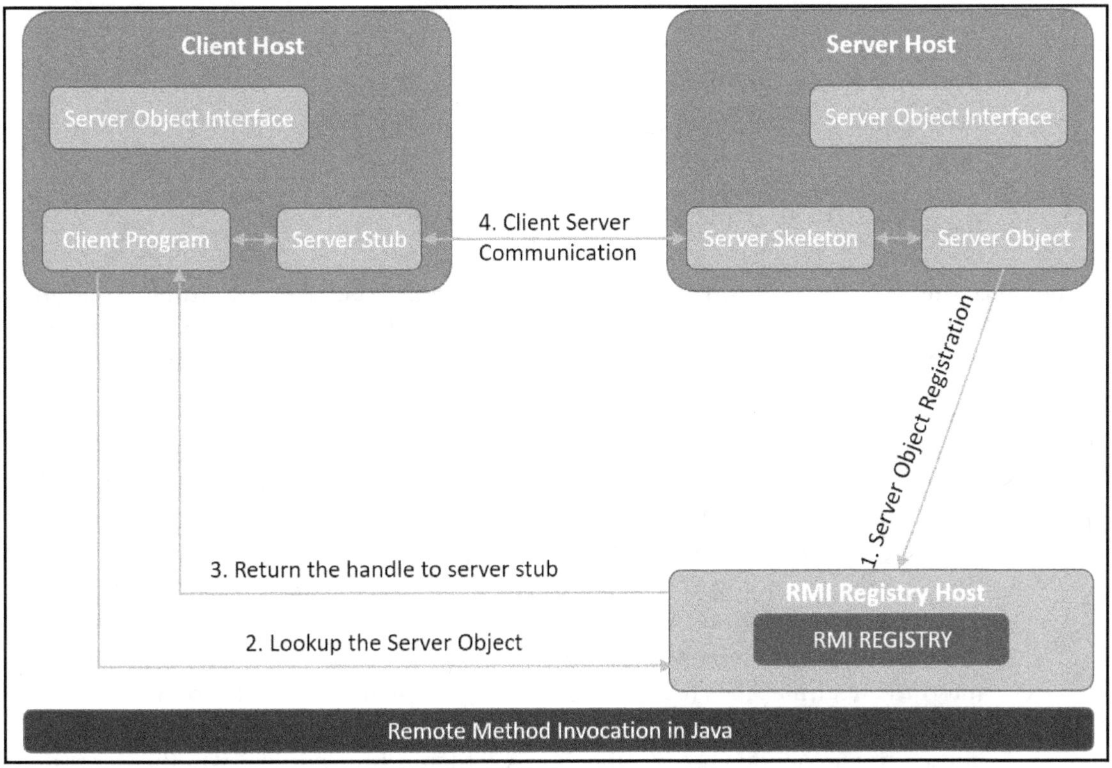

RMI for distributed computing

Remote objects are similar to local objects when it comes to method invocation and returning results from methods. A remote object can be typecasted to any of the remote interfaces supported by its implementation, and the `instanceof` operator can be used to verify the type of remote or local object.

Although the aforementioned similarities exist between remote and local objects, they behave differently. While the clients of remote objects can only interact with remote interfaces, not with implementation classes, the clients of local objects can interact with both the interfaces and implementation classes. RMI is passed by a value, whereas a local method invocation can be passed by a reference. In this context, the mandatory remote exceptions must be defined in a local system.

The essential steps that need to be followed to develop a distributed application with RMI are as follows:

1. Design and implement a component that should not only be involved in the distributed application, but also the local components.
2. Ensure that the components that participate in the RMI calls are accessible across networks.
3. Establish a network connection between applications that need to interact using the RMI.

In the preceding list, the most important step, which needs to be taken carefully, is defining the right architecture in the application with clear distinction between the components that act as Java objects available on a local JVM and ones that are remotely accessible. Let's review the implementation steps in detail:

1. **Remote interface definition**: The purpose of defining a remote interface is to declare the methods that should be available for invocation by a remote client. Programming the interface instead of programming the component implementation is an essential design principle adopted by all modern Java frameworks, including Spring. In the same pattern, the definition of a remote interface takes importance in RMI design as well.
2. **Remote object implementation**: Java allows a class to implement more than one interface at a time. This helps remote objects implement one or more remote interfaces. The remote object class may have to implement other local interfaces and methods that it is responsible for. Avoid adding complexity to this scenario, in terms of how the arguments or return parameter values of such component methods should be written.
3. **Remote client implementation**: Client objects that interact with remote server objects can be written once the remote interfaces are carefully defined even after the remote objects are deployed.

Now let's consider a simple example and how we can implement it to stimulate interaction between multiple JVMs using the Java RMI.

Writing an RMI server

Suppose we are building an application to perform diverse mathematical operations. Let's design a project that can sit on a server. Post this, have different client projects interact with this project to pass the parameters and get the computation on the remote object execute and return the result to the client components. This needs the remote interface to be defined first, as discussed in the preceding section.

The following is the definition of the `Calculate` interface that extends the `Remote` interface:

```
package remote;
import java.rmi.Remote;
import java.rmi.RemoteException;
public interface Calculate extends Remote {
  public long add(long parameterOne, long parameterTwo)
    throws RemoteException;
  public long sub(long parameterOne, long parameterTwo)
    throws RemoteException;
  public long mul(long parameterOne, long parameterTwo)
    throws RemoteException;
  public long div(long parameterOne, long parameterTwo)
    throws RemoteException;
}
```

Implementing a remote interface

The next step you need to take to define the remote interface is this: implement the remote interface by a class that could interact in the RMI. When the remote interface is implemented, the constructor of this remote object needs to invoke the superclass constructor and override all the unimplemented methods.

From the infrastructure setup perspective, we should create and install a security manager, create and export one or more remote objects, and register at least one remote object with the RMI registry or Java naming convention and directory interface for reference.

The following is the `CalculateEngine` class implementing the `Calculate` remote interface:

```
package remote;
import java.rmi.RemoteException;
import java.rmi.server.UnicastRemoteObject;
public class CalculateEngine extends UnicastRemoteObject implements
Calculate {
  private static final long serialVersionUID = 1L;
```

```java
public CalculateEngine() throws RemoteException {
  super();
}
@Override
public long add(long parameterOne, long parameterTwo) throws
RemoteException {
  return parameterOne + parameterTwo;
}
@Override
public long sub(long parameterOne, long parameterTwo) throws
RemoteException {
  return parameterOne - parameterTwo;
}
@Override
public long mul(long parameterOne, long parameterTwo) throws
RemoteException {
  return parameterOne * parameterTwo;
}
@Override
public long div(long parameterOne, long parameterTwo) throws
RemoteException {
  return parameterOne / parameterTwo;
}
}
```

After you define the remote interface and implementation, write the standalone Java program through which you will start the remote server, as follows:

```java
package remote;
import java.rmi.Naming;
import java.rmi.Remote;
public class MyServer implements Remote{
  public static void main(String[] args) {
    if (System.getSecurityManager() == null) {
      System.setSecurityManager(new SecurityManager());
    }
    try {
      Naming.rebind("rmi://localhost:5000/calculate",new
      CalculateEngine());
      System.out.println("CalculateEngine bound");
    }
    catch (Exception e) {
      System.err.println("CalculateEngine exception:");
      e.printStackTrace();
    }
  }
}
```

In the preceding program, the `Naming` method `rebind()` is used to bind the remote object with the name. The following is the list of methods `Naming` offers with their description:

Naming method	Description
public static java.rmi.Remote lookup(java.lang.String) throws java.rmi.NotBoundException, java.net.MalformedURLException, java.rmi.RemoteException;	It returns the reference of the remote object.
public static void bind(java.lang.String, java.rmi.Remote) throws java.rmi.AlreadyBoundException, java.net.MalformedURLException, java.rmi.RemoteException;	It binds the remote object with the given name.
public static void unbind(java.lang.String) throws java.rmi.RemoteException, java.rmi.NotBoundException, java.net.MalformedURLException;	It destroys the remote object which is bound with the given name.
public static void rebind(java.lang.String, java.rmi.Remote) throws java.rmi.RemoteException, java.net.MalformedURLException;	It binds the remote object to the new name.
public static java.lang.String[] list(java.lang.String) throws java.rmi.RemoteException, java.net.MalformedURLException;	It returns an array of the names of the remote objects bound in the registry.

Let's review all the steps we have taken to define the remote application:

- We declared the remote interfaces that are being implemented
- We defined a constructor for the remote object
- We provided implementations for each remote method
- We passed the objects in RMI
- We implemented the server's main method
- We created and installed a security manager
- We made the remote object available to the clients

The next step is to generate a client program that would interact with the remote object through the RMI.

Creating a client program

The server program used to perform the calculation is relatively simple compared to the client program, which needs to handle the RMI along with computation calls.

In our example, the client program communicates with the remote program through the remote application naming invocation and by calling the remote interface methods:

```java
package local;
import java.net.MalformedURLException;
import java.rmi.Naming;
import java.rmi.NotBoundException;
import java.rmi.RemoteException;
import remote.Calculate;
public class CalculateClient {
  public static void main(String[] args) {
    try {
      Calculate remoteCalculate = (Calculate)
      Naming.lookup("rmi://localhost:5000/calculate");
      System.out.println("Remote Addition Result : " +
      remoteCalculate.add(4, 5));
      System.out.println("Remote Subtraction Result : " +
      remoteCalculate.sub(4, 3));
      System.out.println("Remote Multiplication Result : " +
      remoteCalculate.mul(3, 6));
      System.out.println("Remote Division Result : " +
      remoteCalculate.div(9, 3));
    }
    catch (MalformedURLException me) {
      System.out.println("MalformedURLException" + me);
    }
    catch (RemoteException re) {
      System.out.println("RemoteException" + re);
    }
    catch (NotBoundException ne) {
      System.out.println("NotBoundException" + ne);
    }
    catch (java.lang.ArithmeticException ae) {
      System.out.println("ArithmeticException" + ae);
    }
  }
}
```

Compiling programs

We can compile programs in the same order as we designed and developed them, that is, interfaces followed by the server and client classes.

Building a JAR file from the interface classes

The first step is to compile the remote interface components and build a JAR file using it. Note that we have provided the commands for both Microsoft Windows and Solaris or Linux in the following sections:

- For Microsoft Windows:

```
cd C:DistributedComputingWorkspacesrc
javac C:DistributedComputingWorkspacesrc*.java
jar cvf calculate.jar
C:DistributedComputingWorkspaceclasses*.class
```

- For Solaris OS or Linux:

```
cd /home/distributedcomputing/workspace/src
javac /home/distributedcomputing/workspace/src/*.java
jar cvf calculate.jar
/home/distributedcomputing/workspace/classes/*.class
```

Building the server classes

The next step is to build the server classes. We have one server class called `CalculateEngine` that implements the `Calculate` remote interface:

- For Microsoft Windows:

```
cd C:DistributedComputingWorkspacesrc
javac -cp C:DistributedComputingWorkspaceclassescalculate.jar
remoteCalculateEngine.java
```

- For Solaris OS or Linux:

```
cd /home/distributedcomputing/workspace/src
javac -cp
/home/distributedcomputing/workspace/classes/calculate.jar
remote/CalculateEngine.java
```

Building the client classes

Once the interfaces and server classes are compiled, build the client implementation class that will communicate an implementation of the `Calculate` interface with the server class:

- For Microsoft Windows:

```
cd C:DistributedComputingWorkspacesrc
javac -cp C:DistributedComputingWorkspacesrccalculate.jar
localCalculateClient.java
mkdir C:DistributedComputingWorkspaceclasses
cp localCalculateClient.class
C:DistributedComputingWorkspaceclasses
```

- For Solaris OS or Linux:

```
cd /home/distributedcomputing/workspace/src
javac -cp /home/distributedcomputing/workspace/src/calculate.jar
local/CalculateClient.java
mkdir /home/distributedcomputing/workspace/classes
cp local/CalculateClient.class
/home/distributedcomputing/workspace/classes
```

Running a remote client program

Between the hosts running the server and client programs, there can be a security manager installed. When you run either a server or client program with a security policy, the associated security policy definition needs to be specified with the instructions to grant security permissions to both the server and the client as they run. The following are example policy files to use with the server program:

- For `server.policy`, the code is as follows:

```
grant codeBase
"file:D://development//eclipseworkspace//CalculateApp//src//remote//" {
  permission java.security.AllPermission;
};
```

- For `client.policy`, the code is as follows:

```
grant codeBase
"file:D://development//eclipseworkspace//CalculateApp//src//local//" {
  permission java.security.AllPermission;
};
```

Starting the server

Ensure that the RMI registry is started before you start the application:

- For Microsoft Windows (use `javaw` if you're unable to start the registry; `port_no` is optional):

```
start rmiregistry <port_no>
```

- For Solaris OS or Linux:

```
rmiregistry <port_no> &
```

- For Microsoft Windows:

```
java -cp
C:DistributedComputingWorkspacesrc;C:DistributedComputingWorkspace
classescalculate.jar -Djava.rmi.server.codebase=
file:C:DistributedComputingWorkspaceclassescalculate.jar -
Djava.rmi.server.hostname=myserver.host.com -
Djava.security.policy=server.policy    remote.CalculateEngine
```

- For Solaris OS or Linux:

```
java -cp
/home/distributedcomputing/workspace/src;
/home/distributedcomputing/workspace/classes/calculate.jar -
Djava.rmi.server.codebase=http:
//myserver/~server/classes/calculate.jar -
Djava.rmi.server.hostname=myserver.host.com -
Djava.security.policy=server.policy
remote.ComputeEngine
```

Invoking the client

Client invocation needs to be done after the registry and host system are up and running. The following are the commands for client invocation:

- For Microsoft Windows:

```
java -cp
C:DistributedComputingWorkspacesrc;
C:DistributedComputingWorkspaceclassescalculate.jar -
Djava.rmi.server.codebase=file:
C:DistributedComputingWorkspaceclasses -
Djava.security.policy=client.policy client.CalculateClient
```

```
myserver.host.com 45
```

- For Solaris OS or Linux:

```
java -cp
/home/distributedcomputing/workspace/src;
/home/distributedcomputing/workspace/classes/calculate.jar -
Djava.rmi.server.codebase=http://myserver/~client/classes/ -
Djava.security.policy=client.policy client.CalculateClient
myserver.host.com 45
```

Common Object Request Broker Architecture (CORBA)

CORBA is the acronym for Common Object Request Broker Architecture. It is an open source, vendor-independent architecture and infrastructure developed by the **Object Management Group** (**OMG**) to integrate enterprise applications across a distributed network. OMG is a nonprofit global software association that sets the distributed object computing standards. CORBA specifications provide guidelines for such integration applications, based on the way they want to interact, irrespective of the technology; hence, all kinds of technologies can implement these standards using their own technical implementations.

When two applications/systems in a distributed environment interact with each other, it is often true that there are quite a few unknowns between those applications/systems, including the technology they are developed in (such as Java/ PHP/ .NET), the base operating system they are running on (such as Windows/Linux), or system configuration (such as memory allocation). They communicate mostly with the help of each other's network address or through a naming service. Due to this, these applications end up with quite a few issues in integration, including content (message) mapping mismatches. As discussed in the socket/remote method invocation programming section, the publisher may not always know the receiver details well.

An application developed based on CORBA standards with standard **Internet Inter-ORB Protocol** (**IIOP**), irrespective of the vendor that develops it, should be able to smoothly integrate and operate with another application developed based on CORBA standards through the same or different vendor. This rule is true even if the applications are run on different operating systems or servers or developed with a different technology and connected over the distributed network.

CORBA standards

The following are the CORBA standards published by the OMG group version-wise (as advised in CORBA's official website at `http://www.corba.org/`):

Version (Month and Year of Release)	Important Features
CORBA 1.0 (October 1991)	Included the CORBA Object model, Interface Definition Language™ (IDL™), and the core set of application programming interfaces (APIs) for dynamic request management and invocation (DII) and Interface Repository. Included a single language mapping for the C language.
CORBA 1.1 (February 1992)	This was the first widely published version of the CORBA specification. It closed many ambiguities in the original specification; added interfaces for the Basic Object Adapter and memory management; clarified the Interface Repository, and clarified ambiguities in the object model.
CORBA 1.2 (December 1993)	Closed several ambiguities, especially in memory management and object reference comparison.
CORBA 2.0 (August 1996)	First major overhaul kept the extant CORBA object model, and added several major features: dynamic skeleton interface (mirror of dynamic invocation) initial reference resolver for client portability extensions to the Interface Repository "out of the box" interoperability architecture (GIOP, IIOP®, DCE CIOP) support for layered security and transaction services datatype extensions for COBOL, scientific processing, wide characters interworking with OLE2/COM Included in this release were the Interoperability Protocol specification, interface repository improvements, initialization, and two IDL language mappings (C++ and Smalltalk).
CORBA 2.1 (August 1997)	Added additional security features (secure IIOP and IIOP over SSL), added two language mappings (COBOL and Ada), included interoperability revisions and IDL type extensions.
CORBA 2.2 (February 1998)	This version of CORBA includes the Server Portability enhancements (POA), DCOM Interworking, and the IDL/JAVA language mapping specification.
CORBA 2.3 (June 1999)	This version of CORBA includes the following new and revised specifications: COM/CORBA Part A and B (orbos/97-09-07), (orbos/97-09-06, 97-09-19) Portability IDL/Java Objects by value (orbos/98-01-18), (ptc/98-07-06) Java to IDL Language Mapping IDL to Java Language Mapping C++ Language Mapping Core and RTF reports (ptc/98-09-04), (ptc/98-07-05), (ptc/99-03-01, 99-03-02)
CORBA 2.4 (October 2000)	This version of CORBA includes the following specifications: Messaging specification (orbos/98-05-05) Core and 2.4 RTF (ptc/99-12-06), (ptc/99-12-07), (ptc/99-12-08) Interoperable Naming service (orbos/98-08-10) Interop 2K RTF report (interop/00-01-01) Naming FTF report (ptc/99-12-02, 99-12-03, 99-12-04) Notification service (formal/00-06-20) Minimum CORBA (orbos/98-08-04) Real-time CORBA (orbos/99-02-12)

From 2001 onward, CORBA has given us standards that are related to security as well:

Version (Month and Year of Release)	Important Features
CORBA 2.5 (September 2001)	This version of CORBA includes the following specifications: Fault Tolerant (ptc/00-04-04) Messaging (editorial changes) Portable Interceptors (ptc/01-03-04) Realtime CORBA (ptc/00-09-02) RTF outputs from CORBA Core, Interop, OTS, etc.
CORBA 2.6 (December 2001)	This version of CORBA includes the following specifications: Common Security (orbos/2000-08-04, ptc/01-03-02, ptc/01-06-09) Core RTF 12/2000 and Interop RTF 12/2000 (ptc/01-06-10, ptc/01-06-08, ptc/01-06-01)
CORBA 3.0 (July 2002)	The CORBA Core specification, v3.0 (formal/02-06-01) includes updates based on output from the Core RTF (ptc/02-01-13, ptc/02-01-14, ptc/02-01-15), the Interop RTF (ptc/02-01-14 ptc/02-01-15, ptc/02-01-18), and the Object Reference Template (ptc/01-08-31, ptc/01-10-23, ptc/01-01-04). The CORBA Component Model™ (CCM™), v3.0 (formal/02-06-65), released simultaneously as a stand-alone specification, enables tighter integration with Java and other component technologies, making it easier for programmers to use CORBA; its initial release number of 3.0 signifies its conformance to this release of CORBA and IIOP. Also with this release, Minimum CORBA and Real-time CORBA (both added to CORBA Core in Release 2.4) become separate documents.
CORBA 3.0.1 (November 2002), CORBA 3.0.2 (December 2002), CORBA 3.0.3 (March 2004)	These versions contain minor editorial updates.
CORBA 3.1 (January 2008)	Reorganization of the CORBA specification took place in January 2008 with the 3.1 version of CORBA. The specification was divided into three separate documents. Part I – Interfaces Part II – Interoperability Part III – Components
CORBA 3.1.1 (August 2011)	Another major event took place with version 3.1.1. This version was formally published by ISO as the 2012 edition standard: ISO/IEC 19500-1, 19500-2, and 19500-3.
CORBA 3.2 (November 2011)	This version is based on the outcome of the DDS4CCM and CCM Revision Task Forces.
CORBA 3.3 (November 2012)	This version of CORBA is also known as CORBA/ZIOP.

CORBA standards help with the integration of versatile systems, from mainframes to mini computers and from Unix systems to handhelds and embedded systems. CORBA is useful when there are huge connecting systems with good hit rate and when you expect high stability and a reliable system.

Except legacy applications, most of the applications follow common standards when it comes to object modeling, for example. All applications related to, say, "HR&Benefits" maintain an object model with details of the organization, employees with demographic information, benefits, payroll, and deductions. They are only different in the way they handle the details, based on the country and region they are operating for.

For each object type, similar to the HR&Benefits systems we discussed in the preceding section, we can define an interface using the **Interface Definition Language** (**OMG IDL**). The contract between these applications is defined in terms of an interface for the server objects that the clients can call. This IDL interface is used by each client to indicate when they should call any particular method to marshal (read and send the arguments). The target object is going to use the same interface definition when it receives the request from the client to unmarshal (read the arguments) in order to execute the method that was requested by the client operation. Again, during response handling, the interface definition is helpful to marshal (send from the server) and unmarshal (receive and read the response) arguments on the client side once received.

The IDL interface is a design concept that works with multiple programming languages that use OMG standards, including C, C++, Java, Ruby, Python, and IDLscript. This is close to writing a program to an interface, a concept we have been discussing that most recent programming languages and frameworks, such as Spring, adopt. This clear separation between the interface and implementation offered by CORBA standards is well empowered by OMG IDL and helps in easy integration of enterprise systems. However, the interface has to be defined clearly for each object. The systems encapsulate the actual implementation along with their respective data handling and processing, and only the methods are available to the rest of the world through the interface. Hence, the clients are forced to develop their invocation logic for the IDL interface exposed by the application they want to connect to with the method parameters (input and output) advised by the interface operation.

The following diagram shows a single-process ORB CORBA architecture with the IDL configured as client stubs with object skeletons, We have written our object (on the right) and a client for it (on the left), as represented in the diagram. The client and server use stubs and skeletons as proxies, respectively. As discussed earlier, the IDL interface follows a strict definition, and even though the client and server are implemented in different technologies, they should integrate smoothly with the interface definition strictly implemented.

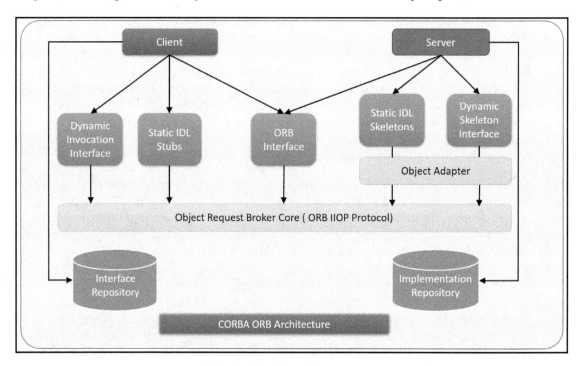

In CORBA, each object instance acquires an object reference for itself with the electronic token identifier. Client invocations are going to use these object references that have the ability to figure out which ORB instance they are supposed to interact with. The stub and skeleton represent the client and server, respectively, to their counterparts. They help establish this communication through ORB and pass the arguments to the right method and its instance during the invocation.

Inter-ORB communication

The following diagram shows how remote invocation works for inter-ORB communication. It shows that the clients that interacted have created **IDL Stub** and **IDL Skeleton** based on **Object Request Broker** and communicated through **IIOP Protocol**.

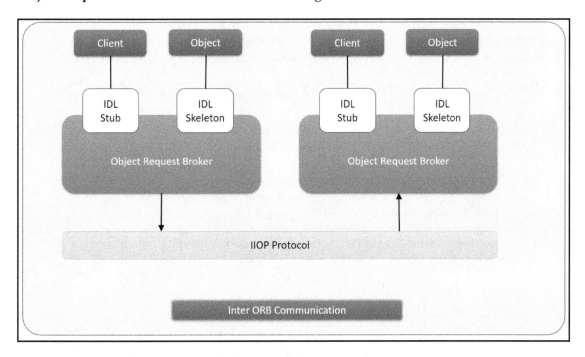

To invoke the remote object instance, the client can get its object reference using a naming service. Replacing the object reference with the remote object reference, the client can make the invocation of the remote method with the same syntax as the local object method invocation. ORB keeps the responsibility of recognizing the remote object reference based on the client object invocation through a naming service and routes it accordingly. This configuration might have been more complex if you would have had cluster and load balancer configurations in place.

Java support for CORBA

Java has great support for using CORBA standards for several reasons, including the following:

- It is an object-oriented programming language
- It supports application portability across multiple platforms
- It provides seamless integration across web applications
- It has a strong component model with features such as enterprise Java beans.

CORBA's high-level object paradigm for distributed objects provided by Java with OMG IDL binding includes the following:

- Interfaces' definition with UML and no knowledge of their future implementations
- Easy integration with other applications developed in a different technology through IDL
- Distributed application integration across the globe
- Ability of the binding to generate code for remote communication
- Accessibility from binding to standard CORBA features

These features further extend the suitability of CORBA for the development of diverse distributed systems.

OMG IDL samples

Now let's review some of the sample programs for the OMG IDL language. We will review IDL interfaces, inheritance, types and constants, structures, exceptions, and other important components in this section.

Interfaces

The purpose of IDL is to define interfaces and their operations. To avoid name clashes when using several IDL declarations together, the module is used as a naming scope. Modules can contain nested modules. Interfaces open a new naming scope containing data type declarations, constants, attributes, and operations:

```
//EmployeeHiring.idl
Module EmployeeHiring {
  interface Employee();
}
```

The process of setting up a reference to one module from another can be defined with `outer::inner` as `::EmployeeHiring::Employee`:

```
Module outer{
  Module inner {
    interface inside{};
  };
  interface outside {
    inner::inside get_inside();
  };
};
```

The `get_inside()` operation is for returning the object reference for the `::outer::inner::inside` interface.

Inheritance

Interfaces can extend one or more interfaces if they want to carry out other interface operations, and in addition to that, declare their own operations as follows:

```
module EmployeeHierarchy {
  interface Person {
    typedef unsigned short ushort;
    ushort method1();
  };
  interface Employee : Person {
    Boolean method2(ushort num);
  };
};
```

In the preceding code, the `Employee` interface extends the `Person` interface and adds `method2()` in addition to `method1()` inherited from the `Person` interface.

The following is an example of one interface inheriting multiple interfaces:

```
interface Clerk: Person, Employee, Associate::Administrator {
};
```

Types and constants

The basic data types advised by the IDL and their corresponding descriptions are given in the following table:

Type Keyword	Description
[unsigned] short	Signed [unsigned] 16-bit 2's complement integer
[unsigned] long	Signed [unsigned] 32-bit 2's complement integer
[unsigned] long long	Signed [unsigned] 64-bit 2's complement integer
float	16-bit IEEE floating point number
double	32-bit IEEE floating point number
long double	64-bit IEEE floating point number
fixed	fixed-point decimal number of up to 31 digits
char	ISO Latin-1 character
wchar	character from other character sets to support internationalization. The size is implementation dependent
boolean	Boolean type taking values TRUE or FALSE
string	variable length string of characters whose length is available at run time
wstring	variable length string of wchar characters
octet	8 bit uninterpreted type
enum	enumerated type with named integer values
any	can represent a valu from any possible IDL type, basic or constructed, object or nonobject
native	Opaque type, representation specified by language mapping

The following is an example that uses data types:

```
interface EmployeeRegistry {
  typedef identification string <10>;
  typedef name string <100>;
  identification getId(in string name);
  name getName(in string id);
};
```

Structures

Structures are used to define reusable data types. Their syntaxes have a keyword struct followed by a variable, which acts as a valid type name.

The basic data types advised by the IDL and their corresponding descriptions are as follows:

```
interface EmployeeRegistry {
  struct address_spec {
    name string <100>;
    salary float;
  };
```

Discriminated unions

Like structures, discriminated unions help as a valid type name in further declarations. They are followed by the type name and then the switch keyword, and they can take parameters of the type int/char/Boolean or enum:

```
. employee_dept {admin, sales, it, business};
union  employee switch (employee_dept) {
  case admin, business : age_spec age;
  cae sales : sales_detail sales;
  default float salary;
};
```

Sequences

Like structures, sequences help you define an element type. A sequence can encapsulate multiple other types of elements. A sequence is an ordered element, and its size can increase during the execution:

```
// "employee" as defined in previous section
typedef sequence <employee> AssignmentOrderSeq;
typedef sequence <employee, 4> QuartelyAssignmentOrderSeq;
typedef sequence <sequence <<employee>, 12> AnnualAssignmentOrderSeq;
typedef sequence <sequence <employee> > CompleteAssignmentOrderSeq;
```

Additionally, arrays, constants, operations, attributes, value types, abstract interfaces, and exceptions can be defined with IDL as well as with this syntax that looks like a pseudocode.

CORBA services

Just like the API libraries in Java that provide some specialized function, CORBA provides services. These services are a set of distributed class libraries known as **Common Object Services**. They provide specific types of objects that are useful to programmers in a distributed environment during a transaction, event service, relationship definition, and even life cycle. Complex distributed applications require additional functionality than just the ability to invoke remote objects. OMG has recognized this requirement and provided a specification for this additional functionality with the basic services; it is called CORBA services. Some of the important CORBA services are as follows:

- **Naming service**: This is helpful in the network system to let the objects in one system point and identify a different set of objects. Its naming context is similar to that of packages in Java. In a given context, names should be unique. Contexts can be nested and can have one context inside other. CORBA naming resembles a lot with the RMI registry's `java.rmi.Naming` interface. The only difference is that RMI does not support the hierarchical naming context and compound object names. It is the most popular service in a CORBA implementation.

- **Trading service**: Trading service helps find a group of objects by referring to a distributed system network. Yellow Pages is the best example of this service. Objects from one system are able to search for another set of objects if they have an entry in the trader service along with the specs for such objects.

- **Notification service**: Notification service is an asynchronous, subscription-based event notification service. If any event occurs on a specific object, then that event information along with the reference are notified to the listening object. If any object wishes to receive such notifications for an event occurring on any other object, they have to register to get automatic event notifications. The best example of this notification service is the coordination between a system and printer. When we give a number of print requests for different documents, they get queued on the spool to get printed. If document printing is complete for one, the printer automatically gets notified about that event to let it start with the next printing task waiting in the print queue.

- **Transaction service**: Transaction service refers to transaction processing for distributed objects. Each object gets the instructions to add or update its state from any other objects. Say, you want to consider a group of operations together to update an object's state that would affect its behavior. During this state-changing operation, if any problem occurs in a part of the transaction of one of the operations, then the object's previous state will be rolled back along with the recovery from the error. This is taken care of by the transaction service.

- **Persistent object state service**: Persistent state service refers to persistent storage of an object state. It acts as an interface between the CORBA application and the object databases or object persistent frameworks.

- **Event service:** Event service enables asynchronous communications between cooperating remote objects. It's similar in nature to message-passing and event-based messaging.

- **Security service**: Security service is a service that provides authentication, authorization, encryption, and other security features. This is a complex service to implement. It consists of security models and interfaces for the implementation of security services, application development, and security administration. The interfaces it provides are as follows:

    - Authentication and credentials generation for principals and exchange of credentials between principals
    - Performing secured transactions
    - Generating secure transactions and performing audit log for tracking and evidence generation

- **Query service**: Query service can be used to query and modify an object collection. An example of this is an interface between CORBA and the databases (relational, hierarchical, object-based, and so on).

Other important services include life cycle, relationships, externalization, concurrency control, licensing, properties, time, and collections.

Sample CORBA program using JAVA IDL

Before we step into a sample Java program for CORBA, let's confirm the minimum environment setup requirements.

For working with CORBA using Java, we need to have the latest JDK installed along with VisiBroker for Java (stable release – 8.5) set up on the computer.

The steps involved while writing a typical CORBA program are as follows:

1. Define the IDL interface.
2. Generate stubs and skeletons by building IDL (done automatically).
3. Implement the interface.
4. Develop the server.
5. Develop the client.
6. Run the service (naming), the server, and the client.

IDL interface specification

In the following example, let's define an IDL interface to work with a client-server application. The client application invokes a method of the server program and gets the response from the server method.

The IDL interface has the interface name followed by the `.idl` extension:

```
//Employee.idl
module org {
  module admin {
    module hr {
      module employee {
        interface Registry {
          string register();
        };
      };
    };
  };
};
```

Compiling the IDL

The next step is to compile the IDL interface definition from the preceding step so that it can generate the stub and skeleton using the following command:

```
prompt> idl2java -strict -root_dir generated Employee.idl
```

This should generate the following Java classes:

```
Registry.java
RegistryHolder.java        RegistryHelper.java
RegistryStub.java          RegistryPOA.java
RegistryOperations.java    RegistryPOATie.java
```

Client application

A client application definition of the aforementioned communication can be established using the following steps:

- Initialize the CORBA environment and get the reference to ORB
- Get the object reference for the object to invoke the operation
- Invoke the operations and process the result

The following code snippet will generate the Java interface:

```
package org.admin.hr.employee;
public interface Registry extends RegistyOperations, org.omg.CORBA.object,
org.omg.CORBA.portable.IDLEntry
{
}
```

The RegistryOperations interface is defined as follows:

```
package org.admin.hr.employee;
public interface RegistryOperations {
  public java.lang.String register();
}
```

ORB can be initialized using the following code snippet:

```
package org.admin.hr.employee;
import java.io.*;
import org.omg.CORBA.*;
public class Client {
  public static void main(String args[]) {
    try {
      ORB orb = ORB.init (args. Null);
    }
    Catch(Exception e)  {
      System.out.println("Exception " + e);
    }
  }
}
```

An object reference can be obtained in this ORB setup as follows:

```
org.omg.CORBA.Object obj = orb.string_to_object (args[0]);
```

Get the Registry object reference by invoking the narrow () method from the helper class, as follows:

```
Registry reg = RegistryHelper.narrow(obj);
If (reg == null) {
  System.err.println("object reference type fault");
  System.exit(-1);
}
```

Once the object reference is found from ORB as earlier, its method can be invoked as a local Java method itself:

```
System.out.println(reg.register());
```

Compile and execute the Java client program as follows:

```
prompt > javac Client.java
prompt > java org.admin.hr.employee.Client IOR:0002453..2
```

This should give the output as follows:

```
Employee Rohith, is now registered
```

Object implementation

A sample object implementation of the preceding client program is as follows:

```
package org.admin.hr.employee;
import org.omg.CORBA.*;
public class RegisterImpl extends RegisterPOA {
  private String name;
  RegisterImple(String name){
    this.name = name;
  }
  public String register() {
    return "Employee " + name + ", is now registered";
  }
}
```

Compile the preceding `impl` class using the following command:

```
prompt> javac RegisterImpl.java
```

Defining the server

The next step is to implement the server program for ORB, as follows:

```
package org.admin.hr.employee;
import java.io.*;
import org.omg.CORBA.*;
import org.omg.PortableServer.*;
public class Server {
  public static void main(String[] args) {
    if(args.length < 1 ) {
      System.out.println("Usage : java org.admin.hr.employee <name> ");
      System.exit(-1);
    }
    try {
      ORB orb = ORB.init(args, null);
      //make java object
      RegisterImpl regImpl = new RegisterImpl (args[0]);
```

```
    //make CORBA object
    POA poa =
    POAHelper.narrow(orb.resolve_initial_references("RootPOA");
  };
  poa.the_POAManager().activate();
  //get the object reference
  Org.omg.CORBA.Object obj = poa.servant_to_reference (regImpl);
  //print the object reference
  System.out.println( orb.object_to_string(obj));
  );
  //wait for the requests to receive
  orb.run();
}
Catch(InvalidName e){
  System.out.println(e);
}
Catch(UserException e){
  System.err.println(e);
}
Catch(SystemException e) {
  System.err.println(e);
}
}
}
```

Compiling and starting the server

Following commands helps in compiling and executing the Server component:

```
prompt> javac Server.java
prompt> java org.admin.hr.employee.Server Rohith
```

This should print stringified IOR, as follows:

```
IOR:000044589
```

This standard output can be saved in a file with the following command:

```
prompt> java org.admin.hr.employee.Server Rohith > shw.ior
```

Executing the client

Now that the server is ready, the client program can be executed as follows:

```
prompt> java org.admin.hr.employee.Client 'Ram shw.ior'
```

JavaSpaces

Building a distributed application invites many new challenges that include partial failure, latency, synchronization, OS compatibility, data consistency, and so on. To address these issues, JavaSpaces was introduced. It provides a powerful and high-level tool for developing robust distributed applications. It works as per shared-network-based space that saves both object storage and exchange area.

Overview

JavaSpaces provides a distributed, persistent object system that is inspired by an earlier shared memory system called LINDA. JavaSpaces is different from other technologies used for distributed computing, such as sockets, message passing, RMI, and so on. It offers the persistent object exchange spaces through which java remoting process manage and exchange data. It is a group of execution processes that work along with the object process execution through the flow of objects to and from the object space. It provides the following design goals:

- It provides a simple platform for distributed system design and development
- The client side should be lightweight with few classes (for simplicity and less downloading time)
- The client side should run with bare minimum runtime memory as client machines may have constrained memory allocation
- Different styles of system design and development need to be allowed
- Duplicate JavaSpaces service generation needs to be allowed

Some of the important properties of JavaSpaces are as follows:

1. They are shared. Multiple remote processes interact with an object space concurrently.
2. They are persistent. They provide reliable storage for objects.
3. They are associative. Objects in a space are located via associative lookup, not by memory location or an identifier. Object search is based on its complete or partial content without knowing its name, ID, source, and so on.
4. They support secured transactions. JavaSpaces makes use of Jini's transaction service to ensure that an operation on space is atomic.
5. They support exchange of executable content. Objects shared through JavaSpaces can be further modified or executed by the process that receives it.

6. Objects are passive data. They are not updated or modified and any of their methods is executed as long as they are in the space

How it works

Different processes within application components make use of the persistent storage space provided by JavaSpaces to store, communicate, and coordinate actions. Direct interaction between objects is not established.

The following are the methods available for the processes to communicate with JavaSpaces:

- `write()`: This is to write new objects to the space.
- `take()`: This is to retrieve and remove objects from the space.
- `read()`: This is to read objects from the space that matches the template.
- `notify()`: An object gets notified if any new entry is introduced in the space that has the same rules as that of the template.
- `readIfExists()` and `takeIfExists()`: These are inherited methods for `read()` and `take()`. At any given instance, if the object state needs to be identified, these methods can be invoked. They help in case a transaction is used to understand the state of objects at different points of time.

All the entries carried out by JavaSpaces must belong to the set of objects referred to within a component implementing the `net.jini.core.entry.Entry` interface. At any point in time, the lookup for an entry can be carried out. The entry lookup operation is carried out to have exact matching with the predefined set of instructions and values through a template. If there exist any additional fields other than the matched (not part of lookup) fields, such kinds of fields can be considered wildcard search entries.

Sample JavaSpaces code

The following code indicates how to write the `Message` object and how to use it in your code:

```
//Message.java
package org.hr.communication;
import net.jini.core.entry.*;
public class Message implements Entry {
  public String details;
  public Message() {
  }
```

```
    public Message(String details) {
      this.details = details;
    }
    public String toString() {
      return "MessageContent: " + details;
    }
  }
```

In the following code, the client makes use of the Message object to store data in the space and then retrieve it as and when required:

```
package org.hr.communication;
import net.jini.space.JavaSpace;
public class SpaceUser {
  public static void main(String args[]) {
    try {
      Message message = new Message();
      message.content = "Hi ";
      //Searching for Java Space
      Lookup searcher = new Lookup(JavaSpace.class);
      JavaSpace jSpace = (JavaSpace) searcher.getService();
      //A Java Space is found
      //Writing a message to space
      jSpace.write(message, null, 60 * 60 * 500);
      Message tmpl = new Message();
      //Reading a message from the space
      Message rslt = (Message) jSpace.read(tmpl, null,
      Long.MAX_VALUE);
      //Print the message content
      System.out.println("The message read is: " + rslt.content);
    } catch (Exception e) {
      e.printStackTrace();
    }
  }
}
```

How Java 9 adds value

New features in Java 9, such as JEP 143, 193, 197, 199, and 295, help in performance improvisation of distributed frameworks, such as JavaSpaces and CORBA. JEP 376, 222, 164, and so on help in the development of modular and easy-to-maintain applications. JEP 158, 266, and 254 help in having better controlled and easy-to-maintain concurrent systems with ease of performing a root cause analysis through application logs.

Some of the nice features in Java 9 that help in enhancing a distributed system's performance are as follows:

JEP	Feature	Benefit	Challenges	Description
158	Unified JVM logging	This is for performance improvisation and better tracking.	NA	Provide an infrastructure for JVM logging for better identification of the root cause of crashes or performance issues. These features are adopted from JRockit--the industry's highest performing JVM (part of Oracle Fusion Middleware).
102	Process API updates	This is for better monitoring, control, and management of native processes.	NA	In a distributed environment, we may have systems with different operating systems. Using this feature developer can monitor native processes and control them through a uniform API.
110	HTTP/2 client	This is to replace the existing problematic API `HttpURLConnection` with the new HTTP client.	NA	This is an existing `HttpURLConnection` API designed for outdated protocols (FTP, gopher, and so on). It supports HTTP/1.1, which is too abstract. It's hard to use and maintain, and many features are not documented. It supports one thread per request/response (blocking mode).

JEP	Feature	Benefit	Challenges	Description
143	Improve contended locking	This is to significantly benefit real-world applications in addition to industry benchmarks.	Needs to provide performance gain without offsetting performance regressions.	This project will explore performance improvements in the following areas related to contended Java monitors: 1. Field reordering and cache line alignment. 2. Speed up `PlatformEvent::unpark()`. 3. Quicker Java monitor enter operations. 4. Quicker Java monitor exit operations. 5. Quicker Java monitor notify/notifyAll operations.
158	Unified JVM logging	Provides easy and faster root cause analysis in the case of a JVM crash or sluggishness in the distributed environment.	This may impact: • Compatibility • Security • Performance/scalability • User experience • No support for I18N • Need for documentation	This logging framework will provide the following features: • Tags: To classify information • Levels: To control the amount of information written to logs in different environments • Decorations: Here, the logged message will be decorated with predefined information, such as date, time, and process/thread identifier • Output: Three types would be supported, namely stdout, stderr, and text file • Command-line options • Control at runtime

JEP	Feature	Benefit	Challenges	Description
165	Compiler control	Compiler testing is possible while it's running. Developing a workaround for bugs and encapsulation of compiler options is also good hygiene. This provides better control in distributed computing.	NA	JVM compilers can be controlled at runtime using certain flags (called directives).
193	Variable handles	With the increasing trend in concurrent and parallel programming, this feature will help programmers achieve atomic and ordered operations on variables defined in the code and have better control over them.	Ensure safety, integrity, performance, and usability.	Variable handle is a reference to a variable under different access modes (static, instance, array elements, array views, byte or char array, and so on). This requires library enhancements.
197	Segmented code cache	Provides performance improvement through separation of specialized code. Provides better control of JVM memory footprint. From a distributed computing perspective, this will improve the management of heterogeneous code (GPU code) and AOT-compiled code.	Having a fixed size per code heap leads to a potential waste of memory in case one code heap is full and there is still space in another code heap. This will cause problems for very small code cache sizes. An option for turning it off is required.	Instead of having a single code heap, the code cache is divided into distinct code heaps; each heap contains compiled code of a particular type. Three top-level types are JVM internal (non-method), profiled, and non-profiled code.

JEP	Feature	Benefit	Challenges	Description
199	Smart Java compilation, phase 2	This improves build speed and allows incremental builds.	At present, the quality of the code and stability of the tool are not poor and not publicly releasable.	This improves the `sjavac` tool so that it can be used by default in the JDK build. It also generalizes it so that it can be used to build large projects other than the JDK.

200	The modular JDK	Compliance with JSR 376.	Should address all the important use cases.	Divide the JDK into a set of modules that can be combined at compile time, build time, or runtime into a variety of configurations as follows: full Java SE platform, the full JRE, the full JDK, compact profiles, and custom configurations.
				The modular structure proposed is as follows:
				• Standard modules that are governed by JCP will start with Java.
				• All other modules will start with JDK.
				• Other JEPs that supplement project jigsaw are as follows:
				  ○ 201: Modular source code
				  ○ 220: Modular runtime images
				  ○ 260: Encapsulate most internal APIs
				  ○ 261: Module system; see JSR 376 as well
				  ○ 282: jlink, which is the Java linker

Summary

In this chapter, you learned about the communication between client-server applications with the help of RMI. You also learned about the standards and definitions of CORBA along with IDL concepts. You also gained knowledge of implementing the CORBA standards using Java. We finished this chapter with an understanding of JavaSpaces and Java 9 support for these concepts.

In the next chapter, you will learn about asynchronous messaging and how it contributes to distributed computing and demonstrates the examples for such programming model in detail.

4
Enterprise Messaging

Large distributed systems are often overwhelmed with complications caused by heterogeneity and interoperability. Heterogeneity issues may arise due to the use of different programming languages, hardware platforms, operating systems, and data representations. Interoperability denotes the ability of heterogeneous systems to communicate meaningfully and exchange data or services. With the introduction of middleware, heterogeneity can be alleviated and interoperability can be achieved. Middleware is a layer of software between the distributed application and the operating system and consists of a set of standard interfaces that help the application use networked resources and services.

In this chapter, we will cover the following topics:

- Enterprise Messaging System (EMS)
- Asynchronous communication
- Synchronous communication
- Java Messaging Service (JMS)
- The publish/subscribe messaging paradigm
- The Point-To-Point messaging paradigm
- JMS interfaces
- Developing a JMS application
- Publish-Subscribe (Topic) Programming
- Point-To-Point (Queue) Programming
- Web services
- Web service architecture
- SOAP web services
- RESTful web services

- Programming SOAP web services
- Programming RESTful web services
- Enterprise integration patterns

EMS

EMS, or the messaging system, defines system standards for organizations so they can define their enterprise application messaging process with a semantically precise messaging structure. EMS encourages you to define a loosely coupled application architecture in order to define an industry-accepted message structure; this is to ensure that published messages would be persistently consumed by subscribers. Common formats, such as XML or JSON, are used to do this. EMS recommends these messaging protocols: DDS, MSMQ, AMQP, or SOAP web services. Systems designed with EMS are termed **Message-Oriented Middleware (MOM)**.

Let's review the behavior offered by both asynchronous and synchronous communication on the part of applications while messaging.

Note the following about asynchronous communication:

- Both the applications need not be active when they communicate
- No "message received" acknowledgments are required
- Provides nonblocking calls
- Useful when massive communication processing is required
- Allows efficient usage of hardware resources

Note the following about synchronous communication:

- Both the applications need to be active when they communicate
- The sender receives a confirmation (acknowledgment/response) from the receiver
- Provides blocking calls
- Useful when an immediate response is required during message processing/communication

Take a look at the following diagram:

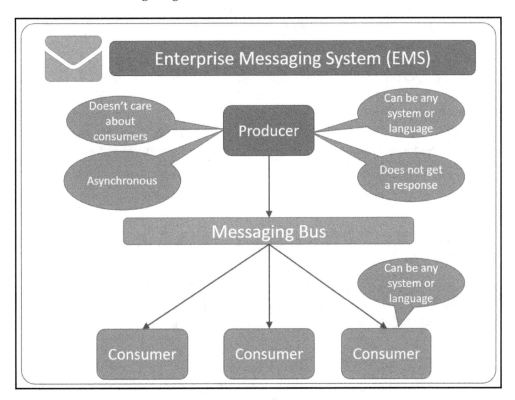

While designing a system with enterprise messaging standards, consider the following points:

- **Application security**: If the systems are integrated over public interfaces or in the enterprise with more than one messaging system, they should be encrypted. Two-way SSL is another recommended security feature that should be considered to ensure that messages are sent and received between known application names and servers.
- **Routing**: Message routing rules carry great importance with regard to safely passing through the routing system and delivering only those messages the subscribing system is subscribed for. Different message headers, message types, or XPath rules need to be considered while defining routing rules.

- **Metadata**: Metadata helps greatly in defining additional information that we want to send along with the message to help the receivers uniquely identify the message along with the publisher information; the message body should only contain the actual message transformed into the receiving system's format.
- **Subscription**: Each system needs to have a set of subscription rules and the ability to define its own subscription policy with rules to route the messages toward them. A single message may be delivered to more than one subscriber based on the commonality in the subscription rules they set up for routing.
- **Policy**: EMS's need to define a common policy across messages that would define the message access levels at the field level for each component and user role.

JMS

Java's implementation of an EMS in the **Application Programming Interface** (**API**) format is known as JMS.

JMS allows distributed Java applications to communicate with applications developed in any other technology that understands messaging through asynchronous messages. JMS applications contain a provider, clients, messages, and administrated objects.

Before JMS, each MOM vendor provided application access to its product through its product-specific (proprietary) API, making it available to different programming languages, including Java. JMS changed this notion by providing a standard, portable way for Java programs to send/receive messages through a MOM product. Any application written in JMS can be executed on any MOM that implements the JMS API standards. The JMS API is specified as a set of interfaces as part of the Java API. Hence, all the products that intend to provide JMS behavior will have to deliver the provider to implement JMS-defined interfaces. With programming patterns that allow a program to interface, you should be able to construct a Java application in line with the JMS standards by defining the messaging programs with client applications to exchange information through JMS messaging. Refer to the following diagram:

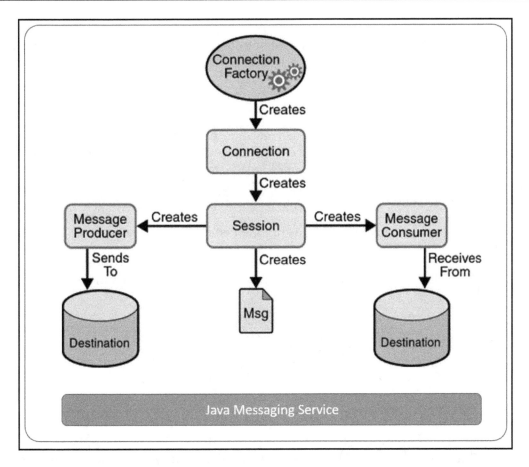

A **JMS provider** is a messaging server that supports the creation of connections (multithreaded virtual links to the provider) and sessions (single-threaded contexts for producing and consuming messages).

A JMS client is a Java program that either produces or consumes messages.

JMS messages are objects that communicate information between JMS clients and are composed of a header, some optional properties, and an optional body.

Administered objects are preconfigured JMS objects, such as a connection factory (the object a client uses to create a connection to a provider) and a *destination* (the object a client uses to specify a target for its messages).

JMS applications are usually developed in either the publish/subscribe or Point-To-Point paradigm.

As you may already know, there are quite a few enterprise messaging products available on the market today that are both open source and licensed. They have all contributed to the definition and development of the JMS concept. JMS defines a common set of features during the implementation of its products and the behavior expected by a matured enterprise application.

The following are the objectives of JMS, as highlighted in its specification:

- Defining a common collection of messaging concepts and features
- Minimizing the number of concepts a developer should learn to develop applications as EMS's
- Improving the application messaging portability
- Reducing the effort involved in implementing a provider
- Providing client interfaces for both Point-To-Point and pub/sub domains

The publish/subscribe messaging paradigm

The publish/subscribe messaging paradigm is built with the concept of a topic, which behaves like an announcement board. Consumers subscribe to receiving messages that belong to a topic, and publishers report messages to a topic. The **JMS provider** retains the responsibility for distributing the messages that it receives from multiple publishers to many other subscribers based on the topic they subscribe to. A subscriber receives messages that it subscribes to based on the rules it defines and the messages that are published after the subscription is registered; they do not receive any messages that are already published, as shown in the following diagram:

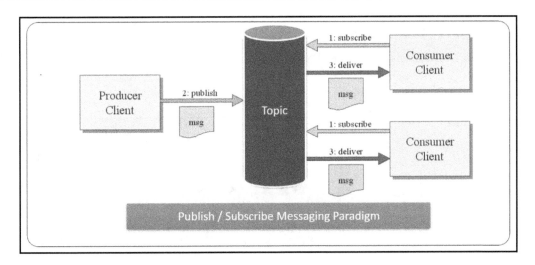

For example, consider there are two publishers: **Publisher 1** publishes news (topics) related to politics and **Publisher 2** publishes news (topics) related to sports; they publish to the **Messaging Broker**, as shown in the following diagram. While **Subscriber 1** receives news related to politics and **Subscriber 3** receives news related to sports, **Subscriber 2** will receive both political and sports news as it subscribed to the common topic "**news**."

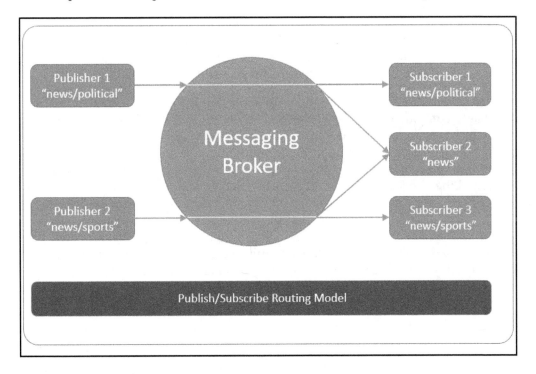

The Point-To-Point Messaging Paradigm

The **Point-To-Point Messaging Paradigm** follows the perception of a queuing system. The senders report the message one after an other to the specific queue, while the receivers take the messages from those queues as shown in the following diagram:

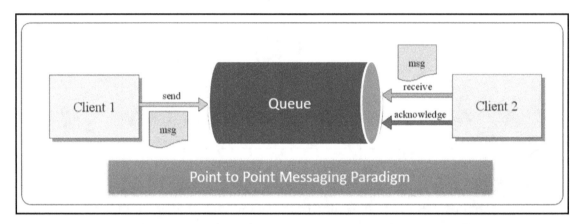

While the publish/subscribe model allows multiple subscribers to receive the same message, the Point-To-Point Messaging Paradigm model may only be used to let one message be consumed by one receiver. Moreover, in the publish/subscribe model, the subscriber receives the messages that are published after the subscription is configured, whereas the Point-To-Point Messaging Paradigm lets the receiver receive messages even after the connection is established, that is, after the sender posts the message on the queue.

Hence, the key features of JMS applications are loose coupling, asynchrony, distributed, message-based communication, resilience, and reliability. JMS applications are loosely coupled, which means both producers and consumers are not obviously conscious of one another but are relatively conscious of the JMS provider. The concept of messaging itself expects application communication to happen through the exchange of information as messages, and the applications should be event-based and asynchronous. Subsequently, messaging clients are independent, and as the provider deals with message distribution, the usage of JMS eases communication beyond the course and system limitations, leading to a distributed application behavior. The JMS API provisions the usage of guaranteed message delivery as well as the choice between using fault-tolerance and load-sharing behaviors, consequently allowing JMS applications to be more reliable and resilient.

JMS interfaces

JMS defines a set of high-level interfaces that encapsulate several messaging concepts. These high-level interfaces are further extended for the Point-To-Point and publish/subscribe messaging domains:

- `ConnectionFactory`: This is an administered object with the ability to create a connection.
- `Connection`: This is an active connection handle to the provider.
- `Destination`: This is an administered object that encapsulates the identity of a message destination where messages are sent to/received from.
- `Session`: This is a single-threaded context for sending/receiving messages. To ensure a simple session-based transaction, concurrent access to a message by multiple threads is restricted. We can use multiple sessions for a multithreaded application.
- `MessageProducer`: This is used to send messages.
- `MessageConsumer`: This is used to receive messages.

The following table shows interfaces specific to both the Point-To-Point and publish/subscribe paradigms enhanced from their corresponding high-level interface:

High Level Interface	Publish Subscribe model Interface	Point to Point model Interface
ConnectionFactory	TopicConnectionFactory	QueueConnectionFactory
Connection	TopicConnection	QueueConnection
Destination	Topic	Queue
Session	TopicSession	QueueSession
MessageProducer	TopicPublisher	QueueSender
MessageConsumer	TopicSubscriber	QueueReceiver, QueueBrowser

Developing a JMS application

A Java program with JMS needs to execute the following steps to be able to produce and consume messages in either publish/subscribe or Point-To-Point:

1. Look up a `ConnectionFactory` object through the **Java Naming and Directory Interface (JNDI)**.

2. Look up one or more `Destination` objects through the JNDI.

3. With the reference of the `ConnectionFactory` object, create a `Connection` object.

4. With the help of the `Connection` object, create one or more `Session` objects.

5. With the help of the `Session` and `Destination` objects, create the required `MessageProducer` and `MessageConsumer` objects.

6. Start `Connection`.

Once you execute the preceding steps, the program will be able to exchange the messages and receive, process, and send messages as designed. Let's review a few more API components before we write sample programs to exchange messages.

JMS offers numerous message types for diverse forms of content; however, all such messages originate from the `Message` interface. `Message` contains the header, properties, and body, which are the essential parts in a Message. Refer to the following points:

- **Message header**: This carries important information related to the message. Some important attributes of a message header include `JMSMessageID`, `JMSDestination`, `JMSDeliveryMode`, `JMSTimestamp`, `JMSExpiration`, `JMSPriority`, `JMSCorrelationID`, `JMSReplyTo`, `JMSType`, and `JMSRedelivered`.

- **Message properties:** JMS has defined a set of standard properties for `Message` to uniquely define a message, including `JMSXUserID`, `JMSXApplID`, `JMSXDeliveryCount`, `JMSXGroupID`, `JMSXGroupSeq`, `JMSXProducerTXID`, `JMSXConsumerTXID`, `JMSXRcvTimestamp`, `JMSXState`, and `JMSX_<vendor_name>`.

- **Message body:** Based on the different types of message content to be carried, the following are the interfaces that extend the `Message` interface:
  - `StreamMessage`: This comprises a stream of Java primitive values stored and read successively with standard Java I/O stream operations
  - `MapMessage`: As the name suggests, this message can contain a set of name-value pairs with string names and Java primitive values
  - `TextMessage`: This simple form of `Message` stores it as a `java.lang.String`
  - `ObjectMessage`: This stores a serializable Java object as its content
  - `BytesMessage`: This stores a stream of uninterpreted bytes that can encode a body to match the existing message format

- **Message transactions:** A JMS transaction is an atomic unit of work that assembles a set of produced/consumed messages. If an error/exception occurs during the execution of a transaction, the entire message production/consumption that is considered part of this transaction should be rolled back. `Session` objects control transactions, and a `Session` object may be denoted as transacted when it is created. A transacted `Session` object always has a current transaction, that is, there is no `begin()`, `commit()`, and `rollback()`; it always ends one transaction and automatically begins another. With the help of the **Java Transaction API (JTA)** `XAResource` API, distributed transactions are supported; however, not all providers support XA transactions. I have had the experience of working with the Apache ActiveMQ, IBM WebSphereMQ, and the Solace message queue systems. Solace system, though the latest of all, is not entirely comfortable with XA transactions.

- **Message acknowledgment:** When a message consumer receives a message and processes it successfully, it can inform the provider about the processing status. If the `Session` object receiving the message is transacted, an acknowledgment is handled automatically. If it is not transacted, then the type of acknowledgment is determined when `Session` is created. There are essentially three types of acknowledgment mode:

    - `Session.DUPS_OK_ACKNOWLEDGE`: This is a lazy acknowledgment of message delivery. It allows duplicate messages to pass through and hence should be selected only if duplicates are expected and can be handled.
    - `Session.AUTO_ACKNOWLEDGE`: In this mode, message delivery is automatically acknowledged to the provider upon completion of the method execution that receives the message.
    - `Session.CLIENT_ACKNOWLEDGE`: In this mode, message delivery is explicitly acknowledged by calling the `acknowledge()` method on `Message`.

There's an important task with the `CLIENT_ACKNOWLEDGE` mode that needs to be performed: advising your clients not to have a huge number of unacknowledged messages before they begin processing the messages. This situation is called as resource exhaustion; in this case, the processing of the resources that are temporarily blocked might fail.

The `recover` method of `Session` can be called by the client to request the provider to stop a session and restart it by sending the first unacknowledged message before terminating the session with the `recover` method. With this option, the session's message queue is reset to a point after its last acknowledged message. The order/series of messages the provider delivers after the recovery may be different from those that were delivered before. This is due to message expiration and the arrival of new high-priority messages. A `Session` must set the `redelivered` flag of the messages that the provider is redelivering due to a recovery being called.

Publish-Subscribe (topic) programming

As discussed in the previous sections, interfaces extending core JMS interfaces for `Topic` help build publish-subscribe components.

Please remember that, to be able to execute the following example programs, you need the message queue environment.

The following is a sample program to publish messages to the Publish-Subscribe topic:

```java
package pubsub;

import java.io.BufferedReader;
import java.io.InputStreamReader;

import javax.jms.Session;
import javax.jms.TextMessage;
import javax.jms.Topic;
import javax.jms.TopicConnection;
import javax.jms.TopicConnectionFactory;
import javax.jms.TopicPublisher;
import javax.jms.TopicSession;
import javax.naming.InitialContext;

/**
 * Program to publish messages to the topic
 * @author Raja
 *
 */
public class PubSubTopicPublisher {

  public static void main(String[] args) {
    PubSubTopicPublisher publisher = new PubSubTopicPublisher();
    publisher.publishMultipleMessages();
  }
```

```
public void publishMultipleMessages() {
  BufferedReader inlineReader = new BufferedReader(
  new InputStreamReader(System.in));
  try {

    //Prompt for the JNDI topic connection factory name
    System.out.println("Enter the Publish Subscribe
    Topic Connection     Factory name:");
    String connectionFactoryName = inlineReader.readLine();

    // Prompt for topic name for the Pub Sub
    System.out.println("Enter the Publish Subscribe Topic name:");
    String pubsubTopicName = inlineReader.readLine();

    // Look up for the administered objects of Pub Sub
    InitialContext context = new InitialContext();
    TopicConnectionFactory topicConnFactory =
    (TopicConnectionFactory)
    context.lookup(connectionFactoryName);
    Topic pubsubTopic = (Topic) context.lookup(pubsubTopicName);
    context.close();

    // Create the JMS objects from administered objects
    TopicConnection topicConnection =
    topicConnFactory.createTopicConnection();
    TopicSession topicSession =
    topicConnection.createTopicSession(false,
    Session.AUTO_ACKNOWLEDGE);
    TopicPublisher topicPublisher =
    topicSession.createPublisher(pubsubTopic);

    // Publish multiple text messages entered one after the other
    String messageContent = null;
    while (true) {
      System.out.println("Enter the new message to send or 'abandon'
      to exit the program:");
      messageContent = inlineReader.readLine();
      if ("abandon".equals(messageContent))
      break;
      TextMessage textMessage =
      topicSession.createTextMessage(messageContent);
      topicPublisher.publish(textMessage);
    }

    // Clean Up
    System.out.println("Messages Successfully posted to
    the queue...");
    inlineReader.close();
```

```
            topicConnection.close();
        } catch (Exception e) {
          e.printStackTrace();
        }
      }
    }
```

While the preceding program helps publish messages to the Publish-Subscribe Topic, the following program is used to subscribe to the Publish-Subscribe Topic, which keeps receiving messages related to the Topic until the quit command is given:

```
package pubsub;

import java.io.BufferedReader;
import java.io.InputStreamReader;

import javax.jms.JMSException;
import javax.jms.Message;
import javax.jms.MessageListener;
import javax.jms.Session;
import javax.jms.TextMessage;
import javax.jms.Topic;
import javax.jms.TopicConnection;
import javax.jms.TopicConnectionFactory;
import javax.jms.TopicSession;
import javax.jms.TopicSubscriber;
import javax.naming.InitialContext;

/**
 * Program to subscribe for messages from the topic
 *
 * @author Raja
 *
 */
public class PubSubTopicSubscriber implements MessageListener {
  private boolean quitMessageSubscription = false;
  public static void main(String[] args) {
    PubSubTopicSubscriber pubSubTopicSubscriber =
    new PubSubTopicSubscriber();
    pubSubTopicSubscriber.subscribeTopic();
  }

  public void subscribeTopic() {
    BufferedReader inlineReader =
    new BufferedReader(new InputStreamReader(System.in));
    try {

        // Prompt for the JNDI topic connection factory name
```

```java
        System.out.println("Enter the Publish Subscribe
        Topic Connection Factory name:");
        String connectionFactoryName = inlineReader.readLine();

        // Prompt for topic name for the Pub Sub
        System.out.println("Enter the Publish Subscribe Topic name:");
        String pubsubTopicName = inlineReader.readLine();
        inlineReader.close();

        // Look up for the administered objects of Pub Sub
        InitialContext context = new InitialContext();
        TopicConnectionFactory topicConnFactory =
        (TopicConnectionFactory)
        context.lookup(connectionFactoryName);
        Topic pubsubTopic = (Topic) context.lookup(pubsubTopicName);
        context.close();

        // Create the JMS objects from administered objects
        TopicConnection topicConnection =
        topicConnFactory.createTopicConnection();
        TopicSession topicSession =
        topicConnection.createTopicSession(
        false, Session.AUTO_ACKNOWLEDGE);
        TopicSubscriber topicSubscriber =
        topicSession.createSubscriber(pubsubTopic);
        topicSubscriber.setMessageListener(this);
        topicConnection.start();

        // Keep listening to the pub sub until
        // the Quit subscription     command
        while (!quitMessageSubscription) {
          Thread.sleep(1000);
        }

        // Clean Up
        System.out.println("Messages successfully listened so far,
        Quitting Subscription!");
        topicConnection.close();
    } catch (Exception e) {
        e.printStackTrace();
    }
}
public void onMessage(Message message) {
    try {
        String messageContent = ((TextMessage) message).getText();
        System.out.println(messageContent);
        if ("quit".equals(messageContent))
        quitMessageSubscription = true;
```

```
      } catch (JMSException e) {
        e.printStackTrace();
        quitMessageSubscription = true;
      }
    }
  }
```

Point-To-Point (queue) programming

As discussed in the previous section, interfaces that extend the core JMS interfaces of Queue help build Point-To-Point components.

Please remember that to be able to execute the following example programs, you need the message queue to have been set up.

The following is a sample program to send messages to the Point-To-Point Queue:

```
package pointtopoint;

import java.io.BufferedReader;
import java.io.InputStreamReader;

import javax.jms.Queue;
import javax.jms.QueueConnection;
import javax.jms.QueueConnectionFactory;
import javax.jms.QueueSender;
import javax.jms.QueueSession;
import javax.jms.Session;
import javax.jms.TextMessage;
import javax.naming.InitialContext;

/**
 * Program to send messages to the queue
 * @author Raja
 *
 */
public class QueueMessageSender {
  public static void main(String[] args) {
    QueueMessageSender messageSender = new QueueMessageSender();
    messageSender.enqueueMessage();
  }

  public void enqueueMessage() {
    BufferedReader inlineReader = new BufferedReader(
    new InputStreamReader(System.in));
    try {
```

```java
      // Prompt for the JNDI Queue connection factory name
      System.out.println("Enter the Queue Connection Factory name:");
      String queueConnFactoryName = inlineReader.readLine();
      System.out.println("Enter the Queue name:");
      String queueName = inlineReader.readLine();

      // Look up for the administered objects of the Queue
      InitialContext context = new InitialContext();
      QueueConnectionFactory queueConnFactory =
      (QueueConnectionFactory)
      context.lookup(queueConnFactoryName);
      Queue queueReference = (Queue) context.lookup(queueName);
      context.close();

      // Create the JMS objects from administered objects
      QueueConnection queueConnection =
      queueConnFactory.createQueueConnection();
      QueueSession queueSession =
      queueConnection.createQueueSession(false,
      Session.AUTO_ACKNOWLEDGE);
      QueueSender queueSender =
      queueSession.createSender(queueReference);

      // Enqueue multiple text messages entered one after the other
      String messageContent = null;
      while (true) {
        System.out.println("Enter the new message to send or 'abandon'
        to exit the program:");
        messageContent = inlineReader.readLine();
        if ("abandon".equals(messageContent))
        break;
        TextMessage textMessage =
        queueSession.createTextMessage(messageContent);
        queueSender.send(textMessage);
      }

      // Clean Up
      System.out.println("Messages Successfully
      posted to the queue...");
      inlineReader.close();
      queueConnection.close();
    } catch (Exception e) {
      e.printStackTrace();
    }
  }
}
```

While the preceding program can send messages to the Point-To-Point queue, the following program will keep receiving messages from the queue until the `stopReceivingMessages` command is received:

```java
package pointtopoint;

import java.io.BufferedReader;
import java.io.InputStreamReader;

import javax.jms.JMSException;
import javax.jms.Message;
import javax.jms.MessageListener;
import javax.jms.Queue;
import javax.jms.QueueConnection;
import javax.jms.QueueConnectionFactory;
import javax.jms.QueueReceiver;
import javax.jms.QueueSession;
import javax.jms.Session;
import javax.jms.TextMessage;
import javax.naming.InitialContext;

/**
 * Program to receive messages from the queue
 * @author Raja
 *
 */
public class QueueMessageReceiver implements MessageListener {
  private boolean stopReceivingMessages = false;

  public static void main(String[] args) {
    QueueMessageReceiver queueMessageReceiver =
    new QueueMessageReceiver();
    queueMessageReceiver.startReceivingMessages();
  }

  public void startReceivingMessages() {
    BufferedReader inlineReader = new BufferedReader(
    new InputStreamReader(System.in));
    try {

      // Prompt for the JNDI Queue connection factory name
      System.out.println("Enter the Queue Connection Factory name:");
      String queueConnFactoryName = inlineReader.readLine();
      System.out.println("Enter the Queue name:");
      String queueName = inlineReader.readLine();

      // Look up for the administered objects of the Queue
      InitialContext context = new InitialContext();
```

```
      QueueConnectionFactory queueConnFactory =
      (QueueConnectionFactory)
      context.lookup(queueConnFactoryName);
      Queue queueReference = (Queue) context.lookup(queueName);
      context.close();

      // Create the JMS objects from administered objects
      QueueConnection queueConnection =
      queueConnFactory.createQueueConnection();
      QueueSession queueSession =
      queueConnection.createQueueSession(false,
      Session.AUTO_ACKNOWLEDGE);
      QueueReceiver queueMessageReceiver =
      queueSession.createReceiver(queueReference);
      queueMessageReceiver.setMessageListener(this);
      queueConnection.start();

      // Keep receiving the messages from the queue until the stop
      // receiving messages command is received
      while (!stopReceivingMessages) {
        Thread.sleep(1000);
      }

      // Clean Up
      System.out.println("Messages successfully received so far,
      Stop receiving messages!");
      queueConnection.close();
    } catch (Exception e) {
      e.printStackTrace();
    }
  }
}

public void onMessage(Message message) {
  try {
    String messageContent = ((TextMessage) message).getText();
    System.out.println(messageContent);
    if ("stop".equals(messageContent))
    stopReceivingMessages = true;
  } catch (JMSException e) {
    e.printStackTrace();
    stopReceivingMessages = true;
  }
 }

}
```

Web services

The next generation application interaction after the message queue is an open standard protocol called web services. It allows applications to communicate based on XML/SOAP/HTTP methodologies for information exchange. A simple individual application can be converted into a web application interacting with other applications using web services.

A web service can be defined as a collection of open protocols and standards for exchanging information among systems or applications. Enterprise applications developed in diverse technologies and languages and executed on different platforms can make web services a common technology to exchange information across system networks (internet/intranet), a kind of interprocess communication within a single computer. This interoperability (for example, between .Net and Java or Linux and Windows) is possible by following open standards.

Not all services performed by an application can be described as a web service. A service can be treated as a web service if:

- The service is discoverable through a simple lookup
- It uses a standard XML format for messaging
- It is available across internet/intranet networks.
- It is a self-describing service through a simple XML syntax
- The service is open to, and not tied to, any operating system/programming language

By following the aforementioned standards, web services attribute the loosely coupled, coarse grained, and synchronous/asynchronous information exchange between applications. Take a look at the following diagram:

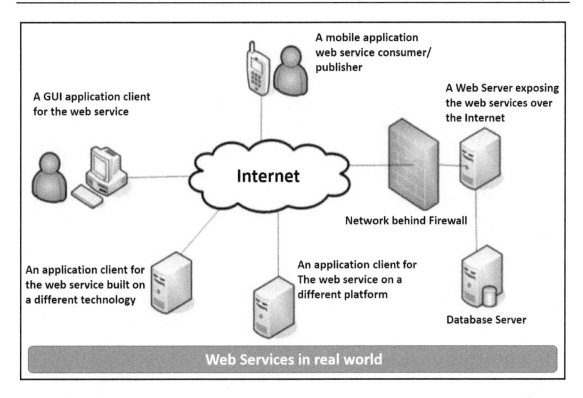

SOAP and RESTFUL are the two main types of web service.

The beauty of web services is that you can build them in two ways: either define the interface with which the individual application will implement its application behavior or expose the existing application functionality as a web service. These are termed top-down or bottom-up approaches, respectively.

Web service architectures

As part of a web service architecture, there exist three major roles. We discuss them next.

Service Provider is the program that implements the service agreed for the web service and exposes the service over the internet/intranet for other applications to interact with.

Service Requestor is the program that interacts with the web service exposed by the Service Provider. It makes an invocation to the web service over the network to the Service Provider and exchanges information.

Service Registry acts as the directory to store references to the web services.

The following are the steps involved in a basic SOAP web service operational behavior:

1. The client program that wants to interact with another application prepares its request content as a SOAP message.
2. Then, the client program sends this SOAP message to the server web service as an HTTP POST request with the content passed as the body of the request.
3. The web service plays a crucial role in this step by understanding the SOAP request and converting it into a set of instructions that the server program can understand.
4. The server program processes the request content as programmed and prepares the output as the response to the SOAP request.
5. Then, the web service takes this response content as a SOAP message and reverts to the SOAP HTTP request invoked by the client program with this response.
6. The client program web service reads the SOAP response message to receive the outcome of the server program for the request content it sent as a request.

SOAP web services

Simple Object Access Protocol (**SOAP**) is an XML-based protocol for accessing web services. It is a W3C recommendation for communication between two applications, and it is a platform- and language-independent technology in integrated distributed applications.

While XML and HTTP together make the basic platform for web services, the following are the key components of standard SOAP web services:

- **SOAP**: This is an XML-based protocol for accessing web services. It is also a W3C recommendation for application integration over networks. Being an XML-based implementation, SOAP is a platform- and language-independent technology. Applications developed in different languages, such as Java, PHP, or .Net, can use this technology.
- **Universal Description, Discovery, and Integration** (**UDDI**): UDDI is an XML-based framework for describing, discovering, and integrating web services. It acts as a directory of web service interfaces described in the WSDL language.
- **Web Services Description Language** (**WSDL**): WSDL is an XML document containing information about web services, such as the method name, method parameters, and how to invoke the service. WSDL is part of the UDDI registry. It acts as an interface between applications that want to interact based on web services.

The following diagram shows the interaction between the UDDI, Service Provider, and service consumer in SOAP web services:

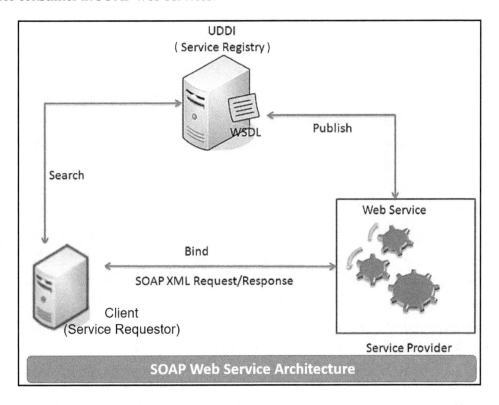

The characteristics of SOAP web services are as follows:

- **Web Service Security**: SOAP web services are considered a secured web service with its security implementation termed as "WS-Security."
- **Language and platform independence**: SOAP web services can be developed using diverse programming languages and can be deployed on any platform. They also allow seamless integration.
- **Performance**: Being an XML-based protocol and carrying multiple standards in its development, SOAP web service interaction requires more network bandwidth and resource allocation compared to other web services.
- **WSDL**: This is the only standard mechanism to define and discover SOAP web services.

Spring Web Services (**Spring-WS**) is a product of the Spring community that is focused on creating document-driven web services. Spring-WS aims to facilitate contract-first SOAP service development, allowing the creation of flexible web services using one of the many ways to manipulate XML payloads. The product is based on Spring itself, which means you can use Spring concepts, such as dependency injection, as an integral part of your web service.

RESTful web services

REST stands for **Representational State Transfer**. RESTful web services are considered a performance-efficient alternative to the SOAP web services. REST is an architectural style, not a protocol. Refer to the following diagram:

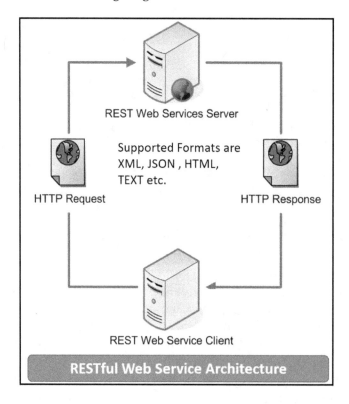

The characteristics of RESTful web services are as follows:

- **Performance**: RESTful web services give better performance efficiency compared to SOAP web services as they don't have strict specifications, unlike SOAP. RESTful web services consume less network bandwidth and resource allocation for information exchange.
- **Language and platform independence**: RESTful web services can be developed using diverse programming languages and can be deployed on any platform. They also allow seamless integration.
- **Support for versatile data formats**: A RESTful web service allows multiple data formats for information exchange, including simple text, HTML, XML, and JSON.

While both SOAP and RESTful support efficient web service development, let's check out the difference between these two technologies in the following table:

SOAP	REST
SOAP is a protocol.	REST is an architectural style.
SOAP stands for Simple Object Access Protocol.	REST stands for REpresentational State Transfer.
SOAP can't use REST because it is a protocol.	REST can use SOAP web services because it is a concept and can use any protocol like HTTP, SOAP.
SOAP uses services interfaces to expose the business logic.	REST uses URI to expose business logic.
JAX-WS is the java API for SOAP web services.	JAX-RS is the java API for RESTful web services.
SOAP defines standards to be strictly followed.	REST does not define too much standards like SOAP.
SOAP requires more bandwidth and resource than REST.	REST requires less bandwidth and resource than SOAP.
SOAP defines its own security.	RESTful web services inherits security measures from the underlying transport.
SOAP permits XML data format only.	REST permits different data format such as Plain text, HTML, XML, JSON etc.
SOAP is less preferred than REST.	REST more preferred than SOAP.

JAX-WS and JAX-RS are the two main APIs defined by Java to develop applications based on SOAP and RESTful web service:

- JAX-WS: This is the API provided by Java for developing SOAP web services. RPC style and Document style are the two different styles of writing SOAP web services using the JAX-WS API. While RPC-style web services use the method name and parameters to generate an XML structure, the Document style sends SOAP message as a single document.
- JAX-RS: This is the API provided by Java for developing RESTful web services. Jersey and RESTEasy are the two prominent implementations of the JAX-RS API.

Take a look at the following diagram:

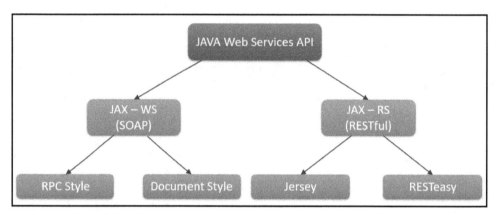

Now let's review how we can write a simple application for each of the aforementioned styles of web service.

Building a SOAP web service using the JAX-WS API in RPC Style

To build a JAX-WS-based SOAP web service, to perform the following coding steps:

1. Define the remote interface.
2. Implement the remote interface as a remote web service.
3. Write the Java component (publisher) that would expose the web service.
4. Write the client program to consume this web service.

5. Define the remote interface. Let's define a remote interface that defines the methods that act as web service methods:

```
//Remote Server Interface
package jaxws.rpc;

import javax.jws.WebMethod;
import javax.jws.WebService;
import javax.jws.soap.SOAPBinding;
import javax.jws.soap.SOAPBinding.Style;
//Service End point Interface
@WebService
@SOAPBinding(style = Style.RPC)
public interface RPCServer{
  @WebMethod String getRPCServerName(String name);
}
```

6. Implement the preceding remote interface that is defined as a remote implementation of the web service:

```
//Remote Server implementation
package jaxws.rpc;

import javax.jws.WebService;
//Service Implementation for the interface
@WebService(endpointInterface = "jaxws.rpc.RPCServer")
public class RPCServerImpl implements RPCServer {

  @Override
  public String getRPCServerName(String name) {
    return " JAX-WS RPC Server is : " + name;
  }

}
```

7. Write the Java component (publisher) that exposes the web service; the `publisher` class exposes the previously defined remote implementation component as a web service with WSDL in the defined URL:

```
//Web Service publisher
package jaxws.rpc;

import javax.xml.ws.Endpoint;

//End point publisher
public class RPCPublisher {
  public static void main(String[] args) {
```

```
        Endpoint.publish
        ("http://localhost:7779/jaxws/rpcservice", new
        RPCServerImpl());
    }

}
```

8. Write the client program to consume this web service. Once the aforementioned remote publisher is run and the web service is available at the WSDL URL exposed by the publisher, you can write and run the following RPC client program to contact the web service from the client system:

```java
package jaxws.rpc;

import java.net.URL;
import javax.xml.namespace.QName;
import javax.xml.ws.Service;

public class RPCClient {

    public static void main(String[] args) throws Exception {
        URL url = new URL("http://localhost:
        7779/jaxws/rpcservice? wsdl");

        //1st argument is the service URI as per the wsdl
        //2nd argument is the service name as per the wsdl
        QName qname = new QName("http://jaxwsrpcsoapservice.com/",
        "RPCServerImplService");
        Service service = Service.create(url, qname);
        RPCServer rpcWebService =
        service.getPort(RPCServer.class);
        System.out.println(rpcWebService.getRPCServerName(
        "Packt RPC"));
    }

}
```

Building SOAP web service using the JAX-WS API in Document style

To build a SOAP web service based on JAX-WS, we need to follow the same procedure as in the RPC style. However, change the SOAPBinding annotation as follows:

```java
//SOAP Binding annotation for document style
@SOAPBinding(style = Style.DOCUMENT)
```

Building a RESTful web service using the JAX-RS API (using the Jersey implementation)

There is a set of annotations defined by JAX-RS under the javax.ws.rs package that you can use to build RESTful web services. The following table defines of some important annotations:

Annotation	Purpose
Path	This annotation identifies the URI path. It can be specified on class or method.
PathParam	This annotation represents the parameter of the URI path.
GET	This annotation specifies the method responds to GET request.
POST	This annotation specifies the method responds to POST request.
PUT	This annotation specifies the method responds to PUT request.
HEAD	This annotation specifies the method responds to HEAD request.
DELETE	This annotation specifies the method responds to DELETE request.
OPTIONS	This annotation specifies the method responds to OPTIONS request.
FormParam	This annotation represents the parameter of the form.
QueryParam	This annotation represents the parameter of the query string of an URL.
HeaderParam	This annotation represents the parameter of the header.
CookieParam	This annotation represents the parameter of the cookie.
Produces	This annotation defines the media type for the response such as XML, PLAIN, JSON etc. It defines the media type that the methods of a resource class or MessageBodyWriter can produce.
Consumes	This annotation defines the media type that the methods of a resource class or MessageBodyReader can produce.

To build a RESTful web service based on JAX-RS, perform the following steps:

1. Define the remote server component.
2. Implement the deployment descriptor configurations.
3. Write the web component that is the default home page of the web service application.

4. Write the client program to consume the web service.

5. The first step is to define the remote server component for the RESTful web service, which is as follows:

```java
package jaxrs;

import javax.ws.rs.GET;
import javax.ws.rs.Path;
import javax.ws.rs.Produces;
import javax.ws.rs.core.MediaType;

@Path("/restws")
public class RESTServer {

  // This method is invoked if the request is
  // not for HTML or          XML
  @GET
  @Produces(MediaType.TEXT_PLAIN)
  public String getServerResponse() {
    return "REST Server plain text response";
  }

  // This method is invoked if XML content is requested
  @GET
  @Produces(MediaType.TEXT_XML)
  public String getXMLServerResponse() {
    return "<restws>REST Server xml response</restws>";
  }

  // This method is invoked if HTML content is requested
  @GET
  @Produces(MediaType.TEXT_HTML)
  public String getHtmlServerResponse() {
    return "<html> " + "<title>" +
    "REST Server Response" + "</title>"
    + "<body><h1>" + "REST Server HTML response" + "</h1>
    </body>" + "</html> ";
  }
}
```

6. Implement the deployment descriptor configurations. Once the remote server for the RESTful web service is defined, the `web.xml` deployment description should have a reference to this component through the provider package, as follows:

```
<?xml version="1.0" encoding="UTF-8"?>
<web-app xmlns:xsi="http://www.w3.org/2001/
XMLSchema-instance"
xmlns="http://java.sun.com/xml/ns/javaee"
xsi:schemaLocation="http://java.sun.com/xml/ns/javaee
http://java.sun.com/xml/ns/javaee/web-app_3_0.xsd"
id="WebApp_ID" version="3.0">
 <servlet>
   <servlet-name>Jersey REST Web Service</servlet-name>
     <servlet- class>
       org.glassfish.jersey.servlet.ServletContainer
     </servlet-class>
     <init-param>
       <param-name>
         jersey.config.server.provider.packages
       </param-name>
       <param-value>jaxrs</param-value>
     </init-param>
     <load-on-startup>1</load-on-startup>
   </servlet>
   <servlet-mapping>
     <servlet-name>Jersey REST Web Service</servlet-name>
     <url-pattern>/rest/*</url-pattern>
   </servlet-mapping>
 </web-app>
```

7. Write the web component that is the default home page of the web service application; being a web application, the default welcome page is `index.html` and can be defined as follows:

```
<!DOCTYPE html>
<html>
<head>
<meta charset="ISO-8859-1">
<title>REST Web Service</title>
</head>
<body>
    <a href="rest/restws">Invoke the REST Web Service</a>
</body>
</html>
```

8. Write the client program to consume the web service; once the preceding application is up-and-running on `4444` as the `jaxrsrestful` project, the RESTful web service is started and made available for the client program to invoke. The following is a client program that can invoke a remote web service for different media-type responses:

```java
package jaxrs;

import java.net.URI;
import javax.ws.rs.client.Client;
import javax.ws.rs.client.ClientBuilder;
import javax.ws.rs.client.WebTarget;
import javax.ws.rs.core.MediaType;
import javax.ws.rs.core.UriBuilder;
import org.glassfish.jersey.client.ClientConfig;

public class RESTClient {
  public static void main(String[] args) {
    ClientConfig config = new ClientConfig();
    Client client = ClientBuilder.newClient(config);
    WebTarget target = client.target(getBaseURI());
    //Invoke the REST Web Service for
    // different media type responses
    System.out.println(target.path("rest")
    .path("restws").request()
    .accep t(MediaType.TEXT_PLAIN)
    .get(String.class));
    System.out.println(target.path("rest")
    .path("restws").request()
    .accept(MediaType.TEXT_XML)
    .get(String.class));
    System.out.println(target.path("rest")
    .path("restws").request()
    .accept(MediaType.TEXT_HTML).get(String.class));
  }

  private static URI getBaseURI() {
    //server is deployed on 4444 port as the
    // jaxrsrestful project
    return UriBuilder.fromUri(
    "http://localhost:4444/jaxrsrestful").build();
  }
}
```

Enterprise integration patterns

Their features, and the similarities in messaging system' design and architecture, are together conceived as enterprise integration patterns. These patterns include the concept of messaging channels, validation filters, routing components, transformers, and adapters, as shown in the following diagram:

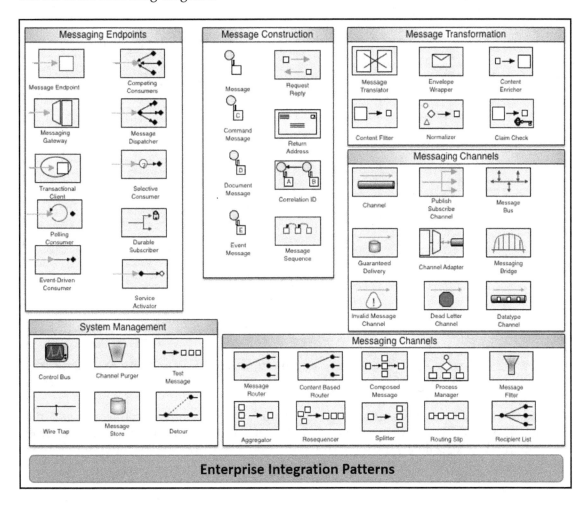

From the set of patterns defined for each requirement, a user can choose a pattern that meets most of their requirements and incorporate it in their application. The following diagram shows the integration of two applications using enterprise integration patterns for each of their requirements (messaging endpoint, message construction, messaging channels, message routing, message transformation, and system monitoring):

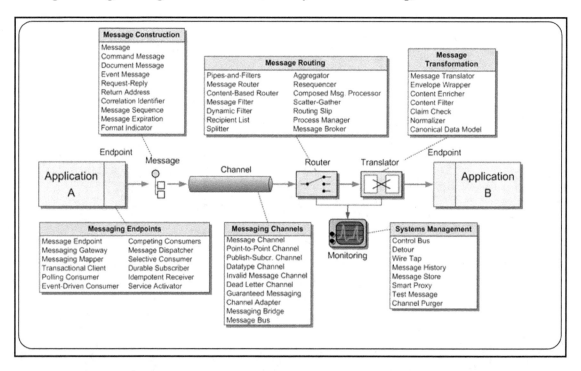

While there are quite a few proprietary and open source implementations of enterprise integration patterns, the Spring Integration framework is the most relevant and consistent framework based on enterprise integration patterns. I strongly recommend that you learn these patterns and at least one good implementation of it, such as Spring Integration, which closely adopts most enterprise integration patterns. Do this if you would like to upgrade your enterprise integration skills.

Summary

In this chapter, you learned about essential enterprise messaging concepts and their role in distributed computing. You also learned about the message queue system through the publish/subscribe and Point-To-Point messaging concepts. Then we covered JMS, interfaces in JMS, and the process of developing a JMS application. We also discussed web services and their architecture and implemented different types of web service, such as SOAP and RESTful, with examples. We finished this chapter with an understanding of enterprise integration patterns and how to design a messaging system using these design patterns.

In the next chapter, you will learn about HPC Cluster Computing and how it contributes to distributed computing. We'll do this by demonstrating a few examples in detail.

5
HPC Cluster Computing

Sometimes, the processing requirements of organizational applications may be more than what a regular computer configuration may offer. This can be addressed to an extent by increasing the processor capacity and other resource allocation. While this can improve the performance for a while, it restricts any future computational requirements, such as adding more powerful computational processors; it also involves an extra cost for producing such powerful systems. Also, there is a need to produce efficient algorithms and practices to produce the best results. A practical and economic substitute for these single high-power computers lies in establishing multiple low-power capacity processors that can work collectively and organize their processing capabilities. This means we'll set up parallel computers that would permit processing activities to be distributed among multiple low-capacity computers and obtain the best results. This would result in a powerful system.

In this chapter, we will cover the following topics:

- Era of computing
- Commanding parallel system architectures
- Massively Parallel Processors (MPP)
- Symmetric Multiprocessors (SMP)
- Cache Coherent Nonuniform Memory Access (CC-NUMA)
- Distributed systems
- Clusters
- Network of workstations
- Cluster computing architecture
- Cluster system software and tools
- High-Performance Computing Cluster (HPCC)
- Java support for high-performance computing
- Java support for parallel programming models
- Multithreading
- The Spliterator interface
- Java 9 updates for processing an API

Era of computing

Technological developments happen rapidly in the industry of computing due to advancements in system software and hardware. Hardware advancements happen around processor advancements and their creation techniques, and high-performance processors are being generated at an amazingly affordable price. Hardware advancements are further boosted by network systems with high bandwidth and low latency. **Very Large Scale Integration (VLSI)** as a concept has brought several phenomenal advancements in regard to producing commanding chronological and parallel processing computers. Simultaneously, *system software* advancements have improved the ability of an operating system, using advanced software programming development techniques. All of these advancements were observed in two commanding computing eras: the sequential and parallel era of computing. The following diagram shows the advancements in both the eras in the last few decades and also forecasts what would happen in the next two decades:

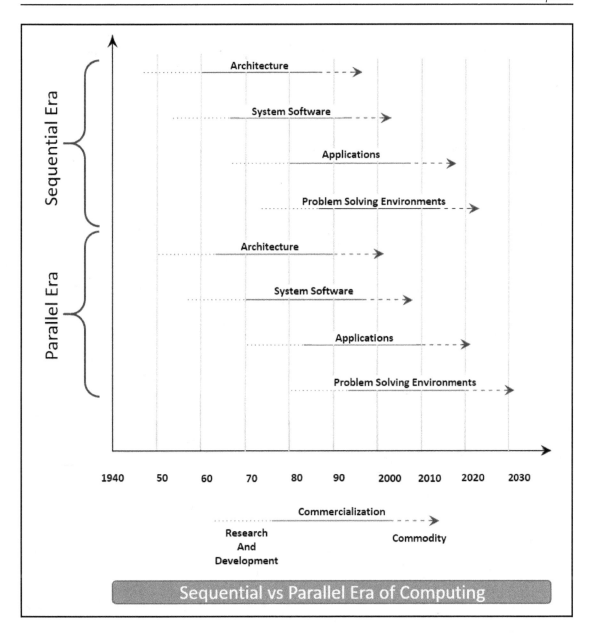

Sequential vs Parallel Era of Computing

In each of these eras, it is observed that the hardware architecture growth is trailed by system software advancements; this means that as more powerful hardware evolved, advanced software programs and operating system capacities correspondingly doubled their strength. Better applications and problem-solving environments were added to systems with the advent of parallel computing; due to this, mini to microprocessor development and the concept of clustered computers emerged.

Now let's review some of the commanding parallel system architectures from the last few years.

Commanding parallel system architectures

In the last few years, multiple varieties of computing models provisioning great processing performance have been developed. They are classified depending on the memory allocated to their processors and how their alignment is designed. Some of the important parallel systems are as follows:

- MPP
- SMP
- CC-NUMA
- Distributed systems
- Clusters

Let's get into a little more detail about each of these system architectures and review some of their important performance characteristics.

MPP

MPP, as the name suggests, is a huge parallel processing system developed in a shared nothing architecture. Such systems usually contain a large number of processing nodes that are integrated with a high-speed interconnected network switch. A node is nothing but an element of computers with a diverse hardware component combination, usually containing a memory unit and more than one processor. Some of the purpose nodes are designed to have backup disks or additional storage capacity.

The following diagram represents the MPP architecture:

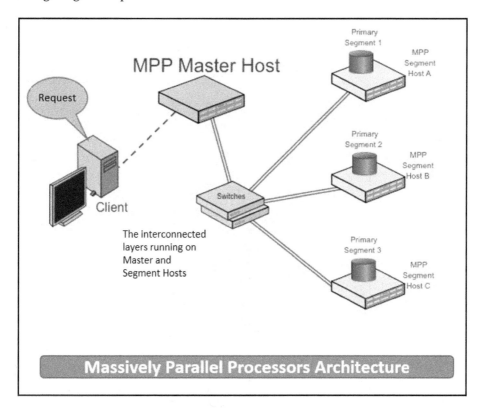

SMP

SMP, as the name suggests, contains a set of a limited number of processors, ranging from 2 to 64, and it shares most of the resources among these processors. An operating system instance operates together with all these connected processors, and these processors commonly share the I/O, memory, and network bus. The essential behavior of SMP is based on the nature of this set of similar connected processors and how they act together on the operating system.

The following diagram depicts the SMP representation:

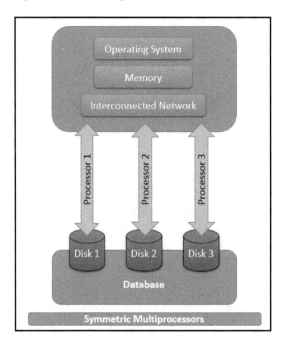

CC-NUMA

CC-NUMA is a special type of multiprocessor system that has mountable processor capability.

In CC-NUMA, the SMP system and the other remote nodes communicate through the remote interconnection link. Each of these remote nodes contains local memory and processors of their own.

The following diagram represents the cache-coherent non-uniform memory access architecture:

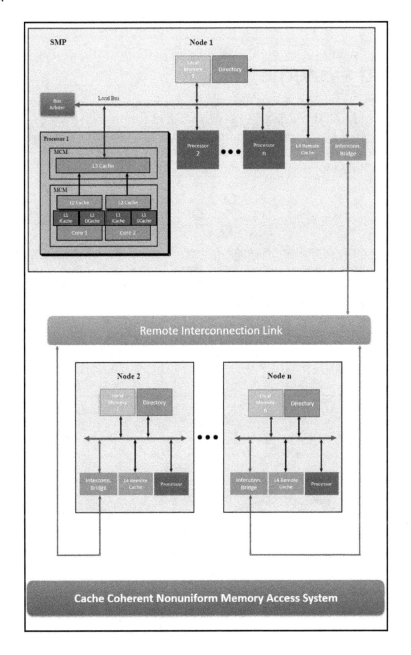

The nature of memory access is non-uniform. Just like SMP, the CC-NUMA system provides a comprehensive insight into an entire system's memory, and as the name suggests, it takes non-uniform time to access either close or distant memory locations.

Distributed systems

Distributed systems, as we have been discussing, are a traditional but individual set of computers interconnected through an Internet/intranet running on their own operating system. Any diverse set of computer systems can make contributions in order to be part of a distributed system if it fulfills this expectation, including a combination of MPP, SMP, distinct computers, and clusters.

Clusters

A cluster is an assembly of terminals or computers that are assembled through internetwork connection to address a large processing requirement through parallel processing. Hence, clusters are usually configured with terminals or computers that have higher processing capabilities connected with high-speed internetwork. Usually, a cluster is considered an image that integrates a number of nodes with a group of resource utilization techniques.

The following diagram is a sample clustered Tomcat server for a typical J2EE web application deployment:

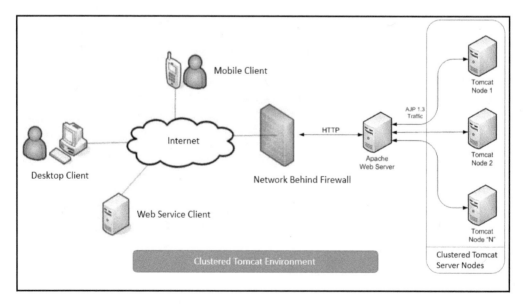

The following table shows some of the important performance characteristics of the different parallel architecture systems discussed so far:

Characteristic	MPP	SMP / CC-NUMA	Cluster	Distributed System
Number of Nodes	O (100) - O (1000)	O (10) - O (100)	O (100) or less	O (10) - O (1000)
Node Complexity	Fine grain or medium	Medium or coarse grained	Medium grain	Wide Range
Internode communication	Message passing/ shared variables for distributed shared memory	Centralized and Distributed Shared Memory (DSM)	Message Passing	Shared files, RPC, Message Passing and IPC
Job Scheduling	Single run queue on host	Single run queue mostly	Multiple queue but coordinated	Independent queues
SSI Support	Partially	Always in SMP and some NUMA	Desired	No
Node OS copies and type	N micro-kernels monolithic or layered Oss	One monolithic SMP and many for NUMA	N OS platforms (homogeneous / micro kernel)	N OS platforms homogeneous
Address Space	Multiple single for DSM	Single	Multiple or single	Multiple
Internode Security	Unnecessary	Unnecessary	Required if exposed	Required
Ownership	One Organization	One Organization	One or more Organizations	Many Organizations

Network of workstations

A network of workstations is a group of resources connected as system processors and as an interface for networks, storage, and data disks that open the space for newer combinations, such as:

- **Parallel computing**: As discussed in the previous sections, a group of system processors can be connected as MPP or DSM, which obtains the parallel processing ability.

- **RAM network**: As a number of systems are connected, each system memory can collectively work as DRAM cache, which intensely expands the virtual memory of the entire system and improves its processing ability.

- **Redundant Array of Inexpensive Disks (RAID)**: As a group of systems are used in the network connected in an array, it improves system stability, availability, and memory capacity with the help of low-cost multiple systems connected to the local area network. This also gives simultaneous I/O system support.
- **Multipath communication**: Multipath communication is a technique of using more than one network connection between a network of workstations to allow simultaneous information exchange among system nodes.

Cluster software can bring the best out of such parallel processing systems. Let's review a bit more about the cluster architecture.

Cluster computer architecture

A cluster is a single system resource that is a collection of distributed or parallel computing systems connecting a group of individual computers for a common processing purpose. The main advantage of such a system is to obtain greater performance through a relatively lower cost setup, when compared to a single high-performance computer. A generic cluster computer architecture is shown in the following diagram:

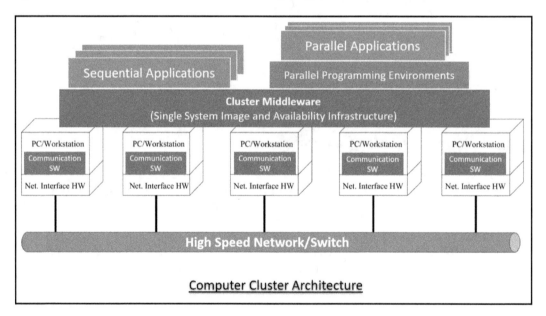

Some of the famous sets of elements that make a cluster computer include the following:

- Numerous effective performing computers (SMP/workstation)
- Sophisticated operating system (layered)
- N/W interface card (NIC)
- N/W of high-speed performing switch (GB Ethernet)
- Effective information exchange protocol (Quick Messaging)
- Cluster middleware (**SSI: Single System Image or System Availability Infrastructure**)
    - System hardware (DEC/DSM/SMP hardware systems)
    - Layered operating system (Solaris MC/Kernel)
    - Software and subsystems, including monitoring tools, DSM file system, LSF/CODINE kind of interface handling, and applications
- Parallel programming environments and software (PVM/MPI)
- Integrated systems (sequential/distributed system/parallel applications)

Network interface hardware is responsible for the information exchange between nodes in a clustered environment.

Communication software is responsible for providing effective and persistent information exchange between cluster nodes.

Cluster Middleware is responsible for bringing all the cluster nodes together to work and appear as a single resource to external resources.

Cluster system software and tools

A set of standard system software programs and tools together have helped the cluster system compute a powerful and workable substitute in parallel computing. The following are some of the programs and tools:

- **Multithreading**: This is an important feature that makes it possible to execute multiple tasks in parallel processing using cluster nodes. Java supports built-in multithreading, which is why the clustered system software and tools can be ported effectively with Java applications.
- **Message Passing Systems**: **Message Passing Interface** (**MPI**) and **Parallel Virtual Machine** (**PVM**) are efficient libraries that allow you to achieve the design goals of portability, functionality, and efficiency. mpiJava is the best example of a Java version of this API.

There exist multiple **Distributed Shared Memory** (**DSM**) systems, such as TreadMarks and Linda; Parallel debuggers and profilers, such as Cray T3E and TotalView; Performance analysis tools, such as AIMS, MPE, and Pablo; and Cluster administration tools, such as Berkeley NOW, SMILE, and PARMON. These have made the cluster environment the best choice for establishing and managing a parallel computing system effectively.

Now, let's understand a high-performance computing cluster that has unique processing abilities.

HPCC

One of the prominent information-centric, open source cluster systems that utilizes big data is developed by LexisNexis Risk Solutions; it is called HPCC. The HPCC system supports two types of processing techniques, as listed in the following points:

- **Thor (parallel batch data processing)**: This is similar to the Hadoop MapReduce platform; it is an information refinery that holds the responsibility of maintaining huge volumes of raw data captured and performs **ETL (extract, transform, and load)** processing through it. Establishing information relations, processing algorithms for complex detail analysis, and identifying the key information for performance improvement are the key strengths of this system. The following is the architecture of the Thor processing cluster:

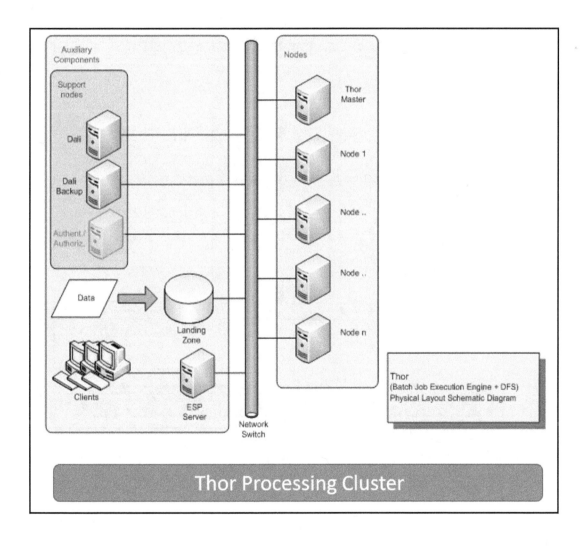

- **Roxie (high-performance online query applications using indexed data files)**: This is like Hadoop with HBase and Hive capabilities added, and it acts as a rapid data delivery engine. This platform is an ideal architecture for data warehouse transportation and numerous online web service requests that have a similarity in their search query and rapid response systems. The following is the architecture of the Roxie platform:

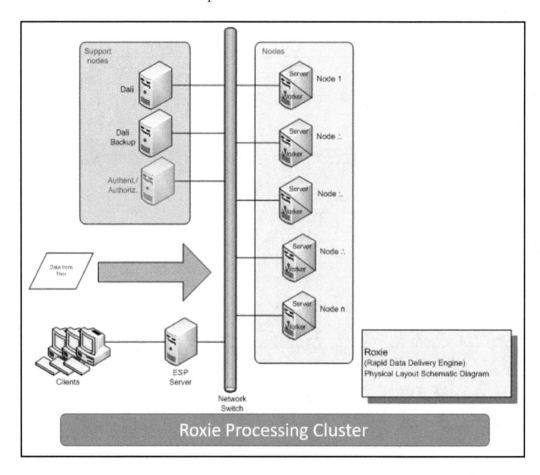

Now let's review how Java as a programming language supports high-performance computing.

Java support for high-performance computing

Java provides numerous advantages to **HPC** as a programming language, particularly with Grid computing. Some of the key benefits of using Java in HPC include:

- **Portability**: The capability to write a program on one platform and port it to run on another operating platform has been the biggest strength of the Java language. This will continue to be the advantage when porting Java applications to HPC systems. In Grid computing, this is an essential feature as the execution environment gets decided during the execution of the program. This is possible since the Java byte code executes in **Java Virtual Machine (JVM)**, which itself acts as an abstract operating environment.

- **Network centricity**: As discussed in the previous chapters, Java provides great support for distributed systems with its network-centric feature of **Remote Procedure Calls (RPC)** through RMI and CORBA services. Along with this, Java support for socket programming is another great support for grid computing.

- **Software engineering**: Another great feature of Java is the way it can be used for engineering solutions. We can produce more object-oriented, loosely coupled software that can be independently added as an API through JAR files in multiple other systems. Encapsulation and interface programming make it a great advantage in such application development.

- **Security**: Java is a highly secure programming language because of the features it provides, such as bytecode verification for limiting resource utilization by an untrusted intruder software or program. This is a great advantage when running an application on a distributed environment with remote communication established over a shared network.

- **GUI development**: Java support for platform-independent GUI development is a great advantage to develop and deploy enterprise web applications over an HPC environment to interact with.

- **Availability**: Java has great support from multiple operating systems, including Windows, Linux, SGI, and Compaq. It is easily available to consume, and you can develop it using a great set of open source frameworks developed on top of it.

While the advantages listed in the previous points are in favor of using Java for HPC environments, some concerns need to be reviewed while designing Java applications, including its numerics (complex numbers, fastfp, and multidimensional), performance, and parallel computing designs.

Java support for parallel programming models

Java provides numerous built-in patterns for parallel programming patterns, including multithreading, **Remote Method Invocation** (**RMI**), Sockets, and message passing or shared memory designs.

Multithreading

In parallel programming models, Java can run multithreaded programs on both single and multiple JVM models. In a single JVM, multithreading can be achieved by the Java native threads or another shared memory pattern, such as **OpenMP**. When you have multiple JVMs, individual programs execute in the respective JVM, and they can communicate using Java APIs such as RMI or MPJ, as shown in the following diagram:

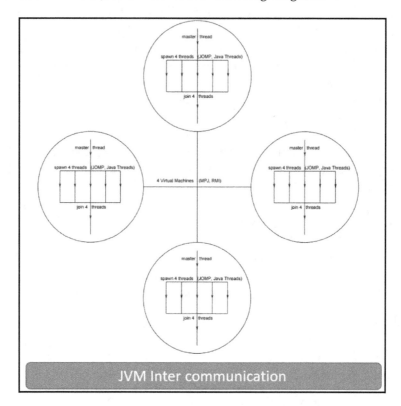

The Java thread class `java.lang.Thread` can produce instances of `Thread` to be able to run, spawn, and fork/join multiple threads, as shown in the following example that consists of five threads:

```java
package threads;

public class SpawningThreads {

  public static void main(String args[]){
    int threadCount = 5;
    Thread threadGroup [] = new Thread[threadCount];
    for(int iter1=0; iter1<threadCount; iter1++){
      threadGroup[iter1] = new Thread(new RunnableComponent(iter1));
      threadGroup[iter1].start();
    }
    for(int iter2=0; iter2<threadCount; iter2++){
      try{
        threadGroup[iter2].join();
      }catch (InterruptedException x){}
    }
    System.out.println("From the Master Thread Execution");
  }
}
class RunnableComponent implements Runnable {
  int iter3;
  public RunnableComponent(int j) {
    this.iter3 = j;
  }
  public void run() {
    System.out.println("From the Spawned Thread Execution");
  }
}
```

Parallelism

In Java multithreading, parallelism is achieved through loop-sharing mechanisms, which is a way to distribute loop iterations effectively between the available system resources. The two commonly available scheduling techniques are block and cyclic distribution; in some systems, they are used together to achieve the best results.

The following is a representation of the block and cyclic distribution technique on a 16-element array to distribute as many as four threads:

Block Distribution   Cyclic Distribution

Synchronization

From the concept of multithreading, joining threads is termed synchronization. Usually, the main thread needs to wait until the processing threads have finished with their execution. Also, multiple threads should be safeguarded not to update a shared resource called **mutual exclusion,** which is achieved with the usage of the keyword called `synchronized`. Statements and methods referred to with the `synchronized` keyword can be accessed and updated by only one process at a time. One thread has to wait for the other to complete the processing of the synchronized block and communicate with the `wait()` and `notifyall()` methods to let other threads know they need to wait and allow this other thread to be executed first.

The following is a sample program for synchronization, using the `synchronized` keyword:

```
package threads;

public class SynchronizeThreads {
```

```
  int threadNumber;
  ThreadCounter threadCounter;
  public SynchronizeThreads(int threadNumber,ThreadCounter
threadCounter) {
    this.threadNumber = threadNumber;
    this.threadCounter=threadCounter;
  }
  public void ThreadBarrier() {
    synchronized (threadCounter) {
      threadCounter.sharedAccessCont++;
      try {
        if(threadCounter.sharedAccessCont != threadNumber) {
          threadCounter.wait();
        } else {
          threadCounter.sharedAccessCont = 0;
          threadCounter.notifyAll();
        }
      }
      catch (InterruptedException e) {
        System.out.println("From Synchronized block execution");
      }
    }
  }
}
class ThreadCounter {
  int sharedAccessCont;
  public ThreadCounter(int sharedAccessCont) {
    this.sharedAccessCont=sharedAccessCont;
  }
}
```

JOMP

JOMP, which is a prototype Java implementation for OpenMP standards, provides a popular parallelism design for Java implementation, without adding the intricacy of Java thread processing. Like Java thread processing, JOMP provides a suitable design for programming a parallel Java application for executing it within a single JVM environment. JOMP contains its own runtime library and compiler; the compiler has the ability to translate Java code that has a directive into the Java code that has the ability to invoke runtime libraries. This is in a way using the concept of Java thread processing for incorporating the concept of parallelism. To bring portability, both the compiler and runtime library need to be implemented using Java.

Java message passing

Message passing is a popularly renowned mechanism to implement parallelism in applications; it is also called MPI. The MPI interface for Java has a technique for identifying the user and helping in lower startup overhead. It also helps in collective communication and could be executed on both shared memory and distributed systems. MPJ is a familiar Java API for MPI implementation. mpiJava is the near flexible Java binding for MPJ standards.

The Spliterator interface

A new interface is added to the `java.util` package called `Spliterator`, which, as the name implies, is a new type of *iterator* that can traverse through a `Collection` object. The `Collection` interface is updated to include a new `spliterator()` method, which returns a `Spliterator` upon `invocation`. The `Spliterator` iterator's strength lies in its ability to *split* the `Collection` object, partitioning off some of its elements as another `Spliterator` component. This gives the ability to perform parallel processing in the `Collection` items; however, `Spliterator` alone cannot supply the ability to process the tasks in parallel. The `Spliterator` ability is to support parallel processing in certain elements of a `Collection` element. Compared to `ArrayList`, this is an added ability to split the content of a collection object, which can be executed in parallel additionally to the split operation.

The fork/join framework of Java is one of the implementations that can be combined with the Spliterator to take a unit of work that can be parallelized. This can be achieved by breaking it into a small set of subtasks separately and aggregating the outcomes of these subtasks for obtaining the final output.

The methods that can perform the split and iteration are shown in the following code snippet:

```
Spliterator<T> trySplit();
boolean tryAdvance(Consumer<? super T> action);
```

The method `trySplit()` performs the split operation on the total list of items and returns a subset of it.

`tryAdvance()` performs the iteration and execution operation; hence, the actual method execution behavior needs to be supplied to this operation.

`forEachRemaining()` is the optimal way of executing the process to the `tryAdvance()` method.

Now, let's review a sample implementation of `Spliterator` to read a large file input and review the processing time.

The first step is to write a base class that implements the Spliterator interface, as shown in the following code snippet:

```
package threads;

import static java.util.Spliterators.spliterator;

import java.util.Comparator;
import java.util.Spliterator;
import java.util.function.Consumer;

public abstract class BaseFixedBatchSpliterator<T> implements
Spliterator<T> {
  private int groupCount;
  private int properties;
  private long estimatedSize;

  // constructor with no paramters
  public BaseFixedBatchSpliterator() {
  // set the behaviour of this component
  this(IMMUTABLE | ORDERED | NONNULL);
}

// constructor with single parameter properties
public BaseFixedBatchSpliterator(int properties) {
  // set the behaviour of this component
  this(properties, 128, Long.MAX_VALUE);
}

// constructor with two parameters, properties and groupcount
public BaseFixedBatchSpliterator(int properties, int groupCount) {
  // set the behaviour of this component
  this(properties, groupCount, Long.MAX_VALUE);
}

// constructor with multiple parameters
public BaseFixedBatchSpliterator(int properties, int groupCount,      long
estimatedSize) {
  this.properties = properties | SUBSIZED;
  this.groupCount = groupCount;
  this.estimatedSize = estimatedSize;
}

static final class HandlingConsumer<T> implements Consumer<T> {
```

```
    Object obj;

    @Override
    public void accept(T obj) {
      this.obj = obj;
    }
  }

    @Override
    public int characteristics() {
      return properties;
    }

    @Override
    public long estimateSize() {
      return estimatedSize;
    }

    @Override
    public Comparator<? super T> getComparator() {
      if (hasCharacteristics(SORTED))
      return null;
      throw new IllegalStateException();
    }

    @Override
      public Spliterator<T> trySplit() {
        final HandlingConsumer<T> holdingConsumer =
        new HandlingConsumer<>();
        if (!tryAdvance(holdingConsumer))
        return null;
        final Object[] consumerBatch = new Object[groupCount];
        int iterator = 0;
        do
        consumerBatch[iterator] = holdingConsumer.obj;
        while (++iterator < groupCount && tryAdvance(holdingConsumer));
        if (estimatedSize != Long.MAX_VALUE)
        estimatedSize -= iterator;
        return spliterator(consumerBatch, 0, iterator,
        characteristics() |     SIZED);
      }
  }
```

The next step is to extend this base component to handle `withBatchSize()`, as shown in the following code snippet:

```
package threads;
```

```
import static java.util.stream.StreamSupport.stream;

import java.util.Spliterator;
import java.util.function.Consumer;
import java.util.stream.Stream;

public class SplitFixedBatchSpliterator<T> extends
BaseFixedBatchSpliterator<T> {
  private final Spliterator<T> iterSpl;

  public static <T> SplitFixedBatchSpliterator<T>
  batchedSpliterator(Spliterator<T> toBundle, int groupCount) {
    return new SplitFixedBatchSpliterator<>(toBundle, groupCount);
  }

  public SplitFixedBatchSpliterator(Spliterator<T> toBundle,
  int groupCount) {
    super(toBundle.characteristics(), groupCount,
    toBundle.estimateSize());
    this.iterSpl = toBundle;
  }

  @Override
  public void forEachRemaining(Consumer<? super T> action) {
    iterSpl.forEachRemaining(action);
  }

  @Override
  public boolean tryAdvance(Consumer<? super T> action) {
    return iterSpl.tryAdvance(action);
  }

  public static <T> Stream<T> withBatchSize(Stream<T> in,
  int groupCount) {
    return stream(batchedSpliterator(in.spliterator(),
    groupCount), true);
  }

}
```

Now it's time to write the main component that reads through the file and reviews the performance, as follows:

```
package threads;

import static java.util.concurrent.TimeUnit.SECONDS;
import static threads.SplitFixedBatchSpliterator.withBatchSize;
```

```
import java.io.IOException;
import java.io.PrintWriter;
import java.nio.file.Files;
import java.nio.file.Path;
import java.nio.file.Paths;
import java.util.stream.Stream;

public class SplitIteratorSample {

  static double drop;
  private static final int NUMBER_THREE = 3, NUMBER_TEN = 10;

  public static void main(String[] args) throws IOException {
    final Path inputFilePath = generateInput();
    for (int i = 0; i < NUMBER_THREE; i++) {
      System.out.println("Begin executing the jdk streams");
      monitoringExeuction(Files.lines(inputFilePath));
      System.out.println("Begin executing the fixed batch streams");
      monitoringExeuction(withBatchSize(Files.lines
      (inputFilePath),NUMBER_TEN));
    }
  }

  private static Path generateInput() throws IOException {
    final Path filePath = Paths.get("fileToRead.txt");
    try (PrintWriter pw =
    new PrintWriter(Files.newBufferedWriter(filePath))) {
      for (int iterC = 0; iterC < 6000; iterC++) {
        final String lineText = String.valueOf
        (System.nanoTime());
        for (int j = 0; j < 15; j++)
        pw.print(lineText);
        pw.println();
      }
    }
    return filePath;
  }

  private static long executeStream(String stream) {
    final long localBeginTimeOfExecution = System.nanoTime();
    double dbl = 0;
    for (int iterA = 0; iterA < stream.length(); iterA++)
    for (int iterB = 0; iterB < stream.length(); iterB++)
    dbl += Math.pow(stream.charAt(iterA), stream.charAt
    (iterB) /     32.0);
    drop += dbl;
    return System.nanoTime() - localBeginTimeOfExecution;
  }
```

```
private static void monitoringExeuction(
Stream<String> streamInput) throws IOException {
  final long beginOfExecution = System.nanoTime();
  try (Stream<String> lineOfExecutions = streamInput) {
    final long overallTimeOfExeuction =
    lineOfExecutions.parallel()
    .mapToLong(SplitIteratorSample::executeStream).sum();
    final double cpuExecutionTime =
    overallTimeOfExeuction, actualTime =
    System.nanoTime() - beginOfExecution;
    final int processors =
    Runtime.getRuntime().availableProcessors();
    System.out.println(" Processors : " + processors);
    System.out.format(" CPU Execution time : %.2f sn",
    cpuExecutionTime / SECONDS.toNanos(1));
    System.out.format(" Actual Execution time : %.2f sn",
    actualTime /     SECONDS.toNanos(1));
    System.out.format("CPU utilization percentage : %.2f%%nn",
    100.0 * cpuExecutionTime / actualTime / processors);
  }
 }
}
```

As you can see, a linear 4x speedup along with the Spliterator implementation can be achieved as compared to single-threaded processing.

Parallel stream processing

Java takes care of the parallel stream with its new stream API and the simplification of creating parallel processing on collections and arrays. Let's have a look at how this works.

Let's say myNumList is a list of integers containing 800.000 integer values. Before Java 8, these integer values were summed up using the for each loop; refer to the following code snippet:

```
for (int i :myList) {
  result+= i;
}
```

Starting from Java 8, we can do the same thing using streams:

```
myList.stream().sum();
```

The next step is to parallelize this processing. We just need to use the `parallelStream()` instead of `stream()` or `parallel()` if we still have a stream, as shown in the following code snippet:

```
myList.parallelStream().sum();
```

The system needs to be reviewed where parallel processes can be performed and the performance of the application can be optimized by introducing parallel processing. Make sure your overall processing task is spawned as parallel processes do not wait for other resources; otherwise, the idea of parallel processing will provide no big advantage.

Java 9 updates for processing an API

Java 9 provides a refined Process API to control and manage the process with better performance in your operating system.

Process control could be made easier by accessing the **process ID (PID)**, username, and resource utilization with the processing path information from the operating system. The multithreaded approach from previous versions is refined to easily deal with process trees and destruct or manage processes that have multiple subprocesses.

The following is an example of retrieving the PID of the current process with this API:

```
private static int getOwnProcessID(){
  return ProcessHandle.current().getPid();
}
```

The following is a code snippet for getting a list of all the processes running on the operating system:

```
private static void listProcesses(){
  ProcessHandle.allProcesses().forEach((h) -> printHandle(h));
}

private static void printHandle(ProcessHandle procHandle) {
  // get info from handle
  ProcessHandle.Info procInfo = procHandle.info();
  System.out.println("PID: " + procHandle.getPid());
  System.out.print("Start Parameters: ");
  String[] empty = new String[]{"-"};
  for (String arg : procInfo.arguments().orElse(empty)) {
    System.out.print(arg + " ");
  }
  System.out.println();
```

```
        System.out.println("Path: " + procInfo.command().orElse("-"));
        System.out.println("Start: " + procInfo.startInstant().
        orElse(Instant.now()).toString());
    System.out.println("Runtime: " + procInfo.totalCpuDuration().
        orElse(Duration.ofMillis(0)).toMillis() + "ms");
        System.out.println("User: " + procInfo.user());
    }
```

In the previous example, we exited the execution of operating-system-dependent applications and regex for the resulting output.

We can also get the handle of a process directly if we know the PID; we can do this by simply calling `ProcessHandle.of(pid)`.

Obviously, this is a much cleaner way than checking the operating system and splitting the String with an appropriate regex. This is more of an operating-system-independent code that makes Java more flexible for distributed and parallel computing processes.

Summary

In this chapter, you learned about the essential parallel systems and their architectures. You also learned about the cluster computing architecture and its implementations.

We also covered Java support for parallel programming models, such as multithreading and the Spliterator interface, and looked at Java 9 updates for processing an API.

In the next chapter, you will learn about distributed computing in databases and demonstrate Java support for such a programming model in detail.

6
Distributed Databases

Global organizations are geographically spread across and would like to maintain their information in the local database, where each database location is situated close to the organization site while making it accessible to global users. This brought the need for the database to have multiple instances and for information to be collated from these multiple systems connected over the communication network and administered through a central system/resource. This central control should allow the applications/users, from the same or different location to the database, to access both local and remote information to effectively support the distributed computing behavior. Such access of the distributed database from the application gets complicated when the application tries to add/update more information across it in a single transaction.

In this chapter, we will cover the following:

- Distributed and decentralized databases
- Distributed database environments
- Homogeneous distributed database environment
- Heterogeneous distributed database environment
- Distributed database setup methodologies
- Replication
- Horizontal partitioning
- Vertical partitioning
- Hybrid Setup
- Distributed DBMS architecture
- Design goals
- Java Database Connectivity (JDBC)
- JTA for distributed transactions
- XA transactions programming

Distributed and decentralized databases

Let's start our discussion by understanding the definitions of distributed versus decentralized databases.

A **distributed database** is a single logical database, which is installed on a set of computers that are geographically located at different locations and linked through a data communication network. Different types of distributed database are classified based on the number of different database management systems operating on each of the remote computers, how these remote DBMS communicate and work together, and if they need a controlling master resource to synchronize the data update requests to each of the database instances.

A **decentralized database** is a database that is installed on systems that are geographically located at different locations but *"not"* linked through a data communication network. This means that it is a group of independent database instances which have no logical connections between them.

Motivation for distributed databases

Let's now review the set of organizational requirements which motivated the need for having distributed databases:

Dispersal and independence of organization units: Global organizations are spread across the continents, countries, and states as different divisions and departments, and each unit of the organization might perform its own business functioning. Hence, it is more certain that individual organization units want to maintain the information and functioning related to the regional organization unit in their local database to have better control and operational capacity within the location. With the trend of mergers and acquisitions, it is more common to integrate and split the database between the units more securely.

Information exchange: More often, the individual organization units need to generate regional information statistics and review specific instance-related information with the global leaders. They should be able to extract such business-critical information from the local organization unit database and share it with the leadership.

Secure information transmission: It is important to transmit the information between the remote databases in a secure and reliable channel through the communication network. It is also important to port the information with minimum costs in less time, and consider different mechanisms to ensure there is no data loss in information exchange. This is why taking regular backups of a database and keeping a copy of information shared for future comparison and records is a part of organizational database maintenance.

Communicating versatile DBMS: When an organization splits into multiple different organizations or when one organization takes over another organization, due to the regional software licensing constraints some organizations tend to maintain different DBMS across different organizational units. Also, applications developed over time tend to start with the latest available DBMS version within the same vendor DBMS. A distributed database should be defined in a way that it can operate based on the reference architecture model and independent of the vendor/application specifics.

Replication and Recovery: Computer systems can collapse anytime due to exceptions and vulnerabilities. It is important to recover the system to the most recent stable version in the minimum time when such an incident happens. Frequent database replication (copy) to another local/remote database is important, as you are able to backup from it during database corruption.

Data mining: It is the process of abstracting the most relevant information related to the criteria to be reviewed from the large set of data. It should be possible to mine both regional and global information as and when needed across the distributed database.

Location Transparency: An organization unit can have the users who need to have access to the information but only specific to a particular location. They should not be able to access/interact with the other location database.

Transaction Management: Some of the global decisions need to be incorporated in each of the organization units, together or in groups. Similarly, the information updated in a specific location can cause a few of the other organization units to get affected. Such kind of information updates should happen together in a single transaction across the distributed database.

Based on the preceding said business requirement, the distributed database can be designed in one of following discussed types.

Distributed database environments

As per the organizational needs and information split and exchange requirements, the distributed database can be designed in one of the following ways, as shown in the following diagram:

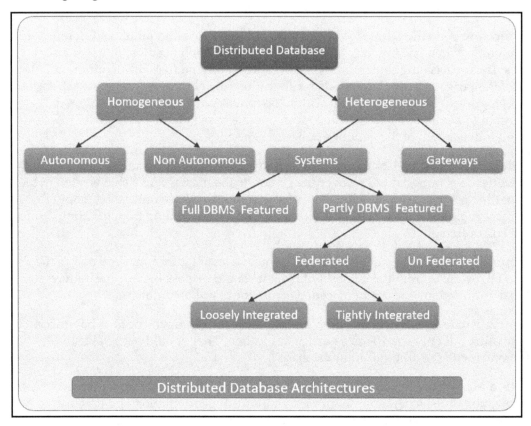

Homogeneous distributed database environment

When setting up a distributed database environment, if the same database management system is used for all the database nodes which take part in this distributed database, then it is termed as a **homogeneous distributed database environment**.

This environment can be represented as in the diagram here:

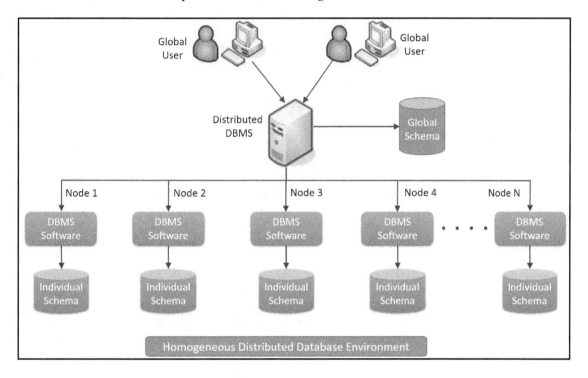

The following are some of the characteristics of the homogeneous distributed database environment:

- Information is distributed between all the individual database management system's nodes
- Across all the remote databases, the same database management system is used
- All the information is controlled by the distributed database management system, which will ensure that there is no region-specific information in an individual database
- Every global user must access the information from the same global schema controlled by the distributed database management system
- A combination of all the individual database schemas makes the global schema

The homogeneous distributed database environment is divided into two types, namely, *autonomous* and *non-autonomous*.

An **autonomous** distributed database environment is one that has each of the individual database management systems with the ability to function autonomously and communicate with the other remote database management systems to exchange the information.

A **non-autonomous** distributed database environment is one that has a master/central database management system, which synchronizes the database access and communicates with the individual nodes to update the information.

Even though organizations want to maintain a homogenous distributed database environment, due to the previously discussed restrictions such as regional licensing constraints, takeovers, application development, or upgrade lifecycles, mergers and splits are difficult to do. Hence, they end up having different database management systems or application software in some of the individual location systems, as discussed in the following section.

Heterogeneous distributed database environment

When setting up a distributed database environment, if possibly a diverse database management system is used for some of the nodes that take part in this distributed database, then it is termed as a heterogeneous distributed database environment.

This environment can be represented as in the diagram here:

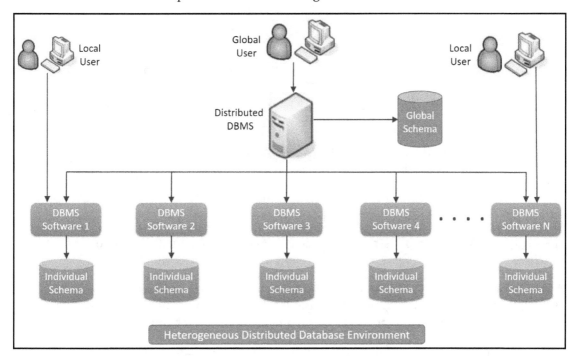

The following are some of the characteristics of the heterogeneous distributed database environment:

- Information is distributed between all the individual database management system's nodes
- A versatile database management system can be installed across the individual database systems
- Local users, who may want to interact with one of the individual database, can be given access to that individual database management system and the individual schema corresponding to it
- Users who want to access the global information can communicate with the distributed database management system, which has a global schema. It is a combination of all the individual database schemas

The heterogeneous distributed database environment is divided into two types, namely, *systems* and *gateways*.

The systems distributed database environment is the one that has full or partial functionality and belongs to a logical database, which is supported.

This environment is further categorized into *Full DBMS Featured* and *Partly DBMS Featured* distributed database environments.
A *Full DBMS Featured* distributed database environment is the one that has complete support for the entire functionality of a distributed database.
A *Partly DBMS Featured* distributed database environment is the one that has support for some of the distributed database features.

A *Partly DBMS Featured* distributed database environment is further categorized into *Federated and Unfederated* distributed database environments.

A *Federated* distributed database environment is the one that supports access provision to an individual database for specific information requests from the individual database.

A *Federated DBMS Featured* distributed database environment is further categorized into *loosely integrated and tightly integrated* distributed database environments.

A *loosely integrated* distributed database environment is the one with each of the individual databases that has its own individual schema. Each individual database management system should be able to interact with all the other individual schemas.

A *tightly integrated* distributed database environment is the one that has a global schema to define the entire information across all the individual databases.

An *unfederated* distributed database environment is the one that needs complete access to the central database component.

A *gateways* distributed database environment is the one that has connectivity to other databases through a simple path and does not support the logical database.

Distributed database setup methodologies

The process of setting up the distributed database environment involves a thorough analysis and design. A review of ongoing and future information maintenance should be made, if it needs a **synchronous** (information across all the nodes should be kept in sync all the time) or **asynchronous** (information is replicated at multiple nodes to make it available for other nodes, instead of accessing through the network when it is required) setup.

Once the analysis for a specific distributed database environment is made, the setup can be performed in one of the following ways:

- Replication
- Horizontal partitioning
- Vertical partitioning
- Hybrid setup

Replication

Replication is the mechanism through which a separate copy of the database instance is made to create the distributed database environment.

It is considered as an easy and minimum risk process as the information is copied from one instance to another without a logical separation. Also, each of the individual nodes having the complete information, is more efficient in accessing the information without having network traversals and reduces the risk of network security.

However, it consumes more storage space having a replica of the entire information from each of the node at all the other nodes, and it takes longer to sync all the nodes when the information across all the nodes needs to be updated.

Snapshots that pull a real-time replication for each transaction are some of the techniques used in data replication.

Horizontal partitioning

Horizontal partitioning is the process of splitting the rows of a table or a relation between two or more databases to form a distributed database. With this setup, each individual database has a set of rows that belong to the table or relation that belongs to the specific individual database.

As the data specific to the location is stored locally, the information access is more efficient, and optimal performance can be expected as the local data is only stored in a specific database. It is also more secure, as the information belonging to the other location is not stored in the database.

However, if a user wants to access some of the other nodes or a combination of node information, the access latency varies across. Also, if there is a problem with a node or a network, the information related to that node becomes inaccessible to the users.

Vertical partitioning

Vertical partitioning is like the normalization process followed in a database setup. The information belonging to a table or relation is split with a certain number of columns between each of the database nodes, while keeping a copy of the base column (primary column) to uniquely identify each record.

Vertical partitioning is more helpful if each of the organizational units located in different geographies have separate operations. It is a more logical partitioning of information based on the behavior and function that each node performs.

However, the aggregation of the data involves complex queries with joins across the location database, as no replication is made for non-primary columns.

Hybrid setup

A hybrid distributed database setup involves a combination of each of the preceding said processes. Some of the information is replicated across the database nodes; if there exist departments exist that are common to multiple nodes, horizontal partitioning is made for those entities and individual departments can have a vertical partitioning for their information.

Data administrators play a crucial role in this setup to choose the right combination. This ensures that the data integrity and security are met, while following specific business needs.

The following table shows a comparison of the distributed database design approaches:

Approach	Reliability	Future Scope of Expansion	Information Exchange	Maintenance	Data Consistency
Centralized	**POOR:** Highly dependent on central server	**POOR:** Limitations are barriers to performance	**VERY HIGH:** High traffic to one site	**VERY GOOD:** One, monolithic site requires little coordination	**EXCELLENT:** All users always have same data
Replicated with snapshots	**GOOD:** Redundancy and tolerated delays	**VERY GOOD:** Cost of additional copies may be less than linear	**LOW to MEDIUM:** Not constant, but periodic snapshots can cause bursts of network traffic	**VERY GOOD:** Each copy is like every other one	**MEDIUM:** Fine as long as delays are tolerated by business needs
Synchronized replication	**EXCELLENT:** Redundancy and minimal delays	**VERY GOOD:** Cost of additional copies may be low and synchronization work only linear	**MEDIUM:** Messages are constant but some delays are tolerated	**MEDIUM:** Collisions add some complexity to manageability	**MEDIUM to VERY GOOD:** Close to precise consistency
Integrated partitions	**VERY GOOD:** Effective use of partitioning and redundancy	**VERY GOOD:** New nodes get only data they need without changes in overall database design	**LOW to MEDIUM:** Most queries are local but queries which require data from multiple sites can cause a temporary load	**DIFFICULT:** Especially difficult for queries that need data from distributed tables, and updates must be tightly coordinated	**VERY POOR:** Considerable effort; and inconsistencies not tolerated
Decentralized with independent partitions	**GOOD:** Depends on only local database availability	**GOOD:** New sites independent of existing ones	**LOW:** Little if any need to pass data or queries across the network (if one exists)	**VERY GOOD:** Easy for each site, until there is a need to share data across sites	**LOW:** No guarantees of consistency, in fact pretty sure of inconsistency

Distributed DBMS architecture

As part of the distributed database setup, we need to configure a distributed database management system, which can synchronize the information retrieval and/or update each of the individual schemas. While each individual system can have its own database management system to control its respective database, having a distributed **Database Management System (DBMS)** takes care of the following purposes:

- Monitoring the data setup in the distributed database, so that individual users and applications see the distributed database as one logical instance of database and schema
- Govern the information by locating it during retrieval and updating requests from individual applications and users

- Taking the requests for individual database nodes, and retrieving the information from other remote databases as well, if the requested information is not available in the local database
- Ensuring that the distributed database access is following the roles of universal query optimization, concurrent, and deadlock management, information security, and automatic exception handling and recovery
- With the help of features such as multiphase commit protocol, ensuring the information across all the distributed database nodes is consistent
- Abstract the globally distributed database as one rational database with the primary key governance to ensure, the entities distributed across the individual database can be joined and related with diverse primary keys

The following diagram illustrates the distributed database management system architecture:

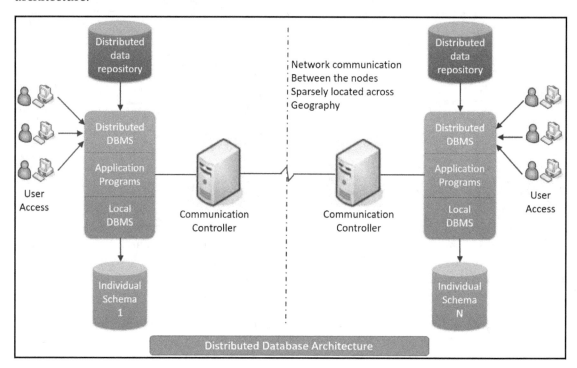

In the preceding architecture diagram, each of the individual systems have their own database management system (local DBMS) to manage the database installed with the information warehoused in that respective system. Along with the local DBMS, each of the individual systems carries a replica of the distributed DBMS along with the distributed data repository association. The purpose of having the distributed data repository is to maintain that the reference for the entire information is stored across the distributed database network and their definitions. Each application or user request for the information will first be reviewed within the local database; if not found, it will be forwarded to the global database with the help of the distributed DBMS. If the requested information is available within the local system, it can be populated by a *local transaction*, and if the information is retrieved from across the network of databases with the references reviewed from the distributed data repository, it is termed as a *global transaction*.

The design goals of the distributed database include:

- **Location Transparency**: Applications and users should be able to populate the information from the network of databases as if they are interacting with a single database.
- **Replication/Fragmentation Transparency**: Applications and users should be able to visualize the information as a single unit/existence of information even though it is replicated across nodes for distributed management.
- **Failure Transparency**: Ensure that a complete set of operations are part of a single transaction and should be either committed, or none of them are committed, across the networked database nodes.
- **Commit Protocol**: A process to ensure that the failure transparency is achieved through transaction management on global transactions. A renowned commit protocol for this purpose is the two-phase commit, wherein the transaction is committed only after the updates at all the nodes are successful through lock – update – notify and commit operations.
- **Concurrency Transparency**: Multiple simultaneously executing transactions should be organized to showcase an individual transaction status and the result of simultaneous execution must be the same as if those transactions are performed in sequential order.
- **Security**: Data and transport security should be adopted with the help of encryption and SSL communication protocols.

Eminent organizations have their own products for distributed database management with the above mentioned design goals, including:

- *IBM*: DB2 Data Propagator, Distributed Relational Database Architecture (DRDA), and Data Joiner
- *Sybase*: Replication Server
- *Oracle*: SQL Anywhere Studio, Table Snapshot, and Symmetric Replication options
- *Computer Associates*: Advantage Ingres Enterprise Relational Database Replicator Option
- *Microsoft:* SQL Server 2005

Let's now review how to communicate the individual database with the renowned Java way JDBC, before reviewing the communication with the distributed database.

Java Database Connectivity

Java Database Connectivity (JDBC) is Java's API for interacting with the relational databases. JDBC is a specification interface, while individual database vendors develop the drivers library adhering to JDBC.

The following is the syntax for a simple database connection and query execution to obtain the results into the object called `ResultSet`:

```
Connection dbConn = DriverManager.getConnection(databaseURL, username,
password);
Statement qryStmt =
dbConn.createStatement(ResultSet.TYPE_SCROLL_INSENSITIVE,
ResultSet.CONCUR_UPDATABLE);
ResultSet queryResults = qryStmt.executeQuery("SELECT <COLUMNS TO RETRIEVE>
FROM <TABLES / VIEWS ALONG WITH CRITERIA>");
```

Here is the sample program for an `UpdatableResultSet` to retrieve, update, delete, and add a new row into an Oracle database:

```
package resultset;

import java.sql.Connection;
import java.sql.DriverManager;
import java.sql.ResultSet;
import java.sql.SQLException;
import java.sql.Statement;

public class UpdatableResultSet {
  public static void main(String[] args) {
    try (
      //Load Driver class
      Class.forName("oracle.jdbc.driver.OracleDriver");
      // Oracle Connection
      Connection databaseConn = DriverManager.getConnection
      ("jdbc:oracle:thin:@myhost:1521:orcl", "scott", "tiger");
      // TYPE_SCROLL_INSENSITIVE: Indicates the ResultSet is scrollable
      // but not sensitive to the data changes
      // that underlies the ResultSet.
      // CONCUR_UPDATABLE: Resultset concurrency mode is updatable
      Statement queryStmt = databaseConn.createStatement(
      ResultSet.TYPE_SCROLL_INSENSITIVE, ResultSet.CONCUR_UPDATABLE);
    ) {
      // Disable auto-commit before executing the query
      databaseConn.setAutoCommit(false);
      ResultSet resultSet = queryStmt.executeQuery(
      "select * from department");
      // To update a row using the result set
      resultSet.last();
      System.out.println("*** Updating the row using ResultSet ***");
      System.out.println(
      resultSet.getRow() + ": " + + resultSet.getInt("deptId") +
      ", " + resultSet.getString("deptName") + ", " +
      resultSet.getString("manager") + ", "
      + resultSet.getDouble("productivity") + ", " +
      resultSet.getInt("effortHours"));
      resultSet.updateDouble("productivity", 99.99);
      // update a field value by its column name
      resultSet.updateInt("effortHours", 99);
      resultSet.updateRow(); // update the row in the database
      //Print the row information after update operation
      System.out.println(
      resultSet.getRow() + ": " + + resultSet.getInt("deptId") + ", "
      + resultSet.getString("deptName") + ", "
      + resultSet.getString("manager") + ", "
```

```
                + resultSet.getDouble("productivity") + ", "
                + resultSet.getInt("effortHours"));

          // Delete a row using the result set
          resultSet.first();
          System.out.println("*** Delete the row using ResultSet ***");
          System.out.println(
          resultSet.getRow() + ": " + + resultSet.getInt("deptId") + ", "
          + resultSet.getString("deptName") + ", "
          + resultSet.getString("manager") + ", "
          + resultSet.getDouble("productivity") + ", "
          + resultSet.getInt("effortHours"));
          resultSet.deleteRow();
          // delete the current row in the database

          // A updatable ResultSet has feature to stage a
          // row before inserting into the database
          resultSet.moveToInsertRow();
          resultSet.updateInt(1, 758);
          // Update fields using the column number instead of column name
          resultSet.updateString(2, "Human Resources");
          resultSet.updateString(3, "Trump");
          resultSet.updateDouble(4, 55.40);
          resultSet.updateInt(5, 65);
          resultSet.insertRow();
          // row is inserted into the database

          // Move the cursor to the starting of the ResultSet.
          resultSet.beforeFirst();

          databaseConn.commit(); // commit
      } catch(SQLException ex) {
        ex.printStackTrace();
      }
    }
  }
```

The **ResultSet** has a bigger hierarchy to support additional features, as shown in the following diagram:

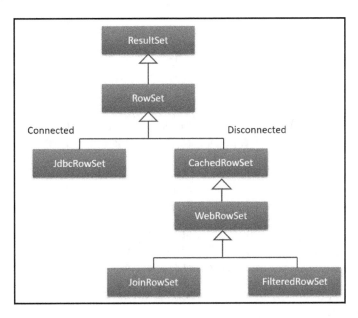

Each implementation of **ResultSet** shown in the preceding hierarchy adds its own new feature to it, as mentioned below.

RowSet implements the **ResultSet** interface. **RowSet**, along with the **ResultSet** behavior, it is scrollable, updatable, and supports the Java bean component model.

JdbcRowSet is a connected **RowSet** and a wrapper component for the scrollable and updatable **ResultSet**.

CachedRowSet and its subcomponents have the ability of disconnected access; they can also reconnect to the data source to capture the updates that happened during disconnect.

WebRowSet is an XML-based **CachedRowSet**.

JoinRowSet can perform the join operation such as SQL, even without connecting to the data source during join.

FilteredRowSet can filter the rows from the result, even without connecting to the data source during filter.

Let's now review how the distributed transactions are managed by JDBC with the help of JTA API from Java to interact with the distributed database.

JTA for distributed transactions

If the applications should interact with multiple databases in a distributed environment at the same time, it is important to handle the persistent data communication to commit the database transaction. This is called multi-phase transaction. The XA transaction is the standard mechanism for distributed transactions. Each individual transaction in a distributed transaction (also termed global transaction) is termed as a transaction branch.

A money transaction is the best example for such distributed transactions. Let's say we want to transfer money from account A to account B. The amount should be deducted from account A, only then if can it be successfully credited in account B, and vice versa.

JDBC supports the distributed transaction based on the connection pooling and open XA standards, and the transaction is handled by **Java Transaction API (JTA)**. Many standard vendors offer the XA transactions, including Oracle.

Key components that take part in XA functionality include *XADataSource, XAConnection, XAResource,* and Xid (transaction IDs).

When an application is establishing a connection to the database, it is initially made with `NO_TXN` mode; however, based on the operation it is executing, it can switch between either of the following modes:

- `NO_TXN`: This means that no transaction is currently consuming this connection.
- `LOCAL_TXN`: This means that a local transaction on a database is consuming this connection. Additionally, `auto_commit` could be disabled. In this mode, applications are not supposed to invoke the prepare, commit, rollback, forget, or end operations on an *XAResource*; if invoked, it can throw an *XAException*.
- `GLOBAL_TXN`: This means that a global transaction for a distributed system is currently consuming the connection. In this mode, applications are not supposed to invoke the `commit`, `rollback`, `rollback(Savepoint)`, `setAutoCommit(true)`, or `setSavepoint` commands on a `java.sql.Connection`. Additionally, the applications are not supposed to invoke the `OracleSetSavepoint` or `OracleRollback` commands on an `oracle.jdbc.OracleConnection`; if invoked, it can throw an `SQLException`.

Switching between the transaction modes

Let's now review in what scenarios the connection transaction mode changes from one mode to another mode in an Oracle database.

From	To NO_TXN	To LOCAL_TXN	To GLOBAL_TXN
NO_TXN	Same mode	When the auto-commit mode is disabled and a DML (data manipulation language) statement is executed.	When the start method is invoked on an *XAResource* obtained from the *XAconnection* that provided the present connection.
LOCAL_TXN	When any of the following happens: - A DDL (data definition language) statement is executed. - A Commit operation is invoked. - A Rollback operation is invoked, but without parameters.	Same mode	When the start method is invoked on an *XAResource* obtained from the *XAconnection* that provided the present connection. This feature is enabled from Oracle 12.1.0.2 database version.
GLOBAL_TXN	- If within a global transaction open command is called on this connection, end command is called on an *XAResource* obtained from the *XAconnection* that provided this connection.	NEVER	Same mode

Key Oracle components that take part in XA transactions are as follows:

- **OracleXADataSource**: This acts as the data source for the XA transaction; it is the producer of the XA connections. It implements the **XADataSource** interface. Additionally, it extends the `OracleConnectionPoolDataSource` class that extends the `OracleDataSource` class.
- **OracleXAConnection**: This acts as an instance of the pooled connection for the database. It implements the **XAConnection** interface that extends the `PooledConnection` interface. Additionally, it extends the `OraclePooledConnection` class.

- **OracleXAResource**: This is the handle for the transaction manager to organize each transaction. It implements the XAResource interface. *OracleXAResource* is available in both the client and server packages to act as both types of resource.
- **OracleXid**: This acts as transaction identifiers for the transaction manager to organize the transactions. It implements the **Xid** interface.
- **OracleXAException**: This is the exception thrown by XA methods if an exception occurs during the transactions. It is a subclass of the **XAException**.

Sample program for the XA transaction

Let's now see a sample program that communicates with two Oracle database instances through an application with XA transaction.

The following is the series of steps to be executed by this program:

1. Begin the transaction division on database DB1 and then on DB2.
2. Perform a DML query execution on DB1 and then on DB2.
3. Complete the transaction execution on DB1 and then on DB2.
4. Prepare the completion on DB1 and then on DB2.
5. Commit the transaction on DB1 and then on DB2.

The following is the program for XATransaction on two Oracle databases. Don't forget to include ojdbc.jar to your project when you are writing this example:

```
package distributedtransaction;

//You need to import the java.sql package to use JDBC
import java.sql.Connection;
import java.sql.ResultSet;
import java.sql.SQLException;
import java.sql.Statement;

import javax.sql.XAConnection;
import javax.transaction.xa.XAException;
import javax.transaction.xa.XAResource;
import javax.transaction.xa.Xid;

import oracle.jdbc.pool.OracleDataSource;
import oracle.jdbc.xa.OracleXAException;
import oracle.jdbc.xa.OracleXid;
import oracle.jdbc.xa.client.OracleXADataSource;
```

```
class XATransaction {
  public static void main(String args[]) throws SQLException {
    if (args.length != 3) {
      System.out.println("usage: java XATransaction <host>
      <port> <service_name>");
      System.exit(0);
    }

    String dbHostName = args[0];
    String dbPort = args[1];
    String dbServiceName = args[2];

    try {
      String dbURL1 = "jdbc:oracle:oci:@";
      String dbURL2 = "jdbc:oracle:thin:@(description=(address=
      (host=" + dbHostName + ")(protocol=tcp)
      (port=" + dbPort + "))(connect_data=
      (service_name=" + dbServiceName + ")))";
      // Set the URL for database # 1
      try {
        String url1FromProperties = System.getProperty("JDBC_URL");
        if (url1FromProperties != null)
        dbURL1 = url1FromProperties;
      } catch (Exception e) {
        // If there is any security exception, ignore it and use the
        // default URL (dbURL1)
      }
      // Set the URL for database # 2
      try {
        String url2FromProperties = System.getProperty("JDBC_URL_2");
        if (url2FromProperties != null)
        dbURL2 = url2FromProperties;
      } catch (Exception e) {
        // If there is any security exception, ignore it and use the
        // default URL (dbURL2)
      }

      // Create a OracleDataSource instance and set properties
      OracleDataSource dataSource1 = new OracleDataSource();
      dataSource1.setUser("HR");
      dataSource1.setPassword("hr");
      dataSource1.setURL(dbURL1);

      Connection dbConn1 = dataSource1.getConnection();

      // Prepare a statement to create the table
      Statement stmt1 = dbConn1.createStatement();
```

```
// Create another OracleDataSource
OracleDataSource dataSource2 = new OracleDataSource();
dataSource2.setUser("HR");
dataSource2.setPassword("hr");
dataSource2.setURL(dbURL2);
Connection dbConn2 = dataSource2.getConnection();

Statement stmt2 = dbConn2.createStatement();

try {
  stmt1.execute("delete from jobs where job_id = 'SC_STUFF'");
} catch (SQLException e) {
  // Ignore an error here
}

try {
  stmt2.execute("delete from regions where region_id > 100");
} catch (SQLException e) {
  // Ignore an error here
}

// Create a XADataSource instance
OracleXADataSource xaDataSource1 = new OracleXADataSource();
xaDataSource1.setURL(dbURL1);
xaDataSource1.setUser("HR");
xaDataSource1.setPassword("hr");

OracleXADataSource xaDataSource2 = new OracleXADataSource();
xaDataSource2.setURL(dbURL2);
xaDataSource2.setUser("HR");
xaDataSource2.setPassword("hr");

// Get a XA connection to the underlying data source
XAConnection xaConn1 = xaDataSource1.getXAConnection();

// We can use the same data source
XAConnection xaConn2 = xaDataSource2.getXAConnection();

// Get the Physical Connections
Connection sqlConn1 = xaConn1.getConnection();
Connection sqlConn2 = xaConn2.getConnection();

// Get the XA Resources
XAResource xaR1 = xaConn1.getXAResource();
XAResource xaR2 = xaConn2.getXAResource();

// Create the Xids With the Same Global Ids
Xid xid1 = createXid(1);
```

```
Xid xid2 = createXid(2);

// Start the Resources
xaR1.start(xid1, XAResource.TMNOFLAGS);
xaR2.start(xid2, XAResource.TMNOFLAGS);

// Do something with conn1 and conn2
insertDataDB1(sqlConn1);
insertDataDB2(sqlConn2);

// END both the branches -- THIS IS MUST
xaR1.end(xid1, XAResource.TMSUCCESS);
xaR2.end(xid2, XAResource.TMSUCCESS);

// Prepare the RMs
int prepareMode1 = xaR1.prepare(xid1);
int prepareMode2 = xaR2.prepare(xid2);

System.out.println("Prepare mode chosent for xid 1 is "
+ prepareMode1);
System.out.println("Prepare mode chosent for xid 2 is "
+ prepareMode2);
// Same boolean variable commitAcceptance is used to confirm with
// both the database
// Only if both database give the acceptance it will start commit
// operation,
// either of them are not accepted, it will
// rollback transactions on
// both the database.
boolean commitAcceptance = true;

if (!((prepareMode1 == XAResource.XA_OK) ||
(prepareMode1 == XAResource.XA_RDONLY)))
commitAcceptance = false;

if (!((prepareMode2 == XAResource.XA_OK) ||
(prepareMode2 == XAResource.XA_RDONLY)))
 commitAcceptance = false;

System.out.println("commitAcceptance from both the database is "
+ commitAcceptance);
System.out.println("Is resource manager
same for both the XAResources? " + xaR1.isSameRM(xaR2));

// Commit / Rollback on DB1 based on the prepareMode and
// commitAcceptance
if (prepareMode1 == XAResource.XA_OK)
if (commitAcceptance)
```

```
    xaR1.commit(xid1, false);
else
    xaR1.rollback(xid1);

// Commit / Rollback on DB2 based on the prepareMode and
// commitAcceptance
if (prepareMode2 == XAResource.XA_OK)
if (commitAcceptance)
xaR2.commit(xid2, false);
else
xaR2.rollback(xid2);

// Close all the connections
sqlConn1.close();
sqlConn1 = null;
sqlConn2.close();
sqlConn2 = null;

xaConn1.close();
xaConn1 = null;
xaConn2.close();
xaConn2 = null;

ResultSet resultSet = stmt1.executeQuery("select job_id,
job_title from jobs");
System.out.println("ncontents of table jobs:n job_id -
job_title");
while (resultSet.next()) {
  System.out.println(resultSet.getString(1) + " - " +
  resultSet.getString(2));
}

resultSet.close();
resultSet = null;

resultSet = stmt2.executeQuery("select region_id,
region_name from regions order by region_id");
System.out.println("ncontents of table regions:
n region_id - region_namen");
while (resultSet.next()) {
  System.out.println(resultSet.getInt(1) + " - "
  + resultSet.getString(2));
}

// Close the resources
resultSet.close();
resultSet = null;
```

```
      stmt1.close();
      stmt1 = null;
      stmt2.close();
      stmt2 = null;

      dbConn1.close();
      dbConn1 = null;
      dbConn2.close();
      dbConn2 = null;

    } catch (SQLException sqlEx) {
      sqlEx.printStackTrace();
    } catch (XAException xaEx) {
      if (xaEx instanceof OracleXAException) {
        System.out.println("XA Error is " + (
        (OracleXAException) xaEx).getXAError());
        System.out.println("SQL Error is " + (
        (OracleXAException) xaEx).getOracleError());
      }
    }
  }

  static Xid createXid(int bids) throws XAException {
    byte[] gid = new byte[1];
    gid[0] = (byte) 9;
    byte[] bid = new byte[1];
    bid[0] = (byte) bids;
    byte[] gtrid = new byte[64];
    byte[] bqual = new byte[64];
    System.arraycopy(gid, 0, gtrid, 0, 1);
    System.arraycopy(bid, 0, bqual, 0, 1);
    Xid xid = new OracleXid(0x1234, gtrid, bqual);
    return xid;
  }

  private static void insertDataDB1(Connection conn)
  throws SQLException {
    // Create a Statement
    Statement stmt = conn.createStatement();

    int rowCount = stmt.executeUpdate("insert into jobs values
    ('SC_STUFF', 'Security Stuff', null, null)");

    System.out.println("No of rows Affected " + rowCount);

    stmt.close();
    stmt = null;
  }
```

```
    private static void insertDataDB2(Connection conn) throws
    SQLException {
      // Create a Statement
      Statement stmt = conn.createStatement();

      int rowCount = stmt.executeUpdate("insert into regions values
      (101, 'Africa')");

      System.out.println("No of rows Affected " + rowCount);

      stmt.close();
      stmt = null;
    }
  }
```

There exists a native API for sending XA commands from different vendors to improve the performance of XA transactions effectively. Oracle is providing OCI Native XA and Thin Native XA as native APIs for this purpose, out of which Thin Native XA (available from Oracle 10g) is more efficient and observed to perform 10 times better than a non-native API.

Summary

Through this chapter, you learned the essential distributed database systems and their architecture. You also learned how to setup the distributed database and a comparison of the techniques. Further, you learned distributed database environments and setup methodologies, replication, distributed DBMS architecture, and XA transactions programming in detail. We finished this chapter with an understanding of the Java Support for the database connectivity (JDBC) and Java transaction API (JTA) support for the distributed transactions in multiple database connections.

In the next chapter, you will learn about distributed computing in Cloud environments and demonstrate the Java support for such distributed models in detail.

7
Cloud and Distributed Computing

Computer networks have been upgraded over the last few decades. From a small group of connected intranet instances to the world of the internet today, networking has come a long way. With the advent of the internet, we've seen numerous novel developments, such as cloud computing and distributed computing models. While both these terms appear different, computing models have been developed to bring them together to build the next generation of computing models that provide rapid execution. The journey from conservative central processing models to the era of distributed cloud computing has been enormously progressive, both in terms of the scale of processing data and resource utilization across internet working models.

In this chapter, we will cover the following:

- What is cloud computing?
- Features of cloud computing
- Cloud versus distributed computing
- Cloud service providers
- Amazon Web Services (AWS)
- Amazon Elastic Cloud Compute (Amazon EC2)
- Amazon Simple Storage Service (Amazon S3)
- Amazon Simple Queue Service (Amazon SQS)
- Amazon CloudFront
- Amazon SimpleDB
- Writing a distributed application on AWS
- Docker Containers as a Service (CaaS)

- Characteristics of Docker CaaS
- Docker CaaS platform components
- Deploying a sample Java application to Tomcat with Docker
- Java 9 support

What is cloud computing?

The **National Institute of Standards and Technology** (**NIST**) has defined cloud computing as a pay-per-use model for enabling convenient, available, on-demand network access to a shared pool of configurable computing resources (networks/servers/storage/services/applications) that can be rapidly provisioned and released with minimal management effort or service provider interaction.

This means that you are going to use the technology when you need it and for as long as you need it, and you pay only for that usage. There is no need to install any software at your end, and you don't need to pay when you are not using the service.

If a cloud infrastructure is set up within an organization's network boundaries, it is termed an *internal cloud*, and if it is set up outside an organization's network and accessed through the internet on the organization's network, it is termed an *external cloud*.

Cloud deployment models

Based on the deployment models and the purpose of usage, cloud computing is categorized into the following types:

- **Private cloud**: A cloud infrastructure that is dedicatedly set up and run for a sole organization and managed by that single organization is called a *private cloud*
- **Community cloud**: A cloud infrastructure set up by a group of organizations that have common requirements of security compliance and understanding and that share features and responsibilities to manage the infrastructure is called a *community cloud*
- **Public cloud**: A cloud infrastructure set up by one organization to sell features and space on the cloud to other organizations that want to maintain their applications on a cloud infrastructure but don't want to own it due to maintenance overheads or cost concerns is called a *public cloud*
- **Hybrid cloud**: A cloud infrastructure that is set up by combining a couple of the preceding cloud infrastructures, based on a common technology or purpose, such as cloud bursting, is called a *hybrid cloud*

The following image depicts the four types of cloud infrastructures we just discussed:

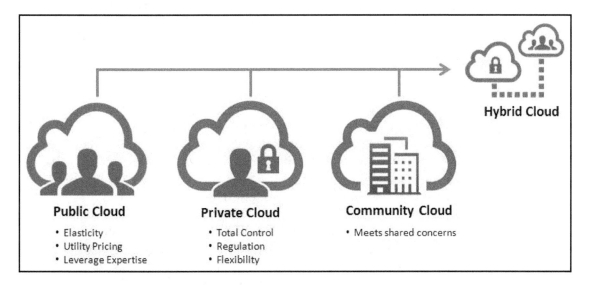

Cloud computing patterns

Cloud computing patterns are the implementation of individual or a combination of different technology mechanisms. Together, these mechanisms provide an extremely concrete view of the cloud architecture layers and individual building blocks. These layers and blocks represent the moving parts that can be assembled in creative ways to leverage cloud environments for business automation. Each design pattern in the cloud computing catalog is associated with one or more mechanisms.

Now let's review a list of different patterns that can be configured on a cloud infrastructure:

- **Storage as a Service**: Storage as a Service, as the name suggests, offers storage space for your applications on a cloud infrastructure that could be remote system storage, which can be used by your applications as single local storage space logically. Storage as a Service is a widely used cloud service; it is used by most of the supplementary cloud components.

- **Database as a Service (DaaS)**: The license for procuring an enterprise database and the overhead to manage it in-house can be very expensive. DaaS offers all the widely used database instances on the cloud (remotely) as shared databases to multiple users who only have to use a single logical instance on their application to access them without the overhead of license and management. You only pay for the users and the space of the specific instance you procured on the cloud database.

- **Information as a Service**: Through this service, an application can host its features as an API on the cloud for other applications so they can interact and receive the required information, for example, information on stocks or railway/airline status, and report it to their application interfaces

- **Process as a Service**: Through this service, an organization can host its specific business process on the cloud as a service offering to other applications so that they can access the information on the go. This helps the organization manage the business process on its own without disturbing other application interfaces.

- **Application as a Service (AaaS)**: Also known as **Software as a Service (SaaS)**, this provides the ability to deploy a specific application on the cloud infrastructure and make itself available to multiple users through different accounts. Examples of this kind of service include Salesforce SFA, Google Docs, Gmail, and Google Calendar.

- **Platform as a Service (PaaS)**: PaaS has the ability to provide the entire software platform on the cloud infrastructure to cater to the needs of application/database/interface development, storage, testing, and other operational infrastructures distributed through a remotely hosted cloud platform for subscribers. Microsoft Azure and Google App Engine are examples of PaaS.

- **Integration Platform as a Service (iPaaS)** and **Data Platform as a Service (dPaaS)** are a couple of specialized applications of PaaS.

- **Blockchain as a Service (BaaS)** is another PaaS specialization offered by a few vendors, such as Microsoft Azure, as part of their PaaS subscription. Some of the projects, such as Docker, have captured the market by packaging the entire software, including code, runtime, system tools, and libraries, so it could be deployed on any cloud platform that procures PaaS as **Container as a Service (CaaS)**.

- **Integration as a Service**: Integration as a Service offers multiple **enterprise application integrations (EAIs)** through the cloud service offering along with the integration interface design. It also offers the managing of the application life cycle as a service.
- **Security as a Service**: Security services, such as identity management and global application security, can be offered as a service through this cloud infrastructure model
- **Management as a Service / Governance as a Service (MaaS/GaaS)**: By enforcing certain policies on other application services and information, GaaS manages other cloud infrastructures on demand
- **Testing as a Service (TaaS)**: Through this service, a cloud platform offers another application/enterprise integration flow testing functionality as a service. You don't even need to install any software or hardware within the organization system for this.
- **Infrastructure as a service (IaaS)**: This can be understood as a data center that provides service through cloud access. This means, instead of setting up a data center in-house, the organization can procure a remote machine and the software installed on that machine for application purposes and pay per usage. A hypervisor, such as Xen, Oracle VirtualBox, Oracle VM, KVM, VMware ESX/ESXi, or Hyper-V, runs virtual machines as guests.
- **Mobile Backend as a Service (MBaaS)**: Some mobile and web applications would want to have both data and services and their interfaces to other social networking applications managed through a cloud platform; this is offered by MBaaS.

Out of these different patterns of cloud architectures, three patterns are important:

- IaaS
- PaaS
- SaaS

Based on the cloud architecture chosen, instead of the on-premise environment, the responsibility of maintenance is shared between the organization and the cloud provider, as shown in the following diagram:

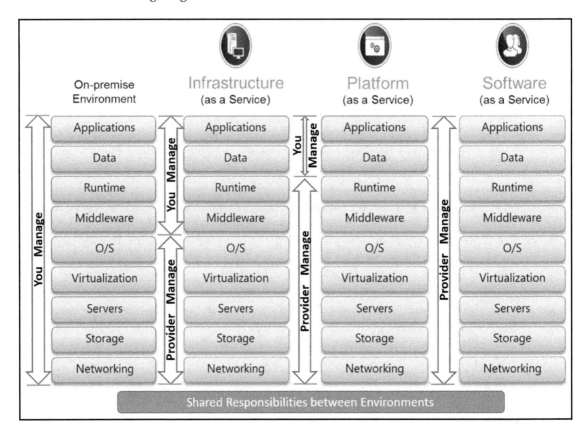

Features of cloud computing

As discussed previously, cloud computing is a pay-per-usage model for empowering convenient, available, and on-demand access to resources such as networks, servers, storage, applications, and services over the network. Besides, it can be established quickly and demolished with nominal administrating effort or interaction with the cloud service provider.

The following are some of the important characteristics of a cloud architecture:

- **On-demand self-service**: As an organization or an administrator of an organization, you can individually establish any of the previously discussed cloud environments without any support from the cloud service provider
- **Global network access**: Cloud platforms are easily accessible by universal network access, and they are supported by any type of device or platform
- **Dynamic resource pooling**: This is a great feature of a cloud environment wherein the provider's computing resources get shared between different customers, based on the demand for the resource of each customer. Customers can logically see the available resources as a single resource, but they are not aware of how many different remote resources make up the resource the consumer is utilizing.
- **Instantaneous elasticity**: The dynamics of a cloud infrastructure can be instantly scaled up or released based on the purchase schemes provided by the customers. This gives great freedom to hold resources that are based on load and memory requirements, which, in turn, is based on the business criteria.
- **Pay per usage**: The billing model of a cloud infrastructure can be managed very dynamically, based on the bandwidth, business, and user count over a given period. Also, organizations can choose to procure global access to pay for all the other locations they would procure the environments for from their base location.

The following diagram represents the benefits of using cloud computing in organizations with the characteristics we just discussed:

Cloud versus distributed computing

While distributed computing provides collaborative resource sharing by connecting multiple resources and users to provide administrative, geographic, and dynamic scalability, cloud computing is aimed at providing on-demand applications or services with set goals of reaching improved scalability, transparency, security, monitoring, and management. Also, in cloud environments, the physical implementation does not constitute or is transparent to the service it is offering to the customers.

The following table shows a comparison of a cloud versus distributed computing architecture:

	Cloud Computing	Distributed Computing
Definition	Cloud computing defines a new way of computing based on the network technology. Cloud computing takes place over the common network like internet. It usually comprises of a collection of integrated and networked hardware, software and internet infrastructure resources.	Distributed computing contains multiple software components from multiple different computers which work together as a single system. Cloud computing can be referred as a virtualization achieved from distributed computing.
Goals	* Reduced Initial Investment and Proportional Costs * Increased Scalability * Increased Availability * Increased Reliability	* Resource Sharing * Openness * Transparency * Scalability
Types	* Public Clouds * Private Clouds * Community Clouds * Hybrid Clouds	* Distributed Computing Systems * Distributed Information Systems * Distributed Pervasive Systems
Characteristics	* It provides a shared pool of configurable computing resources. * An on-demand network model is used to provide access * The clouds are provisioned by the Service Providers. * It provides broad network access.	* A task is distributed amongst different machines for the computation job at the same time. * Technologies such as Remote Procedure calls and Remote Method Invocation are used to construct distributed computations.
Disadvantages	* More elasticity means less control especially in the case of public clouds. * Restrictions on available services may be faced, as it depends upon the cloud provider.	* Higher level of failure of nodes than a dedicated parallel machine. * Few of the algorithms are not able to match with slow networks. * Nature of the computing job may present too much overhead.

Distributed cloud computing is becoming a prominent expression in the IT industry, with a higher number of vendors and system analysts delivering more systems to provide services that would help organizations become more responsive to market conditions while restraining their individual IT costs.

Cloud service providers

With cloud computing becoming a renowned model in the industry, the market for cloud environment providers has increased rapidly. There are a number of cloud service providers available today, but we'll discuss some of the top service providers who have made a remarkable contribution to make the cloud model a successful platform.

Google came up with the PaaS-providing Google App Engine. It uses the Python application language and has tools such as the Google file system and data repositories, so it has a stable environment for running an application platform.

Red Hat OpenShift is another good competitor that provides PaaS providers. It has come up with different patterns such as the OpenShift origin, OpenShift online, OpenShift dedicated, and OpenShift container platform (Enterprise).

Amazon targeted the IaaS platform and became the key competitor in this industry with AWS. The reason for its success is the quality of services and availability it provides to all types of organizations. From the perspective of features, it provides its own hardware and gives you control through the network connection.

Vendors such as GoGrid and Rackspace have come up with the hybrid cloud approach, which represents the way traditional data centers work when supplied through a cloud environment.

Microsoft offers the cloud platform with its own product, called Microsoft Azure. With Azure, Microsoft offers different types of cloud platforms, starting from private clouds to PaaS models.

Oracle is trying to target the cloud market with its SaaS, PaaS, and IaaS services and takeovers, such as NetSuite and its cloud applications. It has a special offering in the Oracle Java Cloud service, which provides easy, rapid, and agile deployment of Java applications with more control and flexibility of the application in the public cloud.

Pivotal Cloud Foundry is another Cloud Provider offering a range of solutions including Private Cloud, it is one of the prominent platform for applications built in Spring and Spring Boot. Spring's micro service patterns and Spring Boot's executable jars are readily available for this platform.

The following diagram shows a bar chart for the most used cloud computing services, based on the provider:

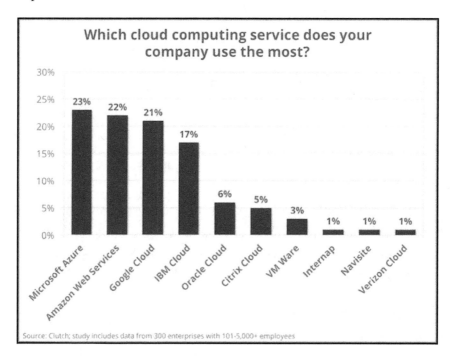

Now let's review different AWS's and their purpose in detail.

AWS

AWS is a broader group of network-based services offered by Amazon. The following are the services it offers:

- Amazon EC2
- Amazon S3
- Amazon SQS
- Amazon CloudFront
- Amazon SimpleDB

While there are a number of service offerings provided by Amazon, Amazon EC2 and Amazon S3 are two important innovations in terms of transaction handling.

The following diagram depicts the AWS architecture with development and application hosting:

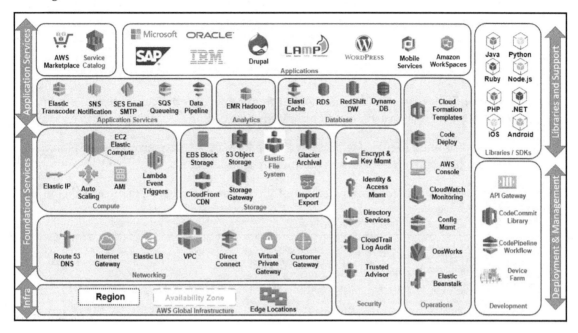

Amazon EC2

Amazon EC2 is the most important feature of Amazon cloud services. It works based on a web services API for establishing, managing, and demolishing the virtual servers that reside in the Amazon cloud. This gives applications that are deployed and accessible through the internet the ability to launch the virtual server present in the Amazon cloud environment using a single web service invocation.

The servers in Amazon EC2 cloud environments run based on a tailored version of the open source Xen hypervisor along with paravirtualization. This provides the ability to dynamically establish and demolish the server capability needed for isolated deployed systems.

Amazon machine image (**AMI**) provides a way to launch a virtual server on the Amazon cloud environment. AMI comes up with the operating system and requested software combination for your application purpose. One can procure a standard AMI with their choice of operating system and convert it as per their software needs and produce a new image; after this, they can establish their servers with these customized images of AMI.

Coming to storage, EC2 provides two types of storage capabilities, as follows:

- Transient storage assigned with a node, which gets expired along with the node
- Block storage, which works as a SAN and continues across time

This feature of providing node-attached storage has given great scope for competitors as well; it provides the ability to use it as a traditional data center operating model.

Another benefit of procuring EC2 servers is that they can access the cloud persistent data store Amazon S3, which is an efficient combination.

Cloud nodes also provide security features with the help of security groups and related rules to facilitate access from a known consumer upon port access.

The following diagram provides an overview of the Amazon EC2 architecture and connects with Amazon S3:

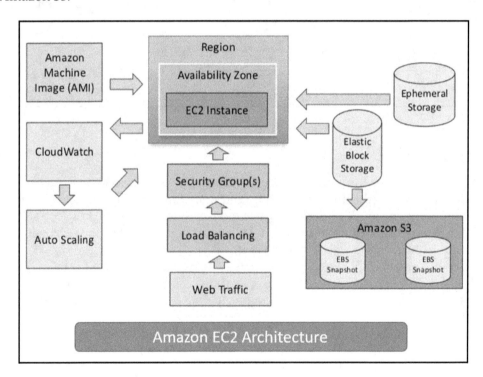

Amazon S3

Amazon's offering for the cloud data storage facility is Amazon S3. It is available through the web services API over the internet. It supports the storage of a number of objects based on the procurement, ranging from 1 byte to 5 GB logically in simple namespace access. Amazon S3 provides persistent storage to store data on the cloud and access it at a later stage. One advantage of cloud storage with S3 is that the storage space is dynamic and could be expanded when you wish to add files to the system based on the chosen plan.

One thing we should remember is that cloud storage is made up of multiple remote system storage systems that combine and act as one logical storage system for each customer. This logical storage system has two levels, called buckets. Buckets are like directories in a file system, but we cannot have a hierarchical bucket structure as we have with directories. You can access Amazon S3 content through web services, which are relatively faster for cloud applications but not as fast as on-premise disk access.

Amazon SQS

Amazon SQS is the foundation of Amazon solutions in the grid computing zone. As discussed in the previous chapters about enterprise asynchronous messaging, with the help of the message queue system, Amazon SQS does a similar job for systems related to cloud integration.

A sending system passes a message to this queue service and continues with its process without waiting for the response from the receiving system. The receiving system takes the message from the queue at a later stage and processes it based on the instruction from the sending system.

This gives great flexibility to the cloud platform in a way that connection systems now need not worry about the exceptions in the connecting systems; they simply pass the message to the queue system and forget about the rest. Another advantage is that both the systems need not be active while sending/receiving the message to the queue, but the queue environment has to be.

With its simple operating model and API requirements, Amazon SQS has become a popular messaging queue model for cloud application communication.

Here's an Amazon SQS Queue representation with message producers and consumers:

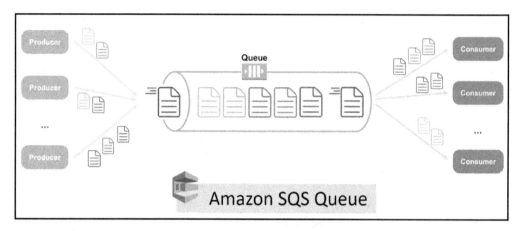

Along with SQS, there are other messaging models offered by AWS, which are presented in the following diagram:

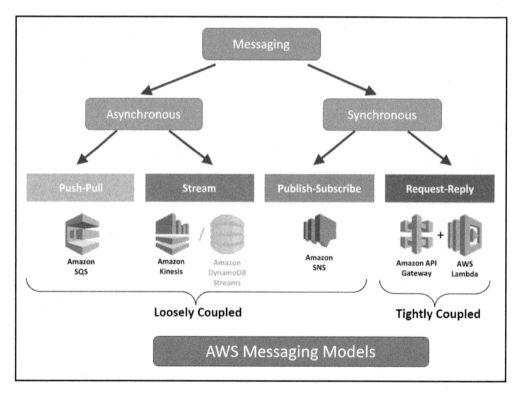

Amazon CloudFront

Amazon CloudFront is a **content distribution network** (**CDN**) offering on the cloud provided by Amazon. When customers place their content on Amazon S3, based on the customer's system location, CloudFront makes that data available at the nearest Amazon site. So, you don't need to access it from a far off remote server termed an edge point. This improves data access efficiency and performance.

Amazon SimpleDB

Amazon SimpleDB serves the purpose of cloud data storage in a structured architecture. It has greater reliability compared to the on-premise Oracle and MySQL data stores. While availability is way higher with this cloud relational data store, it is less complex when it comes to transaction management. Amazon SimpleDB is a better fit for applications that have the web content management requirement.

The features of Amazon SimpleDB include:

- A simple web-service-based data store
- Highly available clustered DBMS
- Highly scalable data storage system
- No need for maintaining an in-house DBA

Amazon SimpleDB is the best fit for NoSQL database access from cloud applications, not for applications with a requirement for powerful relational capabilities.

Writing a distributed application on AWS

Amazon **Simple Workflow Service** (**SWF**) is a workflow service offering that supports building, running, and scaling asynchronous jobs that have parallel or sequential steps as part of their process executions. Amazon SWF can be considered a completely managed state tracker and task coordinator for cloud applications.

An important offering of Amazon SWF for distributed applications is that it enables applications to run as numerous processes, which could be distributed between the number of systems, including Amazon EC2 instances, client computers, and private data centers, that might have different operating systems on each machine. As an example, we can deploy a workflow worker on an Amazon EC2 platform, a workflow starter on a data center system, and the activities on a client desktop system. We could also deploy different activities on different systems.

The following diagram represents a sample workflow setup with Amazon SWF for the program we will review in this section:

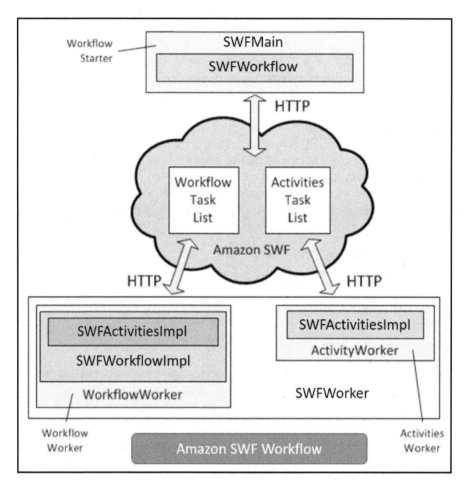

Workflow activities can be denoted as asynchronous methods that get executed and that return a response to permit the workflow to perform further tasks, which are waiting for the activity to get completed.

Workflow starters communicate with workflow workers through an HTTP request, with Amazon SWF helping them to interact. Workflow workers communicate with the activities and workers through an HTTP request, with Amazon SWF helping them to interact.

The AWS Flow Framework for Java and Amazon SWF holds the responsibility of this workflow to work efficiently, which helps developers concentrate on building business logic.

Let's review a sample program to develop an instance of Amazon SWF based on a distributed application. Let's start with a workflow activity interface with the following three methods:

```
package amazonswf;

import com.amazonaws.services.simpleworkflow.flow.annotations.Activities;
import
com.amazonaws.services.simpleworkflow.flow.annotations.ActivityRegistration
Options;

@ActivityRegistrationOptions(defaultTaskScheduleToStartTimeoutSeconds =
300,
                          defaultTaskStartToCloseTimeoutSeconds = 10)
@Activities(version="1.0")
public interface SWFActivities {

  public String getName();
  public String getMessage(String name);
  public void printMessage(String message);
}
```

An implementation of this SWFActivities interface, which acts as the workflow activity's implementation, is as follows. It has methods that were implemented after they were defined in the interface:

```
package amazonswf;

public class SWFActivitiesImpl implements SWFActivities {

  @Override
  public String getName() {
    return "Raja";
  }

  @Override
  public String getMessage(String name) {
    return "Hello " + name;
  }

  @Override
    public void printMessage(String message) {
      System.out.println(message);
    }

}
```

Now, let's define the next component, which is a workflow interface, with a method declaration:

```
package amazonswf;

import com.amazonaws.services.simpleworkflow.flow.annotations.Execute;
import com.amazonaws.services.simpleworkflow.flow.annotations.Workflow;
import
com.amazonaws.services.simpleworkflow.flow.annotations.WorkflowRegistration
Options;

@Workflow
@WorkflowRegistrationOptions(defaultExecutionStartToCloseTimeoutSeconds =
3600)
public interface SWFWorkflow {

    @Execute(version = "1.0")
    public void message();

}
```

The following is the implementation of `SWFWorkflow` that implements the `message()` method that interacts with the workflow activities:

```
package amazonswf;

import com.amazonaws.services.simpleworkflow.flow.core.Promise;

public class SWFWorkflowImpl implements SWFWorkflow {

    private SWFActivities activites = new SWFActivitiesImpl();

    @Override
    public void message() {
        Promise<String> name = activites.getName();
        Promise<String> greeting = activites.getGreeting(name);
        activites.say(greeting);
    }

}
```

Now we can define a `worker` component that would run the workflow `worker` component and make it available to the main component that wants to invoke the worker component and activities built, as follows:

```
package amazonswf;

import com.amazonaws.ClientConfiguration;
```

```
import com.amazonaws.auth.AWSCredentials;
import com.amazonaws.auth.BasicAWSCredentials;
import com.amazonaws.services.simpleworkflow.AmazonSimpleWorkflow;
import com.amazonaws.services.simpleworkflow.AmazonSimpleWorkflowClient;
import com.amazonaws.services.simpleworkflow.flow.ActivityWorker;
import com.amazonaws.services.simpleworkflow.flow.WorkflowWorker;

public class SWFWorker  {

  public static void main(String[] args) throws Exception {
    ClientConfiguration config =
    new ClientConfiguration().withSocketTimeout(70*1000);
    String swfAccessId = System.getenv("AWS_ACCESS_KEY_ID");
    String swfSecretKey = System.getenv("AWS_SECRET_KEY");
    AWSCredentials awsCredentials =
    new BasicAWSCredentials(swfAccessId, swfSecretKey);
    AmazonSimpleWorkflow service =
    new AmazonSimpleWorkflowClient(awsCredentials, config);
    service.setEndpoint("https://swf.sampleworkflow.com");
    String domain = "helloWorldWalkthrough";
    String taskListToPoll = "HelloWorldList";

    ActivityWorker aw =
    new ActivityWorker(service, domain, taskListToPoll);
    aw.addActivitiesImplementation(new SWFActivitiesImpl());
    aw.start();
    WorkflowWorker wfw =
    new WorkflowWorker(service, domain, taskListToPoll);
    wfw.addWorkflowImplementationType(SWFWorkflowImpl.class);
    wfw.start();
  }

}
```

Finally, you can build and deploy the following main component that will interact with the `workflow` methods:

```
package amazonswf;

import com.amazonaws.ClientConfiguration;
import com.amazonaws.auth.AWSCredentials;
import com.amazonaws.auth.BasicAWSCredentials;
import com.amazonaws.services.simpleworkflow.AmazonSimpleWorkflow;
import com.amazonaws.services.simpleworkflow.AmazonSimpleWorkflowClient;

public class SWFMain {

  public static void main(String[] args) throws Exception {
```

```
      ClientConfiguration config =
      new ClientConfiguration().withSocketTimeout(70*1000);
      String swfAccessId = System.getenv("AWS_ACCESS_KEY_ID");
      String swfSecretKey = System.getenv("AWS_SECRET_KEY");
      AWSCredentials awsCredentials =
      new BasicAWSCredentials(swfAccessId, swfSecretKey);
      AmazonSimpleWorkflow service =
      new AmazonSimpleWorkflowClient(awsCredentials, config);
      service.setEndpoint("https://swf.sampleworkflow.com");
      String domain = "helloWorldWalkthrough";
      SWFWorkflowClientExternalFactory factory =
      new SWFWorkflowClientExternalFactoryImpl(service, domain);
      SWFWorkflow workflow = factory.getClient("clientID");
      workflow.message();
   }


   }
```

By deploying the preceding application using Amazon SWF, you will notice that each workflow instance has its own unique run ID for the execution. The same execution ID can be used for other workflow instances, executing one active flow run at a time.

In the preceding example, SWFWorker has the workflow and activity hosted in the same application. For the following approach, we need to run the workflow and activity implementations on separate systems as follows by replacing the just defined SWFWorker with two new components, namely SWFWorkflowWorker and SWFActivitiesWorker:

```
package amazonswf;

import com.amazonaws.ClientConfiguration;
import com.amazonaws.auth.AWSCredentials;
import com.amazonaws.auth.BasicAWSCredentials;
import com.amazonaws.services.simpleworkflow.AmazonSimpleWorkflow;
import com.amazonaws.services.simpleworkflow.AmazonSimpleWorkflowClient;
import com.amazonaws.services.simpleworkflow.flow.WorkflowWorker;

public class SWFWorkflowWorker {
  public static void main(String[] args) throws Exception   {
    ClientConfiguration config =
    new ClientConfiguration().withSocketTimeout(70*1000);
    String swfAccessId = System.getenv("AWS_ACCESS_KEY_ID");
    String swfSecretKey = System.getenv("AWS_SECRET_KEY");
    AWSCredentials awsCredentials =
    new BasicAWSCredentials(swfAccessId, swfSecretKey);
    AmazonSimpleWorkflow service =
    new AmazonSimpleWorkflowClient(awsCredentials, config);
    service.setEndpoint("https://swf.sampleworkflow.com");
```

```
    String domain = "helloWorldExamples";
    String taskListToPoll = "HelloWorldAsyncList";
    WorkflowWorker wfw =
    new WorkflowWorker(service, domain, taskListToPoll);
    wfw.addWorkflowImplementationType(SWFWorkflowImpl.class);
    wfw.start();
  }


}
```

While the earlier SWFWorkflowWorker component handles the workflow worker, the following SWFActivitiesWorker component takes care of the activity worker:

```
package amazonswf;

import com.amazonaws.ClientConfiguration;
import com.amazonaws.auth.AWSCredentials;
import com.amazonaws.auth.BasicAWSCredentials;
import com.amazonaws.services.simpleworkflow.AmazonSimpleWorkflow;
import com.amazonaws.services.simpleworkflow.AmazonSimpleWorkflowClient;
import com.amazonaws.services.simpleworkflow.flow.ActivityWorker;

public class SWFActivitiesWorker {
  public static void main(String[] args) throws Exception {
    ClientConfiguration config =
    new ClientConfiguration().withSocketTimeout(70*1000);
    String swfAccessId = System.getenv("AWS_ACCESS_KEY_ID");
    String swfSecretKey = System.getenv("AWS_SECRET_KEY");
    AWSCredentials awsCredentials =
    new BasicAWSCredentials(swfAccessId, swfSecretKey);
    AmazonSimpleWorkflow service =
    new AmazonSimpleWorkflowClient(awsCredentials, config);
    service.setEndpoint("https://swf.sampleworkflow.com");
    String domain = "helloWorldExamples";
    String taskListToPoll = "HelloWorldAsyncList";
    ActivityWorker aw = new ActivityWorker(service,
    domain, taskListToPoll);
    aw.addActivitiesImplementation(new SWFActivitiesImpl());
    aw.start();
  }


}
```

The following are the steps you need to follow to execute the workflow:

1. Create a runnable JAR file with `SWFActivitiesWorker` as the execution starting point of the runnable JAR.
2. Copy the just-defined JAR file to another system, which may be working on another operating system with support for Java.
3. Ensure that the AWS credentials that have access to your Amazon SWF domain are accessible on this second system.
4. Execute the JAR file to start the workflow.
5. From the development machine, execute `SWFWorkflowWorker` and `SWFMain`, which starts the main workflow and invokes the worker.

Similarly, other cloud providers, such as *Red Hat OpenShift* and *Google App Engine*, support the distributed application running on a cloud platform.

Now, let's review the latest CaaS offering from Docker and its features along with the steps to deploy a Java application with Docker CaaS.

Docker CaaS

Docker is an open source project that helps automate the application deployment process to application containers.

Docker containers package application software within a comprehensive file system that comprises anything and everything that the application would need to run, including the application code, runtime environment, system tools and libraries that you usually request to carry out an installation, on your application server during deployment. With this feature, you ensure the application will execute and behave like any of your other environments, irrespective of the environment it is currently being executed in.

Docker offers an additional feature along with the ability to abstract and automate an OS simulation, both on Windows and Linux operating systems. With the help of the resource isolation feature of Linux--a kernel-like kernel namespace--and cgroups--a union capable file system such as OverlayFS--Docker provides the feature of running independent containers inside one Linux system without having to start and maintain virtual machines.

This ability of Docker is especially helpful for setting up highly distributed systems. Creating and managing containers makes it easy to establish a machine or multiple virtual systems with running multiple applications, scheduled tasks, and any additional processes. Also, the deployment activities of infra teams become easier with Docker instances prepared to be readily deployable to any platform with PaaS-style of deployment.

The following diagram represents Docker's motivation to build, ship, and run distributed applications anywhere:

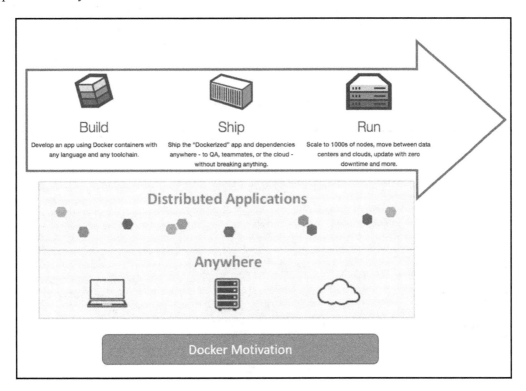

CaaS

CaaS is a secured IT-managed application environment of a particular infrastructure and content where developers can build and deploy applications on their own.

Docker CaaS is a Docker native solution with full support for the Docker API for performing Docker tasks effectively.

Developers and IT operations teams collaborate through the registry, as represented in the following CaaS diagram. This registry service contains a library of secure and signed images. Developers can develop the code and push the content to the registry and pull it from the registry for any future updates; you can pull it after the updates and testing are done, as represented on the left-hand side of the following diagram. The deployment process can also be automated with **Continuous Integration (CI)** tools instead of doing a manual deployment.

The following diagram represents the CaaS workflow:

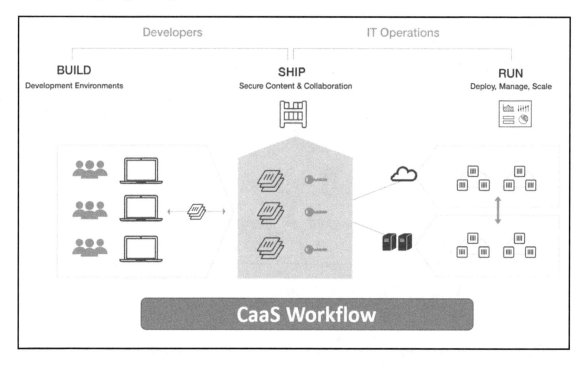

On the right-hand side of the preceding diagram, we have the IT operations team who are responsible for managing different vendor contracts for the production infrastructure, such as compute, networking, and storage. These teams are also responsible for provisioning the compute resources required by the application and monitoring cluster and application behavior during runtime with the help of Docker's Universal Control Plane. Then, the IT operations team can move the applications from one cloud infrastructure to another or scale the services up or down to maintain peak performance for varying system loads.

Characteristics of Docker CaaS

Docker CaaS acts as a basis for organizations to connect with diverse systems, languages, and tools within their individual environments and add a level of control, security, or loose coupling as per their operational or business processes. Docker CaaS streamlines the whole deployment process from the development to the production environment through the container service.

The following are the characteristics of Docker CaaS that will allow developers and IT operations to utilize the software and IDE without having to cross-function the workflow:

- **A tool for development and operations**: The task of CaaS is to quicken the development to production timeline with the unique abilities of the teams utilized consistently throughout the platform to achieve a unified transition between teams.
- **Support for all stages of the application life cycle**: With the right tools for both developers and operations teams, Docker provides great support, starting from CI to delivery. It also provides Devops, which adds innovation cycles to the process of building, testing, and staging the production.
- **Language support**: Docker provides the ability to run multiple versions of a language at the same time. This provides great freedom to the developers to build with whatever language, version, and tooling that is required for the features they are building at that time. This helps teams to concentrate on the business feature development rather than worry about the build and deployment.
- **Operating system flexibility**: While Docker was originally developed to support the Linux operating system, it now provides support for the Windows server as well. This provides you with the freedom to deploy, based on your platform needs.

- **Infrastructure support**: The Docker technology architecture abstracts the infrastructure away from the application, which allows the containers to run anywhere and be portable across any other infrastructure. This gives organizations a facility to run applications between platforms of their choice, such as a private data center, a hybrid cloud environment, or a distributed cloud, with the ability to take a backup and leverage.
- **Flexible to enhance the architecture**: Docker is flexible in regard to adding open APIs, pluggable architectures, and ecosystems to CaaS. This helps organizations customize their platforms based on their legacy and new application needs. This makes it easy to fit Docker into your environment and processes.

Docker CaaS platform components

The Docker CaaS platform offers a suite of integrated software solutions with the ability to perform flexible deployments that meet business requirements, as represented by the following diagram:

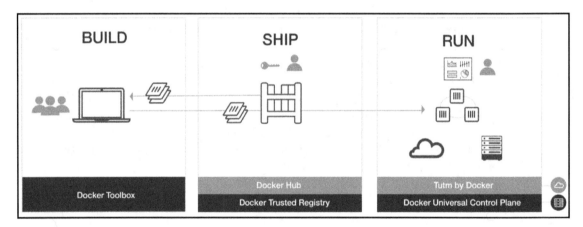

The Docker CaaS platform supports diverse installation types, including in-house and cloud provisioning, as follows:

- **In-house support**: The on-premise environment installation and support of Docker include the *Docker trusted registry* and *Docker Universal Control Plane* deployment processes within the organization's premise/servers. This allows the in-house infrastructure of the organization, including storage, active directory/LDAP, monitoring, and logging solutions, to connect with the environment. The ability to store and manage images within the organization storage infrastructure, including role-based access to these images, is provided by the *trusted registry*. Visibility across the Docker environment, including Swarm clusters, trusted registry repositories, containers, and multicontainer applications, is provided by the Docker's *Universal Control Plane*.
- **Cloud support**: If you want to readily use SaaS solutions, *Docker Hub* and *Tutum* provide a registry service and control plane that are hosted and managed by *Docker*. *Docker Hub* is a cloud registry service to store and manage your images along with user authorizations. *Docker Tutum* provisions and manages the deployment clusters as well as monitors and manages the deployed applications. This gives the flexibility to choose between a cloud infrastructure or deploy the application in our own physical node.

Eclipse integration for a Docker container

The Docker controller of the Eclipse plugin allows us to easily start/stop and deploy a Docker container from within the Eclipse IDE. This is supported in three major operating system platforms: Windows, Linux, and OS X.

This gives a visual outlook in addition to a set of Docker command-line tools and a set of common operations on Docker.

Docker Tooling is available from the Eclipse Neon version onward for easy integration via the Eclipse Marketplace.

In Eclipse IDE, go to **Help** | **Eclipse Marketplace** | **Search** for Docker under Linux tools. You should be able to find **Eclipse Docker Tooling**, as shown in the following screenshot. Install it by following the **Install** instruction from Eclipse:

After installing **Eclipse Docker Tooling**, we should be able to get either of the three perspectives in Eclipse for Docker:

- **Docker Explorer**: This represents a tree view that lists all the available Docker instances, including their images and containers
- **Docker Containers**: This represents a tabular view that lists the containers that belong to a selected Docker connection
- **Docker Images**: This represents a tabular view that lists the images that belong to a selected Docker connection

If you open the Docker Tooling perspective in the Eclipse IDE using the option Windows --> **Show View Perspective**, we can get this explorer, container, and image view.

> To use the plugins, it is assumed that Docker is already installed. You can see Docker's installation guide at `https://docs.docker.com/engine/installation/`; it will tell you how to do this on various platforms.

The following is a snapshot of Docker images from the sample project:

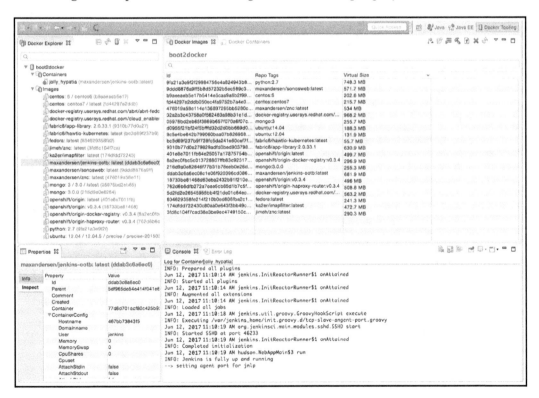

You can observe in the preceding screenshot that Docker Tooling is connected to the local Docker daemon, named `boot2docker`.

Docker Tooling usage includes three important steps, namely *Connect*, *Pull individual images*, and *Run*:

- **Connect**: In this phase, you can connect an existing Docket daemon that is installed in your organization to the Eclipse IDE session by clicking on **Add Connection** under **Docker Explorer**. You will see a wizard as follows. Provide a connection name and host details to connect to a Docker daemon:

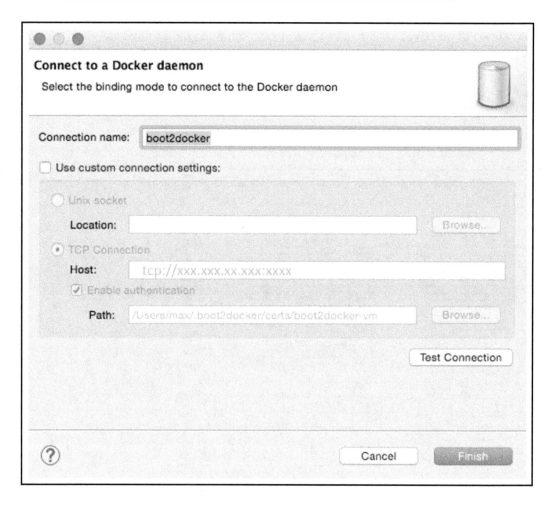

Once the connection is working, you can pull the Docker image as follows:

- Within the Docker image view, using the **Pull Image** option, we can pull an individual Docker image:

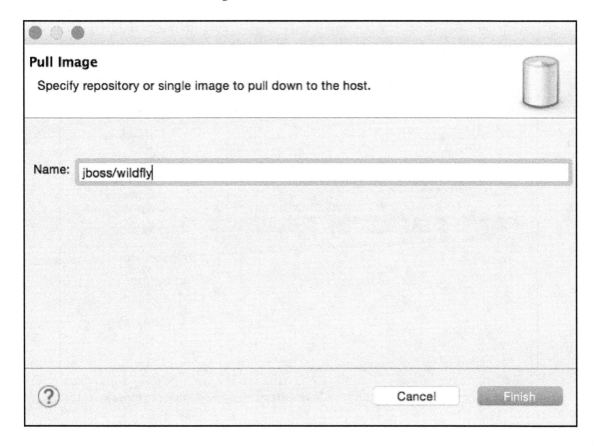

Docker hub has more than 100,000 free apps and public and private registries, including **WildFly,** referred to earlier. You can practice by adding apps from it.

- Once you have connected and pulled the Docker image successfully, you can run **Docker Image** by right-clicking on the image in the **Docker Explorer** view, as follows:

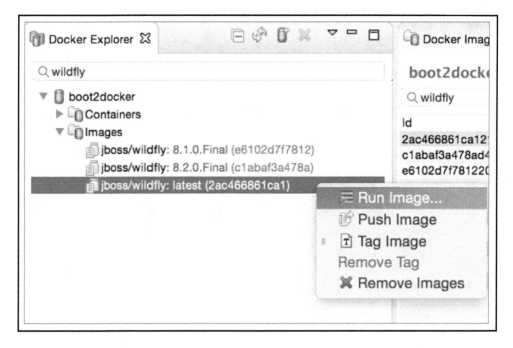

Select the right image under the **Run Image** view and click on **Finish**, as follows:

Run a Docker Image

Docker Container settings

Image: | jboss/wildfly:latest | ⌄ | Search...

Pull this image...

Name:

Entrypoint:

Command: /opt/jboss/wildfly/bin/standalone.sh -b 0.0.0.0

☑ Publish all exposed ports to random ports on the host interfaces

Only publish the selected container ports below to the host:

Container Port	Type	Host Address	Host Port		
☐ 8080	/tcp				Add
					Edit...
					Remove

Links to other containers:

Container Name	Alias		
			Add...
			Edit...
			Remove

☑ Keep STDIN open to Console even if not attached (-i)

☑ Allocate pseudo-TTY from Console (-t)

☐ Automatically remove the container when it exits (--rm)

⑦   < Back   Next >   Cancel   Finish

After the preceding step, the container should start and show the output in a console with the **Docker Containers** view showing the ports used by the application:

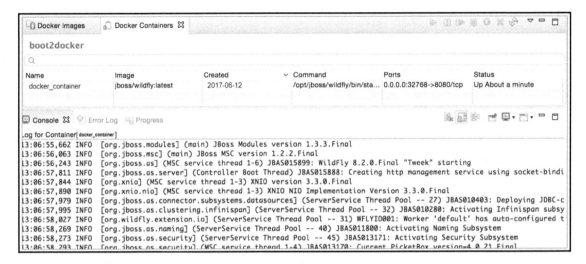

You can run the URL with the port on which the container has started in the browser and see the home page as follows:

Similarly, you can deploy any Java application with another container (such as Tomcat) configuration, with the Docker configuration as an image, and deploy to any other operating system as detailed in the next section.

Deploying a sample Java application to Tomcat with Docker

Now let's review the steps involved in deploying a simple Java application that runs on Tomcat with the help of Docker. For this example, consider an Ubuntu OS and review the commands required for the setup.

The first step is to install Docker on your system that has an Ubuntu OS. Do this with the following commands:

```
//re synchronize the package index files from their sources
sudo apt-get update
//install the package specified
sudo apt-get install linux-image-extra-'uname -r'
//pass advanced options to gpg. With adv --recv-key you can download the
public key.
sudo apt-key adv --keyserver keyserver.ubuntu.com --recv-keys <hashkey>
//execute the following command as interpreted by this program.
sudo sh -c "echo deb http://get.docker.io/ubuntu docker main >
/etc/apt/sources.list.d/docker.list"
//re synchronize the package index files from their sources
sudo apt-get update
//install the package specified
sudo apt-get install lxc-docker
//docker run keeping the stdin open even if not attached and allocate a
pseudo-TTY
sudo docker run -i -t ubuntu /bin/bash
```

The preceding steps should install and start the Docker container on your Ubuntu operating system with `script`.

After the installation, you could add the user to the Docker group with the following commands:

```
sudo groupadd docker
sudo gpasswd -a your_username docker
sudo service docker restart
```

The next step is to set up Java and Tomcat on your Docker container with the following content on the `docker` file:

```
FROM ubuntu:saucy
# Update the Ubuntu with run command
RUN apt-get update && apt-get -y upgrade
# Adding java repository to the container
RUN apt-get -y install software-properties-common
RUN add-apt-repository ppa:webupd9team/java
RUN apt-get -y update
# Accept the Java license for the install
RUN echo "oracle-java9-installer shared/accepted-oracle-license-v1-1
boolean true" | debconf-set-selections
# Install the Java software to the container
RUN apt-get -y install oracle-java9-installer
# Install the tomcat software to the container
RUN apt-get -y install tomcat9
RUN echo "JAVA_HOME=/usr/lib/jvm/java-9-oracle" >>
/etc/default/tomcat9EXPOSE 8080
# Download tomcat homepage
RUN mkdir /var/lib/tomcat9/webapps/ tomcat
RUN wget http://tomcat.apache.org -P /var/lib/tomcat9/webapps/tomcat
# Start Tomcat, after starting Tomcat the container will stop. By using the
below technique, it can be keep running.
CMD service tomcat9 start && tail -f /var/lib/tomcat9/logs/catalina.out
```

Now you can build the container with the `docker build -t tomcat9 .` command. Note . at the end of the command.

The container is now ready to start using the `docker run -p 8080:8080 -d tomcat9` command. This command should ensure port 8080 of the container gets forwarded to the system's local port 8080. After a few seconds, the tomcat page should be available at `http://localhost:8080/tomcat/`.

If you want to see the list of Docker containers, run the following command:

```
$ docker ps -a -s
```

Similarly, you can see the image tree of Docker using the following command:

```
$ docker images -tree
```

The final step is to deploy your sample Java application WAR file through Docker, which can be done using the `wget` command. For the following example, we are using the `sample.war` project available on Tomcat 9's sample projects:

```
RUN wget http://tomcat.apache.org/tomcat-9.0-doc/appdev/sample/sample.war -
P /var/lib/tomcat9/webapps
```

Through these steps, you have built a Docker container application using the `Docker` file, and it should deploy the application that would be accessible through `http://localhost:8080/sample/`.

Similarly, Docker can be integrated into various infrastructure tools, including AWS, Google Cloud Platform, IBM Bluemix, Jenkins, Microsoft Azure, OpenSVC, Oracle Container Cloud Service, and VMware vSphere Integrated Containers.

The big leap of these integrated systems is the ability to build microservices, a variant of the **service-oriented architecture** (**SOA**) style that structures an application as a collection of loosely coupled services. Refer to `http://microservices.io/` for more details about microservices; it has a number of patterns that will provide you information on how to build microservices.

Java 9 support

Java 9 greatly supports the cloud-based distributed application development with its latest features, including *Modular Java Application Packaging* or *Self-Contained Application Packaging*.

Java packaging tools now provide built-in support for multiple formats of self-contained application package development. The basic package contains only one folder on the hard drive that comprises all the required application resources along with the JRE. This package is readily redistributable as is, or we can also build an installable package, such as `exe` or `dmg`.

Self-contained application packages have the following advantages:

- Operations can directly install the applications with the installer that is known to them and launch the application
- We can control the JRE version to be used by the application as it is packaged
- Applications are ready to be deployed on a new system without having to install the JRE separately
- No explicit system admin rights are required to perform the deployment with ZIP or other installer types

- Applications can have file associations
- Applications are deployed as a single self-contained package with support for secondary launchers

However, there are a small set of uncomfortable facts regarding self-contained application packages, including:

- It requires additional steps for deploying applications, for example, applications that allow system security
- With the inclusion of the JRE, the application package size gets larger
- The application needs to be separately packaged, based on the variety of operating systems you may want to deploy
- JRE needs to be explicitly managed and updated with a project package instead of direct system installation

Spring framework observed this move toward the cloud and came up with modules that support the building of distributed applications that were cloud-ready in Java a little earlier. Let's quickly discuss some of the important features these Spring modules (Boot, Cloud, and Cloud Data Flow) offer to build production-ready self-contained cloud applications/microservices.

Spring Boot

Spring Boot enables us to produce standalone, production-ready Spring-based applications that are *ready to run* in micro service architecture. Spring Boot applications need minimum configuration and they provide versatile features, including:

- You can build standalone Spring applications that can be run directly
- You can develop the applications that follow micro service architecture
- Deliver Java Self contained applications ready for cloud deployment
- You can embed servers such as Tomcat and Jetty directly (without having to deploy the WAR files explicitly)
- Spring configurations get configured automatically wherever feasible
- They offer prejudiced `starter` POM files to streamline a Maven-based configuration
- They offer production-ready features, such as metrics, health checks, and externalized configurations
- They provide the ability to deploy with *no code generation* and *no XML configuration*

Spring Cloud

Spring Cloud offers distributed systems a standard approach for generating features based on generic patterns. The implementation of such generic patterns in distributed systems gives the ability to the systems and services to rapidly govern their booting process predominantly in a distributed environment, such as Cloud Foundry.

Spring Cloud builds on top of Spring Boot by providing a much-needed group of libraries that improve the system capabilities.

Spring Cloud Data Flow

Spring Cloud Data Flow is a cloud-based service offering that produces microservice applications with latest runtime systems. This is especially useful in producing applications that can handle big-data-related features, such as data ingest, real-time analytics, and data import/export. It can produce, stream and task/batch microservice applications based on Spring Boot, which can natively run in modern runtimes, such as Cloud Foundry, Apache YARN, Apache Mesos, and Kubernetes.

Summary

In this chapter, you learned important cloud computing features and how they are different from distributed computing; you also learned about different cloud platforms. Then, we discussed the leading cloud service providers on the market today and also checked out various AWS's with an example on how to build a distributed application with Amazon products. You also learned about the latest CaaS offering from Docket and observed the steps in setting up a Java web application with Docker. We finished this chapter with an understanding of Java 9 support for the cloud and distributed application development with self-contained features along with Spring Framework modules that enable self-contained and cloud-based microservice development.

In the next chapter, you will learn about the essential big data technologies and how they help in distributed computing along with the different implementations available and big data concepts, modules, and applications in detail.

8
Big Data Analytics

Big data (as embodied by Hadoop clusters) and Big Compute (as embodied by MPI clusters) provide unique capabilities for storing and processing large volumes of data. Hadoop clusters make distributed computing readily accessible to the Java community, while MPI clusters provide high parallel efficiency for compute-intensive workloads. Bringing the big data and Big Compute communities together is an active area of research. Projects such as Apache ZooKeeper provide a centralized infrastructure and service that enables synchronization across a cluster, which is the way to achieve distributed computing in big data systems.

In this chapter, we will cover the following:

- What is big data?
- Big data characteristics
- NoSQL databases
- Hadoop, MapReduce, and HDFS
- Distributed computing for big data
- ZooKeeper for distributed computing

While technologies such as Hadoop, Hbase, Accumulo, and Cassandra allow us to store, query, and index large volumes of complex data, **Dynamic Distributed Dimensional Data Model (D4M)** provides a uniform mathematical framework for processing structured, semi-structured, and non-structured multidimensional data.

What is big data?

Data is the important constituent in an organization's analytics; each characteristic of an organization's information is maintained in a field that is ubiquitous and aids in capturing, reviewing, transforming, and combining the facts that make business analytical problems. Audit information, in an organization, builds up over time and helps in business forecasting and planning; it is essential in this competitive world. Such information captured across organizations grows rapidly. It becomes difficult for organizations to maintain it in a relational database. With the advent of mobile-based applications and social media networking services, especially in the field of banking and the e-commerce domain, the ability to process data at lightening speed causes it to be both unstructured (data in no format related to RDBMS storage, such as text and multimedia) and semi-structured (data where the format is partly related to RDBMS storage such as CSV, XML, and JSON); this is termed as big data.

The dynamics of big data are in terabytes, petabytes, and exabyte; for some organizations, it could be larger than this. Dispensing and examining such huge volumes of data are extremely strenuous and daunting over time. If you are still planning to use traditional data management and analytical tools to manage big data, you are no more in the race for the market demands. Newer technologies and projects have been evolving to manage such big data, such as Hadoop.

Big data characteristics

Big data maintenance and analysis are formed by the characteristics of data, including the structure or unstructured nature of the data, which helps in obtaining more accurate results from data processing. Big data elements can be referred to as the four V's; they are represented in the following figure:

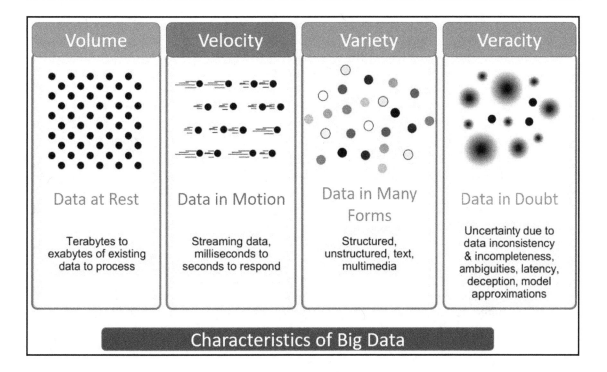

Volume	Velocity	Variety	Veracity
Data at Rest	Data in Motion	Data in Many Forms	Data in Doubt
Terabytes to exabytes of existing data to process	Streaming data, milliseconds to seconds to respond	Structured, unstructured, text, multimedia	Uncertainty due to data inconsistency & incompleteness, ambiguities, latency, deception, model approximations

Characteristics of Big Data

Volume

When organizations collect information over the years, it makes an extremely huge volume of data. Such huge volume a of data may be generated from user information, application-generated audit information, and any unstructured information from the online sources. Analytic tools help in choosing the right set of data to perform the analysis and in recognizing the important metrics, which are appropriate to the perspective you may want to review from that information.

From the organization's perspective, a huge volume of information can be segregated into the following types of information:

- **Business identification data**: Each organization performs certain business activities. The stakeholders carry a unique identification based on the set of fields attributed to them such as a social security number. Collecting such identification information over time and performing big data analytics on it helps in improving the business and targeted customer stake. Additionally, organizations can start reinforcing the marketing efforts to pursue profitable strategies.
- **Descriptive data of unique business identifiers**: The descriptive data of business identifiers includes demographic information such as age, gender, education, profession, and whereabouts. Some of the information may not be maintained in an organization's data store, but can be captured through social media. Such information can be used to promote business and operations tailored to the business needs.
- **Quantitative data about customer engagement**: By reviewing the customer's interest in business and by analyzing information about their previous engagements, prospects can be made for the group of customers. This helps in offering the right set of products to such customers, which changes the way your organization markets its products and reaches the right customers with the right product.
- **Qualitative data**: By performing the right set of analytics, qualitative data such as customer investments and reviews can be extracted in organizations that helps in taking strategic decisions in the business motivations. This information can be extracted from communications, feedback, and other support engagements.

Variety

Based on the sources and form of data collection, such as emails and chat communication, relevant data management tools need to be engaged to handle such complex information to achieve a business advantage. Using the right set of analytic tools, such as Hive and Pig, restructuring the way the information is captured and stored in an organization's data store, and engaging in more agile analytics helps in bringing better results with the variety of information.

Velocity

Organizations are often overwhelmed in accepting huge volumes of information, which are produced in a short span of time due to the collection of application and social network information. This makes it challenging to review all that information and come up with the right business advice. It is essential to engage with the right set of tools and communication to perform such rapid analytics on large volumes of data that are generated in a short span of time.

Veracity

The veracity shows the variance in the consistency in any database following the internet trends in the same field, hence a quantifiable client engagement is the key for alleviating big data imprecisions within your organization data. Veracity is the data ambiguity for the analytics between the slots they capture the information from. This ambiguity, or the speed at which a data trend changes, makes it difficult for any organization to analyze and change based on trends.

NoSQL databases

Data has been increasing rapidly across the world due to various reasons such as transactional, application information, demographic, social networking, and audit information. Organizations have to find newer ways to manage such huge volume of data other than relational databases (such as, MySQL and Oracle) to bring simple design, horizontal scaling, and clustering to ensure better access control and performance. This means that the data stored in a NoSQL database carries a data model, which is different from tabular relations of relational databases. NoSQL means Not Only SQL. The following diagram shows different types of database models:

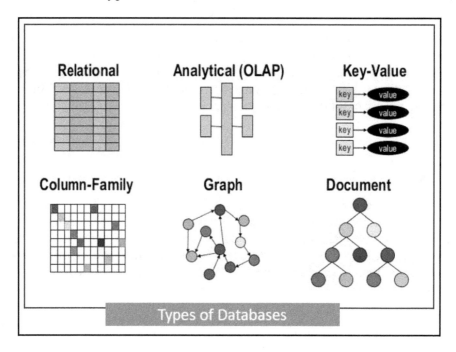

The preceding diagram represents types of databases; relational and analytical databases are treated as SQL databases, while the others are added with NoSQL.

SQL, the structured query language, has been around from the 70s, and is the most frequently used database query language in relational databases with abilities such as **Data Definition Language** (**DDL**) and **Data Manipulation Language** (**DML**).

NoSQL has been around from the 90s, and its key purpose is to achieve a greater performance in large databases. The key-value, column-family, graph, and document data structures makes the faster processes compared to a relational database.

The following table shows the key difference between SQL and NoSQL database models:

Parameter	SQL Database	NOSQL Database
Consistency	Can be configured for strong consistency	Depends on the product. MongoDB offers strong consistency with tunable for reads whereas others like Cassandra offer eventual consistency.
Data Manipulation	Specific language using Select, Insert, and Update statements.	Through object-oriented APIs
Data Storage Model	Individual records are stored as rows in tables, with each column storing a specific piece of data about that record much like a spreadsheet. Related data is stored in separate tables, and then joined together when more complex queries are executed.	Varies based on database type. For example, **key-value** stores function similarly to SQL databases, but have only two columns ('key' and 'value'), with more complex information sometimes stored as BLOBs within the 'value' columns. **Document databases** do away with the table-and-row model altogether, storing all relevant data together in single 'document' in JSON, XML, or another format, which can nest values hierarchically.
Development Model	Mix of open-source (e.g., Postgres, MySQL) and closed source (e.g., Oracle Database)	Open-source
Purpose	Deal with first wave of data storage applications	Deal with limitations of SQL databases, especially scalability, multi-structured data, geo-distribution and agile development sprints
Scaling	Vertically, meaning a single server must be made increasingly powerful in order to deal with increased demand. It is possible to spread SQL databases over many servers, but significant additional engineering is required, and core relational features such as JOINs, referential integrity and transactions are typically lost between them.	Horizontally, meaning that to add capacity, a database administrator can simply add more commodity servers or cloud instances. The database automatically spreads data across servers as necessary.
Schemas	Structure and data types are fixed in advance. To store information about a new data item, the entire database must be altered, and database must be stopped to bring the new changes.	Typically dynamic, with some enforcing data validation rules. Applications can add new fields on the fly, and unlike SQL table rows, dissimilar data can be stored together as necessary.
Transaction support	Yes, updates can be configured to complete entirely or not at all	In certain circumstances and at certain levels like document level vs. database level
Types	SQL Database is of a single type with minor variations	Diverse type of databse including key-value stores, document databases, wide-column stores, and graph databases
Variants	MySQL, Postgres, Microsoft SQL Server, Oracle Database	MongoDB, Cassandra, HBase, Neo4j

Within the NoSQL database, there are multiple types of database based on the content and relationship maintenance. The following table shows the key differences and variants available within NoSQL databases:

Document Database	Graph Database	Key-Value Database	Wide Column Stores
Store data elements in document-like structures that encode information in formats like JSON.	Emphasize connections between dta elements, storing related nodes in graphs to accelerate querying.	Use a simple data model that pairs a unique key and its associated value in storing data elements	It is also called as table style databases. Store data across tables that can have very large number of columns
Common uses include content management and monitoring web and mobile aplications	Common uses include recommendation engines and geospatial applications	Common uses include storing clickstream data and application logs.	common uses include internet search and other large scale web applications
Examples: Couchbase Server, MarkLogic, CouchDB, MongoDB	Exmaples: Allegrograph, IBM Graph, Neo4j	Examples: Aerospike, DynamoDB, Riak, Redis	Examples: Accumulo, Hbase, Hypertable, Cassandra, SimpleDB

Apart from the earlier discussed advantages of different NoSQL databases, having the ability to contain flexible and dynamic schemas, support for distributed database system, automatic database replication, integrated caching, and tunable consistency are their major benefits.

Hadoop, MapReduce, and HDFS

As discussed in the previous sections, the rapidly increasing data storage, analysis, and process requirements are in the necessity of mining the essential information for business needs from such huge volume of data in storage clusters and data-intensive applications. Scalability, high availability, fault tolerance, data distribution, parallel processing, and load balancing are the expected features of such a system.

These features of big data are addressed by the MapReduce program introduced by Google.

Hadoop

Hadoop is the most prevalent and open source execution of the MapReduce programing model. Apache Hadoop is a scalable and reliable software framework for parallel and distributed computing. Instead of depending on expensive resources for storage and processing huge volume of data, Hadoop allows big data parallel processing on inexpensive commodity hardware. The following diagram represents the components of the Hadoop architecture:

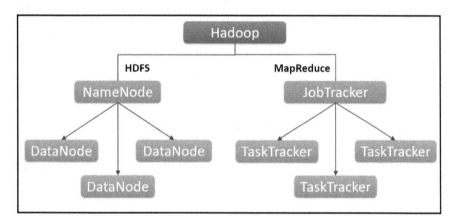

Apache Hadoop contains five diverse modules, each running on its own JVM, namely:

1. NameNode.
2. DataNode.
3. Secondary NameNode.
4. JobTracker.
5. TaskTracker.

NameNode and **DataNode** belong to the **HDFS** layer, storing the data and metadata. **JobTracker** and **TaskTracker** belongs to the **MapReduce** layer, keeping track and executing the job. Hadoop clusters contain a master node and numerous slave nodes.

The Hadoop core architecture contains:

1. Hadoop Distributed File System (HDFS).
2. MapReduce.

HDFS (Hadoop Distributed File System)

HDFS is a self-controlled, distributed filesystem, providing scalable and reliable data storage on commodity hardware with a fault tolerance mechanism. HDFS, in association with MapReduce, manages data storage on a clustered environment by scaling up, based on content and resource consumption. Unlike RDBMS systems, HDFS can store data in multiple formats such as files, images, and videos in addition to the text. In the case of exceptions on one node, HDFS switches between the nodes and transfers information at rapid speed.

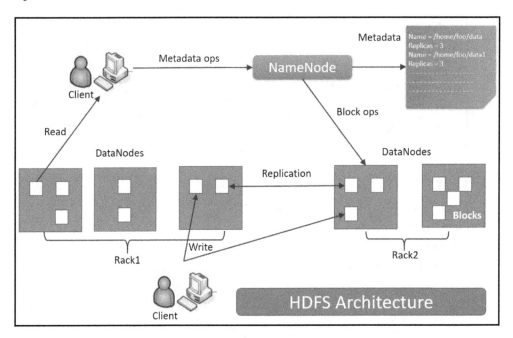

HDFS behaves in the master slave architecture with a single **NameNode** and a number of **DataNodes**. The master (**NameNode**) is responsible for managing the namespace of the filesystem and controling the client file access. The **DataNodes** are responsible for serving read and write requests from the filesystem's clients. The **DataNodes** also perform block creation, deletion, and replication on instructions from **NameNode**.

MapReduce

MapReduce is a programming pattern used by Apache Hadoop. Hadoop MapReduce works in providing the systems that can store, process, and mine huge data with parallel multi node clusters in a scalable, reliable, and error-absorbing inexpensive distributed system. In MapReduce, the data analysis and data processing are split into individual phases called the Map phase and Reduce phase as represented in the following figure:

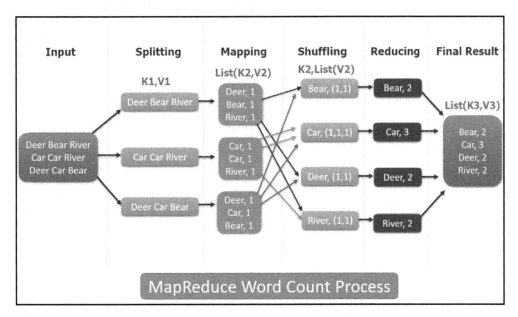

In the preceding diagram, the word count process is handled by MapReduce with multiple phases. The set of words in **Input** are first split into three nodes in the (**K1**, **V1**) process. These three split nodes communicate with the corresponding mapping nodes with **List (K2, V2)**. The **Mapping** nodes take the responsibility of invoking the shuffling process where each word from **Mapping** nodes is passed to the corresponding **Shuffling** nodes as **K2, List(V2)**. From the **Shuffling** nodes, the corresponding **Reducing** phase is invoked where the count is calculated for each word. Finally, the result is captured in the **list (K3, V3)** node.

Let's review how to implement the preceding Hadoop MapReduce example as a program.

 Note: *Make sure you have Hadoop with JDK installed in your system to practice this example.*

1. In Eclipse, create a core Java project as `HadoopMapReduceDemo`.
2. Create a `Hadoop` package under the source directory.
3. Add the following libraries to the project in the project build path: `hadoop-core.jar`, `commons-cli.jar`, and `commons-logging.jar`.
4. The Hadoop libraries can be added to the project using Maven entries from: `https://mvnrepository.com/artifact/org.apache.hadoop`
5. Write the following `MapReduceWordCount` Java program:

```java
package hadoop;

import java.io.IOException;

import org.apache.hadoop.conf.Configuration;
import org.apache.hadoop.fs.Path;
import org.apache.hadoop.io.IntWritable;

import org.apache.hadoop.io.Text;
import org.apache.hadoop.mapreduce.Mapper;
import org.apache.hadoop.mapreduce.Reducer;
import org.apache.hadoop.mapreduce.lib.input.FileInputFormat;
import org.apache.hadoop.mapreduce.lib.output.FileOutputFormat;
import org.apache.hadoop.util.GenericOptionsParser;
public class MapReduceWordCount {
  public static void main(String[] args) throws Exception {
    Configuration config = new Configuration();
    String[] argFiles = new GenericOptionsParser(
    config, args).getRemainingArgs();
    Path inputFilePath = new Path(argFiles[0]);
    Path outputFilePath = new Path(argFiles[1]);
    Job mapReduceJob = new Job(config, "wordcount");
    mapReduceJob.setJarByClass(MapReduceWordCount.class);
    mapReduceJob.setMapperClass(MapperForWordCount.class);
    mapReduceJob.setReducerClass(ReducerForWordCount.class);
    mapReduceJob.setOutputKeyClass(Text.class);
    mapReduceJob.setOutputValueClass(IntWritable.class);
    FileInputFormat.addInputPath(mapReduceJob, inputFilePath);
    FileOutputFormat.setOutputPath(mapReduceJob,
    outputFilePath);
```

```
        System.exit(mapReduceJob.waitForCompletion(true) ? 0 : 1);
    }

    public static class MapperForWordCount extends Mapper<
    LongWritable, Text, Text, IntWritable> {
      public void map(LongWritable key,
      Text wordText, Context context)
      throws IOException, InterruptedException {
        String wordsAsString = wordText.toString();
        String[] wordsAsArray = wordsAsString.split(",");
        for (String word : wordsAsArray) {
          Text hadoopText = new Text(word.toUpperCase().trim());
          IntWritable count = new IntWritable(1);
          context.write(hadoopText, count);
        }
      }
    }

    public static class ReducerForWordCount extends Reducer<
    Text, IntWritable, Text, IntWritable> {
      public void reduce(Text word, Iterable<IntWritable> values,
      Context context)
      throws IOException, InterruptedException {
        int CountOfWords = 0;
        for (IntWritable value : values) {
          CountOfWords += value.get();
        }
        context.write(word, new IntWritable(CountOfWords));
      }
    }
}
```

6. The preceding program contains three classes, the driving component (main class – `MapReduceWordCount`), the Mapper component (`MapperForWordCount`) extending Mapper<KEYIN,VALUEIN,KEYOUT,VALUEOUT>, and Reducer component (`ReducerForWordCount`) extending the Reducer<KEYIN,VALUEIN,KEYOUT,VALUEOUT>.

7. Right-click on the **HadoopMapReduceDemo** project followed by **as Jar**.

8. Generate a text file with words to be counted, and name it `wordCountInput` as follows:

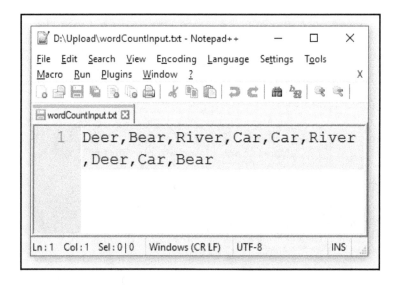

9. Move this file to the Hadoop system through the following terminal command:

```
[practice@localhost ~]$ hadoop fs -put wordCountInput wordCountInput
```

10. To execute the Hadoop MapReduce program, the following command needs to be executed:

```
[practice@localhost ~]$ hadoop jar HadoopMapReduceDemo.jar hadoop.
MapReduceWordCount wordCountInput wordCountOutput
```

11. View the word count output result from the output file with the following command:

```
[practice @localhost ~]$ hadoop fs -cat wordCountOutput/part-r-
00000
    BEAR    2
    CAR     3
    DEER    2
    RIVER   2
```

Cloud computing for Hadoop

Well-known internet-based organizations such as Google, Twitter, and so on, need to perform data processing at the rate of millions and billions of requests per hour. To achieve this, they are moving toward computing for inexpensive resources and better performance in recent times. Organizations need to choose the right combination of components that need to be hosted on cloud to achieve the expected processing and performance in durable services.

Here, you can see the pros and cons of hosting Hadoop in cloud:

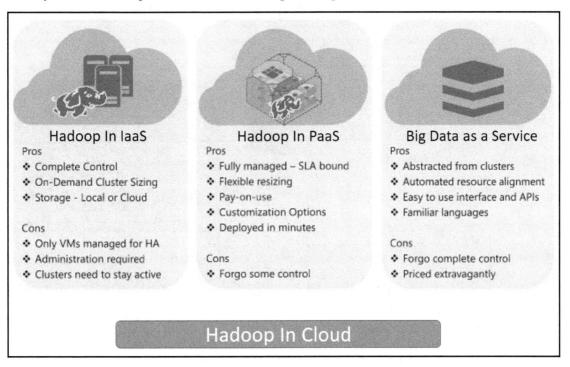

Apache Hadoop is also offering a comprehensive combination of solutions for cloud-based applications. These Linux-based cloud systems are scalable and flexible systems that give the expected performance throughput of big data. In cloud-distributed platforms as well, Hadoop is the chosen solution for efficient performance.

Dynamic Distributed Dimensional Data Model (D4M)

While technologies such as Hadoop, Cassandra, and Accumulo can facilitate the processing of huge data volumes, D4M is a uniform mathematical framework for processing structured/semi-structured/non-structured multidimensional data.

The data model follows the pattern of representing any multidimensional data as a matrix of 0 and 1, which can be seen as follows:

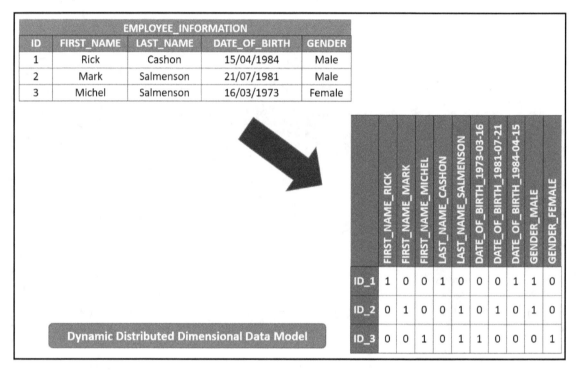

The following are the advantages of representing data in this model:

1. Easy visualization of data storage and retrieval from the database.
2. Competent performance can be achieved in the NoSQL database with compact storage of triplets (key, value) as **1**.

Distributed computing for big data

Distributed computing is not required for all computing solutions. Consider that the business doesn't have any time constraints in system processing and an asynchronous remote process can do the job efficiently in the expected time of processing. Then, why should the business invest in having either a more competent resource or a distributed environment to bring performance improvements in such a process?

Over the past few years, organizations are looking at reducing costs and are investing in critical and essential business needs. This means that, if there is a real need for processing a complex data analysis and the organization has a number of additional resources available, it can make use of distributed computing wherein each computing resource, with its own memory, can process a bit of the complex analysis and contribute to its completion.

Not only that; instead of having a single huge computing resource, if we utilize multiple commodity hardware to act as a distributed system, this also adds load balancing resource optimization with an enormous cluster of nodes.

System software, such as Zookeeper, is discussed in detail in the next section and is available to effectively handle the resource load and fault tolerance with built-in rules. This has changed the *economics* of big data processing by bringing distributed systems into the picture.

Moreover, latency in data analysis and processing with big data impact the results a lot, especially due to ever changing data trends such as social networking. In such scenarios, big data computing processes should have minimum latency to follow market trends in its processing. Distributed systems in such a scenario makes a big difference by introducing multiple scalable resources for computation.

Organizations such as Amazon, Yahoo, Google, and Facebook are on this track, and this is how they can bring you the expected and matching content in fractions of seconds from such a huge database.

ZooKeeper for distributed computing

Zookeeper is the chosen solution for handling big data encounters in Hadoop. It is a performance-efficient distributed coordination service for distributed applications. It offers a simple interface for essential services such as naming, synchronization, configuration management, and group services.

ZooKeeper runs on Java and allows bindings for both C and Java programming.

The following diagram represents the architecture of the ZooKeeper:

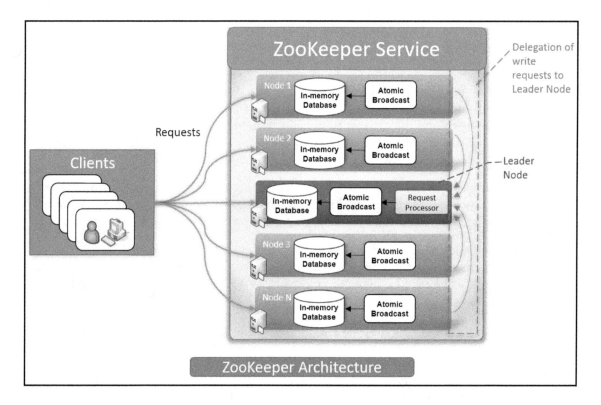

In the preceding diagram, the **Leader Node** is the only node having the write access. All the other nodes shown on the **ZooKeeper Service** are called followers, and they only delegate the requests to the **Leader Node** as represented earlier.

The request processor present in the leader node holds the responsibility for processing the request and handing over the result to the respective follower nodes so that they can take it forward from there in the process chain.

The atomic broadcast component is responsible for broadcasting the changes to all the other nodes.

The in-memory database helps the ZooKeeper nodes to process the respective node responsibilities.

The advantages of this ZooKeeper architecture include:

1. Design simplicity.
2. Quicker processing and process synchronization.
3. Configuration management.
4. Data replication and self election.
5. Reliable messaging system.
6. Atomic and sequential update mechanism.

ZooKeeper can be effectively configured in the queue environment to bring synchronization over distributed environments, cluster environment management, fault recovery, and involuntary leader assortment necessities.

Summary

Through this chapter, you learned the basics of big data and its characteristics. You also learned about various NoSQL databases and their categories. The concepts of MapReduce, Hadoop, and Hadoop Distributed File System with a Java program were also covered. We completed this chapter with an understanding of distributed computing for big data and reviewed the architecture of Apache ZooKeeper for distributed computing.

In the next chapter, we will discuss essential testing, debugging, and troubleshooting aspects of Java-based distributed applications.

9
Testing, Debugging, and Troubleshooting

Software systems are being developed with more advanced features, which needs huge resourcing that is addressed using the distributed systems as discussed in the previous chapters. However, while processing such heavy resourcing systems on multiple small computers and collating the results, it is expected to run such an integrated system providing a greater fault tolerance.

Moreover, the systems used in distributed computing can have their own operating systems and software to perform the respective jobs, while they are part of a large distributed system. Testing of such versatile platform systems is complicated without setting the right approach and solutions.

In this chapter, we will cover the following:

- Challenges in testing distributed applications
- Standard testing approach in software systems
- Cloud distributed application testing
- Latest tools for testing Java distributed applications
- Debugging and troubleshooting distributed applications

Challenges in testing distributed applications

Distributed systems are observed to behave more dynamically compared to the single server systems, and they behave differently at different times. The systems involved in distributed computing can give the results to the tests performed individually.

However, when these small systems are integrated to form a large distributed system, the processing ability and the order of starting these individual processes and responding or returning values change the behavior of the distributed application rapidly. Such varying behavior of a distributed system complicates the testing of such systems.

Moreover, with the multiple different types of systems involved in the distributed system processing, the systems availability, topology, and the execution status highly affect the results of the same tests run at different times, which makes testing and considering such results as the baseline decided by the system behavior.

Maintaining interoperability among different automated business processes and components involved in the integration is an important but challenging task in distributed applications.

The following diagram represents some of the quality requirements of distributed systems:

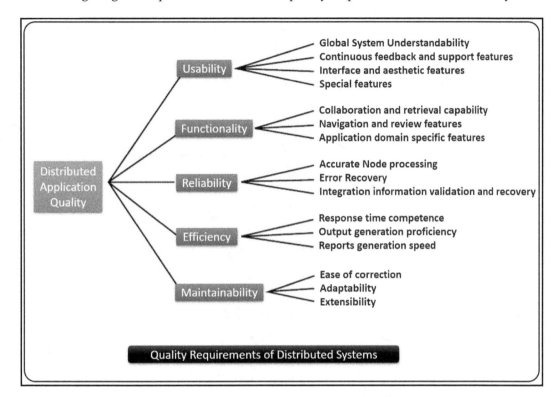

To ensure the distributed applications meet such quality requirements, they should be developed with the quality assurance enabling techniques such as component-based development, adhering to the global development standards and enforcing the right security measures between the components.

Standard testing approach in software systems

The standard testing approach in software systems comprises of the sequence of steps as represented in the following diagram.

In each stage a set of tests are executed, and the results are reviewed. Based on the review, further steps are taken until all the stages are completed.

Starting with Unit Testing by the developers, the application needs to go through the system testing, system integration testing, and **User Acceptance Testing (UAT)**, respectively. Moreover, the technical tests such as load performance testing and failover tests should definitely be included in the test plan.

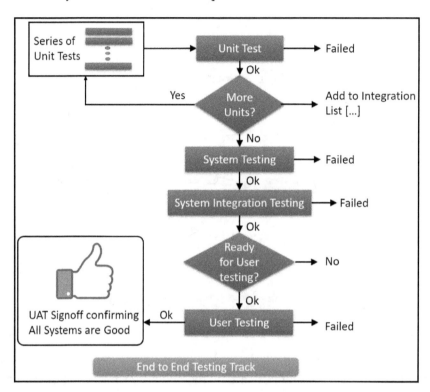

Unit testing

This is the program-based individual component verification process to ensure most of the development artifacts are independently tested for their expected behavior. For example, if you write an application to advise on pensions for the previous employees in an organization, the component that calculates the age of a person based on the date of birth can be developed as an independent component and unit tested for its behavior. Assertions are the essential terminology in which the individual components functionality is validated between the actual and expected behavior, the failing of which is treated as a failure for the component's expectancy.

While setting up the unit test cases for any feature/component takes a considerable amount of time, another challenge is to keep the test cases up to date for changing requirements. Application teams are advised to maintain a set of test artifacts/data that can be used for executing the unit test cases multiple times through the project's life cycle. Moreover, running a test coverage verification to review the amount of code considered by the unit test cases is helpful in uncovering the untested components in the application.

Some of the important applications of unit testing for distributed applications are:

- Mocking the dependencies of a component with the help of the mocking framework
- Continuous integration-based unit test execution
- Test coverage in applications

Mocking the dependencies

While executing the unit test cases on a set of scenarios, it gets complicated when some of your code components are extensively using any framework/dependent API as part of the component building. The following diagram shows how a **Unit** (component) can work with its dependency in real life but with **Mock Dependency** during a **Unit Test**:

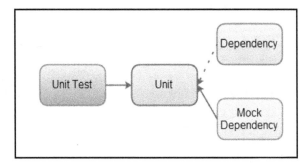

With the help of mock dependency, the key framework/infrastructure dependencies can be mocked and the components targeted for unit testing can be successfully tested without having the actual dependency elements available during the unit test.

Moreover, for the continuous integration processes wherein the unit tests are configured to automatically execute on all the targeted components on the CI job run, the infrastructure dependencies may not be available or accessible to the continuous integration servers. In such scenarios, the mock dependency elements greatly help in overcoming the infrastructure dependencies for the tests to execute, as explained here.

Continuous Integration (CI)-based unit testing

Continuous Integration (**CI**) is the tool-based configuration that automates the build, test, and deploy features. CI is more of a development practice, where developers should integrate the code more frequently into the shared repository. Every time the developer checks-in the code, the whole code base gets verified by an automated build, allowing us to detect the problems in the code base earlier. By integrating regularly, we can detect errors quickly, and address them at the earliest opportunity.

For example, in CI, the Java builder tasks automatically run the unit test cases configured and enabled for the specific application. One good example is the Junit parser which executes the unit test cases and produces a comprehensive report.

The following diagram represents the CI-based application build life cycle:

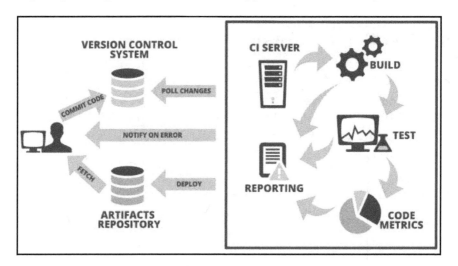

The following steps are involved in the CI-based build process:

1. The developers commit the code to the version control system.
2. The CI server polls the changes from the version control system and invokes the build process.
3. The build process compiles the code and verifies the build status.
4. If the build is failed, immediately it generates the reporting and fails the build. Followed by this, the notification (email) about the error gets generated and sent to the preconfigured set of users.
5. If the build is successful, the process goes to the next stage which is the execution of the regression test suite against the compiled code.

6. If some of the tests are failed, the build can be failed and generates the reports and notification to the users.

7. If all the tests are successful, the code metrics get captured and prepared for the reporting.

8. Once the test reporting is complete, the CI server deploys the components to the artifacts repository and users can fetch the content from there.

9. The CI servers are flexible to configure additional steps such as static code analysis, security analysis, deployment of the compiled code to the test environments along with the integrations to the alerts, and bug tracking systems.

Bamboo and Jenkins are the widely used CI server products in recent times.

System testing

System testing is the process of verification of the modular systems for the functionality they are programmed for. A system consists of a set of units thoroughly unit tested and seamlessly integrated with reusable components and libraries to possess the business requirements for that system. The following diagram shows the integration of elementary components (units) that make a system that should be tested with the request content as input and executing it to get the desired system output:

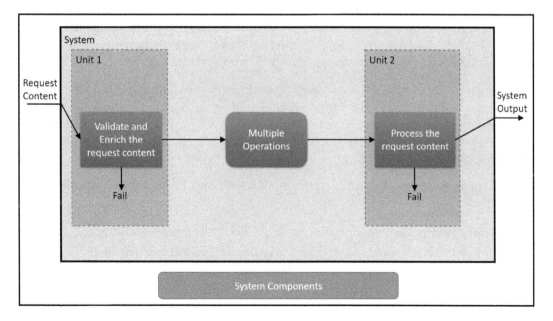

The preceding diagram represents a system components as a series of units integrated with multiple operations to be performed in them. A system receives the request content that needs to be processed by each unit that the request content is sent for; failure at any unit should stop the processing of that message and give a corresponding failure message. Once all the units and operations process the message, it can be given as the output from that system.

With system testing, the system is tested for a set of valid and invalid request content and the behavior is recorded. Based on the failure scenarios and criticality of those defects, the development team needs to fix them based on priority and handover the corrected system for another round of testing.

System integration testing

System integration testing is a broader level of testing the application that is formed by integrating multiple systems thoroughly tested and seamlessly integrated with other systems, based on the agreed contract interface.

The system integration testing includes the validation and verification of the functional behavior of the application along with the performance, load/stress, compatibility, and scalability testing.

At the end of system integration testing, the application can be assessed for its overall richness, in volumetric terms, that it can possess and the latency of the application, along with the container and hardware requirements for that application based on the nonfunctional benchmark requirements expected from that application.

Integration testing also covers the concerns related to the invocation of multiple software components while they are interacting with one another, such as, information exchange between the modules in appropriate mechanisms, and the compatibility between the systems to confirm the behavior of one system not affecting the functionality and performance of the other modules.

System integration is not just limited to the interfacing of multiple software systems, but it also includes:

- Integration of systems developed in different technologies
- Integration of working applications with a set of software products
- Integration of the data with data repositories

- Integration of the communication network
- Integration of new business processes with new technical capabilities brought into the existing environment
- The entrenching of information through newer processes and empowering it with the right technology
- Integration of resource abilities with the newer processes

However, there are set of challenges involved in setting up the right integration of systems that includes:

- Unreliable infrastructure and environments
- System nature being distributed
- Interoperability
- Unpredictable interaction models
- Performance and reliability concerns with the heterogeneous integration

Some of the widely used integration testing approaches in the industry include:

- End-to-end integration testing
- Model-based testing
- Increment or decrement approach
- Coupling-based testing
- Big bang testing
- Open source testing
- V model

User Acceptance Testing

This is the end-to-end testing performed after all the preceding tests are successful. The focus and intention of the User Acceptance Testing is to confirm the application is meeting the business process operation and not just the low-level component behavior.

The following are the series of steps involved in the User Acceptance Testing:

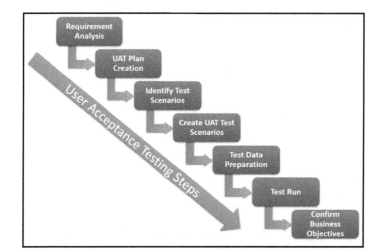

A group of subject matter experts for the application get together and perform the represented series of operations, seen in the preceding diagram, thoroughly to ensure that the application is complying to the strategy.

The key features of User Acceptance Testing include:

- The increased satisfaction of the clients to ensure that the requirements are met, and a boosts the confidence in the product on its real environment behavior and any unforeseen critical issues.
- The functional quality of the product is expected through the earlier phases of implementation.
- It establishes better communication between the implementation and the business teams as the acceptance criteria is improved through the series of user acceptance tests.
- The engineering team gets confidence about the product implementation and any risk of post production/go-live issues.
- Better understanding of the target audience needs through stakeholders' engagement in UAT.

By spending about 5-10% of the project time for UAT, we can save almost 30% of the total waste, which is a good way to ensure a better ROI from the project for the stakeholders.

Cloud distributed application testing

Compared to the on-premise application testing, there are multiple differences in testing the cloud distributed applications. With the variety of cloud implementations and the complicated nature of the topology, testing the cloud-based systems is more important and involves critical intricacies. System performance, application security, and isolation testing are difficult areas to create and replicate the problems.

Hence, it is very important not only to test the end-to-end application, but also to test the cloud infrastructure on which the application is getting deployed in the distributed architecture.

A tangible problem in cloud testing is with testing the capability and reliability of the application from inside the cloud among diverse services offered by the cloud provider. Your application deployed in the cloud is assured by the reliability and performance offered by the cloud solution. Some of the factors involved in affecting the security and reliability of cloud-based applications include the applications running in parallel with your application in the same server and the same hardware.

Tests like load and performance testing are no longer reflect the application level only, but at the cloud infrastructure because the cloud applications are coming up with the scalability and dynamic infrastructure abilities, which can expand based on the system demand and usage. The components need to be thoroughly tested for the failover and temporary disconnect scenarios, as this is the most common behaviors in cloud platforms.

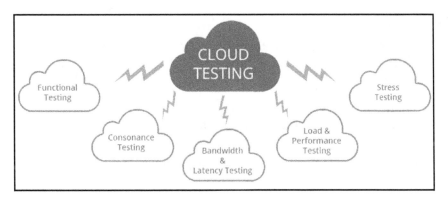

Considering these behaviors, it is recommended to produce certain automated test cases, and load testing while the application is contained in the cloud along with the on-premise application testing.

Thoroughly tested and well-functioned applications can also fail on cloud platforms due to the unexpected changes to the external systems. Hence, a thorough compatibility test is recommended for the cloud distributed applications.

Latest tools for testing Java distributed applications

We will take a look at the tools for testing, one by one.

JUnit

JUnit is a unit testing framework, which played an important role in the development of test-driven development frameworks. The power of JUnit is to reach almost every single statement in your Java program, including conditional statements. It uses annotations to ensure the target method of a Java class gets executed on the selected objects during test execution.

JUnit has been important in the development of test-driven development. JUnit is linked as a JAR at compile-time and can be used to write repeatable tests.

JTest

JTest is an automated Java software testing and static analysis tool; it includes the ability to generate the unit test cases and execute, static code analysis, dataflow static analysis, and metrics analysis, regression testing, and runtime error detection.

It also supports the runtime error detection such as race conditions, exceptions, resource, and memory leaks, and security attack vulnerabilities.

TestNG

TestNG is a testing framework designed to primarily cover a wider range of test categories such as unit, functional, end-to-end integration, and so on. It has introduced the new features to make testing more easy and powerful such as annotations, running tests in big thread pools with diverse policies, code testing in a multithread safe, flexible test configurations, and data-driven testing support for parameters.

Arquillian

Arquillian is an extendible testing platform for JVM, allowing developers to easily create automated integration, and functional and acceptance tests for Java applications. Arquillian allows you to run tests in the runtime, and it can be used to manage the life cycle of the container (or containers), bundle the test cases, dependent components, and resources. It also supports deploying the archive into containers, executing tests in the containers, and capturing the test results and creating reports. It easily integrates with other testing frameworks such as Junit, TestNG running Ant, and Maven test plugins.

The Grinder

The Grinder is a Java load testing framework offering the easy-to-run and distributed testing with multiple load injector machines. The Grinder has the ability to perform load testing on any system having the Java API, including HTTP web servers, SOAP, and REST web services, and application servers and including custom protocols. It is also having a GUI console allowing users to have multiple load injectors to be monitored and controlled, and automatic management of client connections and cookies, SSL, Proxy aware, and Connection throttling.

JWalk

JWalk is a unit testing toolkit for the Java applications supporting a testing paradigm called lazy systematic unit testing. The **JWalkTester** tool can perform the tests on compiled Java classes and is capable of testing conformance to a lazy specification, by static and dynamic analysis, and from hints by the programmer behind the code.

Mockito

Mockito is an open source testing framework allowing programmers to create and test double objects (mock objects) in automated unit tests for **test-driven development** (**TDD**) or **behavior-driven development** (**BDD**). It is useful in testing cloud and CI environments without having dependency on the inaccessible framework or infrastructure resources.

PowerMock

PowerMock is a framework to perform the unit testing on Java source code and works as an extension to other Mocking frameworks like Mockito or EasyMock and enables more powerful capabilities. PowerMock provides a custom classloader and bytecode manipulator to enable the mocking of static methods, removal of static initializes, constructors, final classes and methods, and private methods. PowerMock allows the developers to write powerful test cases extending the existing APIs with a small number of methods and annotations to enable the extra features.

Debugging and troubleshooting distributed applications

Traditional debugging and troubleshooting of on-premise applications is through the IDE-based Java debugger option to run the application in debug mode with the visibility to the executed code path. For example, a desktop application in-house to an organization to manage their employee information can be developed and tested in a single IDE and debugged through the Java debugger option. However, this approach doesn't let us review the application performance, and has a restriction to replicate the production application issues and distributed issues.

One traditional approach to review the issues is through analyzing the log files during the defect timing. This allows the production application logs to be reviewed for identifying the actual issues; however, it is very time consuming having limited scope and visibility with high performance impact based on the IO.

The distributed application debugging and troubleshooting involves the review of concurrent execution issues, including deadlocks, raise conditions, and unexpected complexity. The high data volumes on which the distributed applications are running needs to be considered. They are constantly increasing the impact on multiple resources; however, the resources are very limited and have the risk of starvation.

DevOps is the way to go for next generation cloud distributed applications, with the development and operations teams working together with the real-world tools and techniques to perform the build, deploy, and test the applications on the cloud distributed infrastructure.

AppDynamics is a tool to review the application performance management on the production environments by monitoring the systems to provide the right information rather than reviewing the issue after it has happened.

Summary

Through this chapter, you learned about the important distributed systems testing and the challenges involved in testing the distributed applications. You also learned about the standard testing approaches in software systems with the examples of latest trends, including continuous integration-based test execution. The cloud distributed application testing techniques and importance was also covered. We completed this chapter with an understanding of the debugging and troubleshooting needs of the distributed applications.

In the next chapter, we will discuss the essential security aspects and implementation of the latest security features from Java 9 in distributed applications.

10
Security

As global organizations have started to depend more on the market-leading open systems and cloud environments to increase their reach to the market and improve their business, more online transactions are going on the Internet. As more business transactions are taking place in open networks, it is equally open to the threats from the outside world. While organizations make the most of the marketing information available to the business, they are equally worried about the privacy of the information. Having business-critical applications distributed across, the communication between the clients and applications needs to be established in a more secure way.

In this chapter, we will cover the following:

- Security issues and concerns
- Two-way Secure Sockets Layer (SSL) implementation
- Cloud computing security
- Security as a service (SECaaS)
- Security enhancements in Java 9

Let's start by reviewing security issues and concerns for distributed applications.

Security issues and concerns

Distributed computing is more about the collaboration of multiple different systems to work together in a shared environment. Hence, inter-system communication is prone to one of the following threats that is explained in detail here:

- **Passive Tap**: This is a threat by an intruder to review application interaction and the data being exchanged between systems. It cannot change the data or harm the interaction directly, but it can steal any secured information with the access to view the network data; the intruder can use this information later for improper access. Passive Tap is an easy-to-attack threat for distributed systems.

- **Active Tap**: This is a threat in which the actual message sent from a client to the server is being accessed to obtain secure information and steal or alter the information in the favor of the interloper.

- **Denial-of-Service**: This is the scenario wherein the message in a wrong format is consistently trying to access application server that blocks the access from all other users. This causes serious delay and availability of services.

- **Faking**: Fake messages and replay are the scenarios where the same message, for example, a money transfer, gets triggered multiple times and causes serious business losses. Audit trails are one of the solution for such threats.

- **Traffic analysis**: Traffic analysis is required when the messaging activity is increased and causes dense traffic. The standard mechanism to prevent this scenario is to keep connections loaded with random messages and transfer the content instead of background traffic.

- **Replay accidental access**: This is where users access applications and the access is captured and replayed. Software fault and crossed lines are the standard causes for the accidental access. For example, a caller may have used the service and disconnected the call, while an other caller gets the previous caller session, which causes this issue.

Two-way Secure Sockets Layer (SSL) implementation

While there are multiple security implementations in enterprise systems with distributed architecture, including authentication, authorization, and role-based access, one of the preferred and secured way of establishing the system integration is through a two-way SSL. In this concept, both the client and server shake hands by sending the expected and known **Domain Name System** (**DNS**)-named certificates (server certificate and client certificate) and confirming the system protocol before exchanging any information. Once the known system encryption is established, they start exchanging the information, which is a secured way of communication. The following diagram represents the SSL/**Transport Layer Security** (**TLS**) handshake mechanism between a client and server:

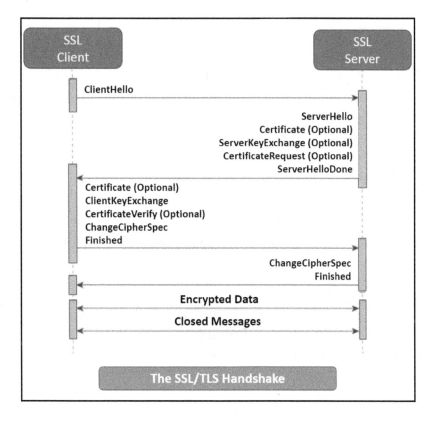

Let's review the steps involved in the SSL/TLS Handshake process here:

- **ClientHello:** In this stage, the client application invokes the server with the details of the highest version of SSL it is supporting and a list of the cipher suites it can support (TLS 1.0 is represented by SSL 3.1). Cryptographic algorithms and key sizes are included in the cipher suite details.
- **ServerHello:** In this stage, the server selects the highest version of SSL and the best cipher suite that both the client and server support, and confirms the details with the client.
- **Certificate (Optional):** The server sends the client a certificate or a certificate chain. It may include the server's public-key certificate, the authority-root certificate, and so on.
- **CertificateRequest (Optional):** If the server authenticating the client is enforced, then the server sends a certificate request to the client.
- **ServerKeyExchange (Optional):** The server sends a server key exchange message to the client, if the public-key details from the certificate are not enough for the key exchange.
- **ServerHelloDone:** The server confirms to the client that the initial conciliation is completed.
- **Certificate (Optional):** The client sends its certificate chain if the server requests one.
- **ClientKeyExchange (Optional):** The client produces the details submitted for key generation and symmetric encryption. The client then encrypts this key information with the server's public key and sends it to the server for RSA.
- **CertificateVerify (Optional):** When this message is used along with the certificate that the client sends the server, the client sends details that it digitally signs using a cryptographic hash function. When the server decrypts this detail with the client's public key, the server can authenticate the client.
- **ChangeCipherSpec:** This message from the client to the server confirms that the server can change to encrypted mode.
- **Finished:** This message from the client to the server confirms that the protocol is ready for secure data communication to be established.
- **ChangeCipherSpec:** This message from the server to the client confirms the client to change to the encrypted mode.
- **Finished:** This message from the server to client confirms that the protocol is ready for secure data communication to establish, and this concludes the SSL handshake process.

- **Encrypted Data:** During the SSL handshake, the client and server interact with symmetric encryption and cryptographic hash function with the secret-key. This is sent by the client to the server in the client-key exchange stage. This process can be repeated during the renegotiation stage.
- **Closed Messages:** Once the communication is completed, the server and client pass `close_notify` message to each other to confirm that the connection is closed.

In general, the secured two-way SSL protocol observes a slight degradation of performance due to this process. The details shared as parameters in SSL handshake can be stored and reused in future handshake to improve the performance.

The two-way SSL communication can be established in multiple communication channels, including Java message service and web services.

For implementing the two-way SSL, the first step is to procure the right set of certificates along with the DNS. This can be achieved with a number of tools and providers such as Venafi.

The KeyTool is a key and certificate management utility for generating and administering the private and public key pairs and associated certificates with the SSL security protocol. It uses a file called KeyStore to stores the keys and certificates, which are secured with a password.

Check the following Oracle document for more information about using the KeyTool utility:

```
https://docs.oracle.com/javase/8/docs/technotes/tools/unix/keytool.html
```

Two-way SSL implementation for web services

KeyStore and TrustStore files need to be generated to pass through the SSL communication between server and client certificates and verified during a two-way SSL handshake.

Allow the secured calls in server application

To allow the two-way SSL-enabled secure calls in your application, you can add a filter for verifying if it is a secure call with a valid client certificate.

If you are deploying a J2EE application, you can do this configuration through the custom filter component with `@WebFilter("/*")`, which ensures each and every request to the application URL gets filtered for the secured SSL call with this **SSLValidationFilter** as follows:

```java
package com;


import java.io.IOException;
import java.security.cert.X509Certificate;

import javax.naming.InvalidNameException;
import javax.naming.ldap.LdapName;
import javax.naming.ldap.Rdn;
import javax.servlet.Filter;
import javax.servlet.FilterChain;
import javax.servlet.FilterConfig;
import javax.servlet.ServletException;
import javax.servlet.ServletRequest;
import javax.servlet.ServletResponse;
import javax.servlet.annotation.WebFilter;

@WebFilter("/*")
public class SSLValidationFilter implements Filter {

  @Override
  public void init(FilterConfig arg0) throws ServletException {
    // TODO Auto-generated method stub
  }

  @Override
  public void doFilter(ServletRequest req,
  ServletResponse resp, FilterChain chain)
    throws IOException, ServletException {

    boolean validSSLCall = false;
    if (!req.getScheme().equals("https")) {
      validSSLCall = true;
    } else {
      X509Certificate[] certificates = (X509Certificate[])
      req.getAttribute("javax.servlet.request.X509Certificate");

      for (X509Certificate clientCert: certificates) {
        System.out.println("Certificate is :
        " + clientCert.toString());
        String distinguishedName =
        clientCert.getSubjectX500Principal().getName();
```

```
            LdapName ln;
            try {
              ln = new LdapName (distinguishedName);
              for (Rdn relativeDN : ln.getRdns()) {
                System.out.println("Relative DN name:
                " + relativeDN.getValue());
                System.out.println("Relative DN Type:
                " + relativeDN.getType());
                //Here you can put number of validations based on
                //relative DN name, type as such.
                if (relativeDN.getType()!= null &&
                "CN".equals(relativeDN.getType())) {
                  validSSLCall = true;
                }
              }
            } catch (InvalidNameException e) {
              // TODO Auto-generated catch block
              e.printStackTrace();
            }
          }
        }
        if(validSSLCall) {
          chain.doFilter(req, resp);
        } else {
          throw new ServletException("Invalid SSL Call");
        }
      }

      @Override
      public void destroy() {
        // TODO Auto-generated method stub
      }
    }
```

Generate a client program as a web service client with a two-way SSL

For the client program to invoke a REST web service with a two-way SSL ability, you need to include the Apache HTTP components (http://hc.apache.org/) dependency to your project. The program should include the following parameters to act as a secure web service client.

- Server TrustStore file name, including the path
- Server TrustStore password

- Client KeyStore file name, including the path
- Client KeyStore password
- Client key password
- target URI

Additionally, from the client program, the following details need to be verified in order to rightly produce the HTTPS client:

1. Verify the URI protocol and confirm for a secured web request.
2. The expected server certificate must be in a trust store and the corresponding KeyTool must report *trustedCertEntry* when listing the contents.
3. The required user key must be in a KeyStore and the corresponding KeyTool must report `PrivateKeyEntry` when listing the contents.
4. Create and register a socket factory for all HTTPS connections.
5. Verify the secure port invocation, which is by default 443 and others are also allowed.
6. After validating all the preceding steps successfully, produce the response.

Once the Server application is started, run the preceding client program to successfully invoke the service and print the response. Note that, the specifics required for the two-way, SSL-enabled web service call are only mentioned in this example, not your web service implementation.

Cloud computing security

Cloud computing security refers to the set of techniques, protection controls, and security policy to secure the application, data, and related infrastructure components on the cloud infrastructure.

While the introduction of cloud computing and big data in organizations helps solve the maintenance overhead of on premise software, platform, and/or infrastructure, this model also reminds us of the security concerns as aforementioned are being maintained on third-party data centers. Even though the cloud application providers are coming up their own security features, application teams should ensure that their components are deployed with application security in the cloud practice.

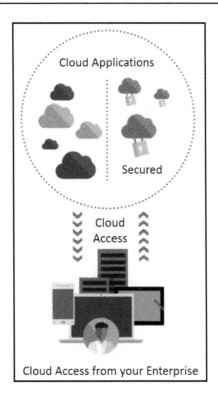

Cloud Access from your Enterprise

Cloud security controls such as deterrent, preventive, detective, and corrective controls are referred by security management to address the cloud security issues.

Different security policies such as identity management (SSO/CloudID) and the physical and privacy policy (data masking / encryption) should be engaged to ensure the cloud applications are secured.

If you are dealing with the data on cloud, the corresponding confidentiality, integrity, and access control policies should be incorporated.

More advanced encryption algorithms are available in the market such as **Ciphertext Policy Attribute Based Encryption (CP-ABE)** / **Key Policy Attribute Based Encryption (KP – ABE)**, **Fully Homomorphic Encryption (FHE)**, and **Searchable Encryption (SE)** with the features like crypto shredding, which can clear the cryptographic keys when the related data usage is complete, which are more appropriate for cloud information exchange.

Services such as **Identity and Access Management** (**IAM**), governance, and authentication should be thoroughly reviewed, and cloud-based solutions should be added to these services. The following diagram shows a glimpse of such services in each area of the application portfolio:

	Identity Management Services	Access Management Services	Privileged Identity Services	Identity Governance Services	Authentication Services
Integration Services	Identity Life Cycle Management	Web Access Management	Privileged Remote Access	Role Engineering and Modeling	Multi Factor Authentication
Directory Services	Access Provisioning	Enterprise Single Sign On	Privileged Session Management	SoD Compliance	Adaptive Authentication
Compliance, Auditing & Reporting		Web Single Sign On			Out Of Band Authentication
Migration Services	Centralized Role Management & Attestations	Federation Service	Privileged Single Sign On	Identity Assurance	Authentication Brokerage
Development Services	Work Flow Design and Implementation	Role Based Access Control	Auditing & Reporting of Privileged Session	Entitlement & Access Certification	Managed Authentication Services
Advisory Services		OS Access Control			

As the cloud infrastructure allows multiple organizations to host their applications and data on a common service provider, the changes made in the secure information of one organization is accessible to other organization's applications, if no proper data isolation and logical storage segregation is engaged.

Security as a service (SECaaS): Cloud service providers are offering security services, including authentication, antivirus/malware/spyware, security events, and intrusion detection and management, and delivering these as a cloud service called as SECaaS.

For the applications on cloud and the ones that are intranet-based, the Internet security services and protection with no additional hardware is the biggest advantage of SECaaS.

Cloudbric, Incapsula, AIONCLOUD, and Cloudflare are some of the cloud security offerings.

While the security solutions can be delivered in gateway, hub, and spoke (Inline/management) models, they can be classified based on the functionality as:

- Identity and access management
- Endpoint security
- Network, messaging, and web security
- Security and vulnerability management

The following diagram shows some of the security solutions for these categories:

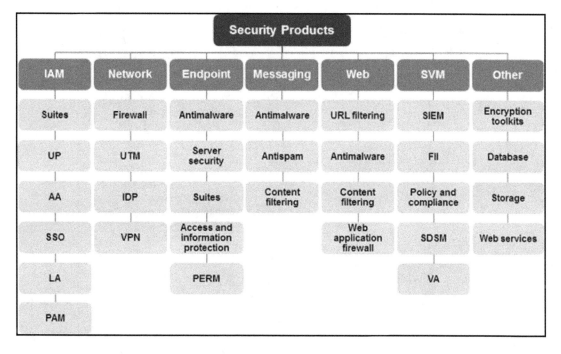

Java 9 comes up with the features that include the enhancements to the security to support cloud and distributed platforms. Let's now review some of the interesting security enhancements in java 9.

Security enhancements in Java 9

The increased usage of distributed network applications has demanded the newer version of programming languages to update their security standards to keep them more secure and robust against any security threats.

Java 9 came up with the following listed security enhancements to keep itself updated with the latest security standards.

Datagram Transport Layer Security

The **Datagram Transport Layer Security** (**DTLS**) works, based on the sequence of message exchange between the client and server through SSLEngine as shown in the following diagram:

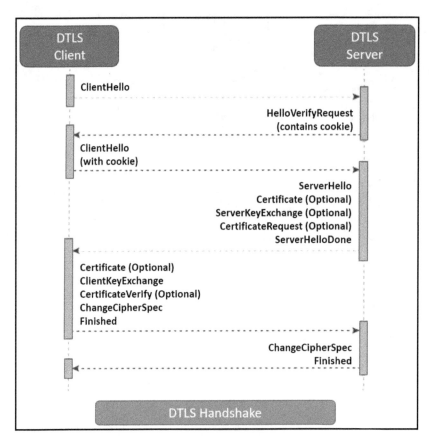

The DTLS empowers the the SunJSSE security provider and the **Java Secure Socket Extension (JSSE)** API for supporting the 1.0 and 1.2 versions of the DTLS protocol.

The following are the set of JSSE components used for the SSLSocket and SSLEngine creation:

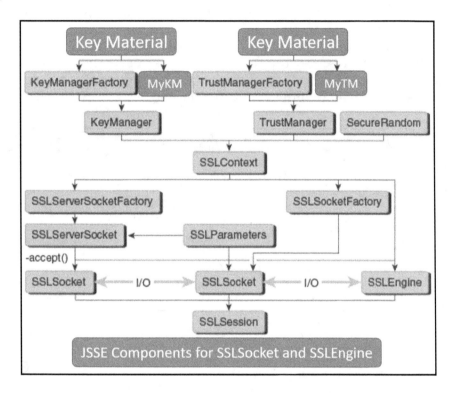

TLS Application Layer Protocol Negotiation Extension

In a TLS connection, the client and server uses the **Application Layer Protocol Negotiation** (**ALPN**) extension to find out the application protocol. In the starting of the TLS handshake, the client takes the help of the ALPN extension for sending the number of application protocols reinforced to the server during the **ClientHello** phase. When the server receives the **ClientHello** message, it selects the preferred protocols from the number of protocols received from the client and informs the client through the **ServerHello** message. Even if no protocol is chosen, the server confirms back to the client in the **ServerHello** message:

Component	Method	Usage
SSLParameters	public String[] getApplicationProtocols();	Client Side and Server Side: This method helps in returning a String array having each protocol set.
SSLParameters	public void setApplicationProtocols([] protocols);	Client Side: This method helps in setting the protocols available for the server to choose. Server Side: This method helps in setting the protocols which are available for the server as an array ordered in rank of the protocols.
SSLEngine SSLSocket	public String getApplicationProtocol();	Client Side and Server Side: This method is used after protocol negotiation to return a String containing the protocol chosen for that connection.
SSLEngine SSLSocket	public String getHandshakeApplicationProtocol();	Client Side and Server Side: This method is used during the handshake for returning a String with the protocol chosen for the connection.
SSLEngine SSLSocket	public void setHandshakeApplicationProtocolSelector(BiFunction,String> selector)	Server Side: This method is used to register a callback function. LIke the protocol or cipher suite, the application protocol value is set in the callback.

Using the preceding set of methods, the communication is established in two stages:

- Client-side protocol negotiation

- Server-side protocol negotiation

Within Server-Side Protocol Negotiation, there is a default and custom negotiation mechanisms. If no negotiated ALPN is decided, the server can throw an exception or ignore the ALPN values sent by the client.

OCSP stapling for TLS

During the client and server handshake with the TLS process, the server certificate revocation status can be verified with the OCSP stapling. **OCSP Responder** takes the request from the server and attaches the OCSP responses to the certificates before returning to the client. The **OCSP Responder** takes the request from server and caches for multiple requests from the client.

The following diagram represents the OCSP stapling for the TLS handshaking:

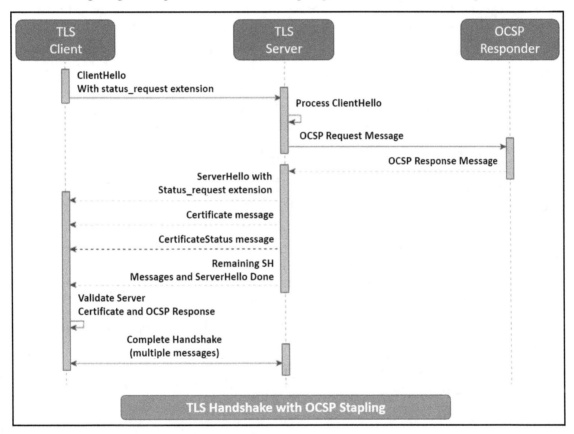

Online Certificate Status Protocol (OCSP): This enables the server to verify the X.509 certificate withdrawal in a TLS connection.

Leverage CPU Instructions for GHASH and RSA: GHASH intrinsics are enhanced using xmul/xmulhi on SPARC and pclmulqdq on the Intel x64 CPU. Using such enhanced GHASH HotSpot essentials, a performance improvement of 34x to 150x range can be achieved in AES/GCM/NoPadding.

Similarly, on the Intel x64 RSA intrinsics apply to the `java.math.BigInteger` class. RSA HotSpot intrinsics achieved a performance improvement to the extent of 50% for the `BigInteger mulAdd` and `BigInteger squareToLen` methods.

In Java 9, significant performance improvement is achieved in such algorithms with the introduction of a new security property `jdk.security.provider.preferred` to configure providers.

DRBG-based secure random implementations: This feature is added to the SecureRandom API for generating the functionality of the **Deterministic Random Bit Generator (DRBG)** mechanism. Latest algorithms such as AES-256 and SHA-512 are used in the DRBG mechanisms with versatile security features and assets.

Create PKCS12 Keystores by Default: The SunJSSE provider gives a comprehensive implementation for the PKCS12 with the `java.security.KeyStore` format. This also provides the ability to read and write the PKCS12 files. The PKCS12 keystores can be created by key and certificate management utilities such as KeyTool.

This feature is changing the default KeyStore type from JKS to PKCS12, which is an extensible, widely supported, and standard format for managing the cryptographic keys. PKCS12 keystores stores the private, public, secret key certificates, and thus improve the confidentiality. Other systems such as Microsoft Internet Explorer, Mozilla, and OpenSSL also have the great support with PKCS12 for interoperability.

SHA-3 Hash algorithms: As per the IST FIPS 202 specification, Java 9 provisions the SHA-3 cryptographic hash function.

SHA3-224, SHA3-256, SHA3-384, and SHA3-512 are supplementary standard algorithms that the `java.security.MessageDigest` API supports.

While the aforementioned security protocols help in establishing a secured connection on distributed systems, it is always recommended to have organization-specific security policies such as application names, message types, and identifiers for the systems interacting to confirm the information is exchanged between the right systems and audited through the interactions.

Summary

Throughout this chapter, you learned about important distributed system security and its aspects of security. You also learned about security issues and concerns for distributed computing. The security implementation for enterprise systems with SSL handshakes and a two-way SSL implementation with an example for web services was also covered. We completed this chapter with a thorough understanding of the new features from Java 9 that support distributed system security.

Index

OracleXAException 180
OracleXAResource 180
OracleXid 180
OutputStreamWriter 48

P

parallel computing
  about 9, 10, 11, 141
  Amdahl's law 12
  versus distributed computing 18
parallel processing 9
parallel systems
  architectures 136
  clusters 140
  distributed systems 140
  Massively Parallel Processors (MPP) 137
  Symmetric Multiprocessors (SMP) 138
patterns, cloud computing
  Application as a Service (AaaS) 190
  Blockchain as a Service (BaaS) 190
  Database as a Service (DaaS) 190
  Governance as a Service (GaaS) 191
  Information as a Service 190
  Infrastructure as a service (IaaS) 191
  Integration as a Service 191
  Integration Platform as a Service (iPaaS) 190
  Management as a Service (MaaS) 191
  Mobile Backend as a Service (MBaaS) 191
  Platform as a Service (PaaS) 190
  Process as a Service 190
  Security as a Service 191
  storage as a Service 189
  Testing as a Service (TaaS) 191
PipedInputStream 49
PipedOutputStream 49
Platform as a Service (PaaS) 190
point-to-point (queue) programming 112, 114
Point-To-Point Messaging Paradigm 104
port 32
PowerMock 260
private cloud 188
Process as a Service 190
process ID (pid) 22
program compiling, RMI server
  about 68

client classes, building 70
  JAR file, building from interface classes 69
  server classes, building 69
public cloud 188
publish-subscribe (topic) programming 108
publish/subscribe messaging paradigm 102
PushbackInputStream 48
PushbackReader 48

R

RAM Network 141
Reducing phase 237
remote application communication
  methods 29
Remote Method Invocation (RMI)
  about 21, 59, 60
  for distributed computing 63, 64
  key terminologies 62
Remote Procedure Call (RPC) 60
replication 169
Representational State Transfer (REST) 120
RESTful web services
  about 120
  building, JAX-RS API used 125, 128
  characteristics 121
ResultSet 177
RMI REGISTRY 61
RMI server
  about 61
  client program, creating 67, 68
  client, invoking 71
  programs, compiling 68
  remote client program, running 70
  remote interface, implementing 65, 67
  starting 71
  writing 65
roles, web service architectures
  Service Provider 117
  Service Registry 118
  Service Requestor 117
RowSet 177
RPC Style
  SOAP web service, building JAX-WS API used 122

S

sample CORBA program, with JAVA IDL
  about 83
  client application 84, 85, 86
  client, executing 87
  IDL interface specification 84
  IDL, compiling 84
  object implementation 86
  server, compiling 87
  server, defining 86
  server, starting 87
sample JavaSpaces code
  about 89
  Java 9 features 90
Searchable Encryption (SE) 271
Security as a Service 191
service-oriented architecture (SOA) 223
setup methodologies, distributed database
  about 169
  horizontal partitioning 169, 170
  hybrid setup 170
  replication 169
  vertical partitioning 170
SHA-3 Hash algorithms 278
Shuffling nodes 237
Simple Object Access Protocol (SOAP) 118
Simple Workflow Service (SWF) 201
skeleton 60
SOAP web service
  building, JAX-WS API used in document style 124
  building, JAX-WS API used in PRC style 122
  characteristics 119
socket 36
  multicasting 45
  programming, for TCP 38
  programming, for UDP 42
  reading from 40
Software as a Service (SaaS) 190
Software Redundant Array of Inexpensive Disks (RAID) 142
software systems
  standard testing approach 249, 250
Spring Boot
  about 224

  features 224
Spring Cloud 225
Spring Cloud Data Flow 225
Spring framework 224
Spring Web Services (Spring-WS) 120
SSL/TLS Handshake process
  steps 266, 267
SSLValidationFilter 268
standard testing approach
  in software systems 249, 250
  system testing 253
  unit testing 250, 251
  User Acceptance Testing 255
Storage as a Service 189
streams 36, 46
stub 60
Symmetric Multiprocessors (SMP) 134, 138
system testing
  about 253
  system integration testing 254, 255

T

TaskTracker 235
test-driven development (TDD) 259
Testing as a Service (TaaS) 191
testing tools, Java distributed applications
  Arquillian 259
  Grinder 259
  JTest 258
  JUnit 258
  JWalk 259
  Mockito 259
  PowerMock 260
  TestNG 258
testing
  in distributed applications, challenges 248, 249
TestNG 258
threads 21
Tomcat
  Java application, deploying with Docker 221, 223
Transport Control Protocol (TCP) 32
  socket, programming 38
Transport Layer Security (TLS) 265
Two-way Secure Sockets Layer (SSL)

www.ingramcontent.com/pod-product-compliance
Lightning Source LLC
LaVergne TN
LVHW081335050326
832903LV00024B/1167